The EQ Edge

EMOTIONAL INTELLIGENCE AND YOUR SUCCESS

THIRD EDITION

Steven J. Stein, Ph.D.
Howard E. Book, M.D.

JOSSEY-BASS
A Wiley Imprint
www.josseybass.com

Library and Archives Canada Cataloguing in Publication Data

Stein, Steven J., 1950–
      The EQ edge : emotional intelligence and your success / Steven J. Stein,
      Howard E. Book.—3rd ed.

Includes bibliographical references and index.

      1. Emotional intelligence. 2. Success—Psychological aspects.
I. Book, Howard E. II. Title.

BF576.S733 2011   152.4   C2011-901439-4

978-0-470-68161-9 (print), 978-0-470-95266-5 (ePDF), 978-0-470-95287-0 (eMobi), 978-0-470-95264-1 (ePub)

Production Credits
Cover and Interior Design: Mike Chan
Typesetting: Laserwords Private Limited
Printer: Printcrafters

John Wiley & Sons Canada, Ltd.
6045 Freemont Blvd.
Mississauga, Ontario
L5R 4J3

Printed in the U.S.A. by Courier Corporation
7 8 9 10 CW 17 16 15 14

To our families for their support
during the long gestation of this book:
Rodeen, Alana, and Lauren
Linda, Josh, and Adam

Contents

About EQ-i 2.0

As our knowledge of emotional intelligence continues to evolve, so does this book on emotional and social intelligence. Just over ten years have passed since we wrote the original *EQ Edge*. The previous revised editions were driven by the huge increase in knowledge, both scientific and experiential, that arose on this new topic. The present revision, while also influenced by new data, is primarily driven by the first major revision of the most widely used test of emotional intelligence in the world, the Emotional Quotient Inventory (EQ-i^{TM}), now referred to as the Emotional Quotient Inventory 2.0 or EQ-i 2.0^{TM}.

Most of the scientific knowledge about emotional and social intelligence that exists today is a result of research studies that rely on tests or measurement. If it were not for tests that measure these attributes, we would only have conjecture and hypotheses about what emotional intelligence is, its significance in our world, and how it can be improved.

Most of the research in the field has been based on either the EQ-i, a self-report measure, or the MSCEIT (Mayer, Salovey, and Caruso Emotional Intelligence Test), an abilities-based measure. These measures are developed through widely accepted standards in psychology that include theory development; refinement of constructs; development of items to measure those constructs; testing out those items with samples of people; refinement of items, then testing thousands of people representative of the population at large; normalization of the data; and continued research on its reliability and validity.

The current revision of the EQ-i 2.0 is a process that took several years to complete and was entirely carried out by the talented staff at MHS (Multi-Health Systems), one of the world's leading assessment companies. Hundreds of thousands of hours were invested in this process by the highly skilled professionals. Why was this necessary? Tests can become dated over time. People change as cultures are changed. Things we reacted to one way many years ago may no longer get the same reaction today. Thus, of necessity, items had to be changed and norms adjusted to respectively determine and verify people's reactions in the contemporary world.

Among this team at MHS we'd like to thank Dr. Derek Mann, Katie Ziemer, Wendy Gordon, Scott Millar, Rick Walrond, Sara Rzepa, Dr. Gill Sitarenios, Deena Logan, Dr. Kevin Williams, Dr. Craig Nathanson, Diana Durek, Daniela Kwiatkowksi, Charlene Colella, Jaroslaw Kunicyn, Heather Coe, Ronald Tumbas, Kelley Marko, Dr. Dana Ackley, Marcia Hughes, Brett Richards, Hile Rutledge, John Elliot, Hazel Wheldon, Thomas Gale, and James Buchanan.

The EQ Edge has been read and put into practice by hundreds of thousands of people in all walks of life. It has also become an integral part of the training of professionals in how to use the EQ-i. In this edition of *The EQ Edge*, our goal is to provide you with helpful information on emotional and social intelligence based on the most up-to-date developments in the field. This edition has been reorganized to fit the new format of the EQ-i 2.0. Based on the input of hundreds of professionals experienced with the original EQ-i, along with our accumulated knowledge of the published research in the field, and unpublished studies that we have been privy to, we will provide you with the most useful information that you can implement in your work, at home, and in your social relations.

Preface

It's hard to believe that 10 years have passed since we first released *The EQ Edge*. The world has changed in dramatic ways since then. We've experienced 9/11, the wars in Afghanistan and Iraq, the 2004 tsunami, earthquakes, 7/7, severe hurricanes in Louisiana and Florida, massacres in Sudan, and a number of other crises.

We were very excited when asked to update our book by the people at Wiley. *The EQ Edge* has continued to sell very well over the years and we receive comments from readers all over the world. We are very pleased that so many people have contacted us with stories of how parts of our book have touched their lives. In some cases people have made dramatic life changes for the better as a result of the examples and exercises provided.

In this update, our goal was to make a few changes based on some comments we've received about what people really liked best about the book. We also wanted to update you on some of the new developments in emotional intelligence since the book was originally written. We've added information on how emotional intelligence has helped play a role in the lives of families of survivors of the 9/11 tragedy; its use in training top police officers from around the world at the FBI Academy; how emotional intelligence played a small part in the reality TV shows *Survivor*, *The Apprentice*, *The Amazing Race*, *Big Brother*, and *From the Ground Up*; and how the top-rated lawyers in Canada measure up, among other stories.

We want to thank Don Loney for his excitement about *The EQ Edge* and for championing the book at Wiley.

Acknowledgments

We wish to thank the hundreds of thousands of people who have taken the Emotional Quotient Inventory (EQ-i and EQ-i 2.0) to date. In the process of validating and conducting research with this instrument we have learned a great deal about emotional intelligence and the role it plays in the lives of so many people, including those who are fulfilled, rich (in life and/or material wealth), famous, successful, less fortunate, unfulfilled, and downtrodden. We hope that you have learned more about yourselves and the areas on which you can focus to greatly enhance your lives.

Many people played key roles in allowing us access to data that would ordinarily have been very difficult to obtain. We want to thank Cmdr. Dean Bailey, former SMO (Senior Medical Officer) of one of the world's most technologically sophisticated aircraft carriers, the USS *George Washington*, for all his assistance in our testing of navy personnel while the ship was on duty in the and EQ-i 2.0 Mediterranean Sea and the Atlantic Ocean. We also thank (former) Lt.-Cmdr. Bill Glasser and (former) Maj. Charley Magruder for making these trips possible. Both provided great camaraderie, along with a good deal of education about the U.S. military.

Many thanks to Larry Tanenbaum, co-owner of the Toronto Maple Leafs hockey team, as well as to (former) Maple Leafs president Ken Dryden, (former) assistant general manager Anders Hedberg, and (former) associate general manager Mike Smith. We have learned a great deal about professional sports, and hockey in particular, through our testing. We were pleasantly surprised at how open these hockey professionals were to the importance of emotional intelligence in the development of their young hockey players.

We also want to thank the "star performers" who gave us permission to use their test scores and their stories. They have added an important dimension to the understanding of emotional intelligence by showing how well-developed emotional skills can lead to success in real life. Only those people whose first and last names are both given in the text are real. Other examples are composites drawn from our experience with clients, relatives, friends, acquaintances, and public figures.

Others we would like to thank include Dr. Gill Sitarenios (director of research, MHS); Jennifer Schipper (Environics) for her lessons on public relations; Lt.-Col. Rich Handley (formerly of the U.S. Air Force); Irene Taylor (Irene Taylor and Associates); the late Dr. Ruth Borchiver (Jewish Vocational Services of Greater Toronto); Hy M. Eiley; Allan Gould; Nomi Morris; Brian Twohey (formerly at Canadian Imperial Bank of Commerce, Global Private Banking and Trust); Shawna Sheldon (former senior editor at MHS); Jennifer Braunton (former graphic designer at MHS); and all the people at MHS who helped out with the research.

Special thanks to our exceptional assistants, Lynn Walker, Francesca Dipasquale, and Donna Penticost, for service above and beyond the call of duty, and to our first editors at Stoddart Publishing, Donald Bastian and Sue Sumeraj.

We also thank Multi-Health Systems for permission to use the material from the *EQ-i Technical Manual*, the *EQ-i 2.0 Technical Manual*, and the *MSCEIT Technical Manual*, and other graphs and research findings. Additionally we thank Dr. Reuven Bar-On for creating the EQ-i, and Drs. Peter Salovey, Jack Mayer, and David Caruso for creating the MSCEIT.

We are pleased to be donating a portion of the income earned on this book to Doctors Without Borders.

Introduction

The appearance in 1995 of Daniel Goleman's *Emotional Intelligence: Why It Can Matter More than IQ* [1] generated a flood of interest in the role that emotional intelligence plays in our lives. Goleman elegantly surveyed years of research into psychological functioning and interpersonal skills, presenting his case to general readers in a coherent and accessible way. The response was seismic. At long last, the so-called soft skills which do so much to determine our success were rescued from the fringe and seriously considered by mainstream educators, business people, and the media.

Meanwhile, to satisfy this burgeoning demand, numerous other books have entered the marketplace. Many, however, lack solid research to substantiate their claims or methods and are dedicated primarily to putting forward their authors' self-serving points of view. These books have threatened to erode confidence in the core concept of emotional intelligence with their expansive promises and one-sided arguments.

But emotional intelligence is not a fad or a trend. Nor is it quite as new as many people believe. It seems novel only because it was shuffled aside, sent into hibernation by the 20th century's fixation on scientific data and rationalism at any cost. Only now are the social sciences catching up and coming to grips with those aspects of personality, emotion, cognition, and behavior which were previously judged incapable of being identified, measured, and fully understood. Now, they're increasingly recognized as crucial to effective functioning, both in the workplace and in our personal lives. Good relationships and coping strategies are key to our success in every area of human activity, from the initial bonding between parent and child to the ability of a manager to bring out the best in his or her employees.

In fact, one of a number of emotional intelligence breakthroughs took place in the 1980s, when the American-born Israeli psychologist Dr. Reuven Bar-On began his work in the field. He was perplexed by a number of basic questions. Why, he wondered, do some people possess greater emotional well-being? Why are some better able to achieve success in life? And—most important—why do some people who are blessed with superior intellectual abilities seem to fail in life, while others with more modest gifts succeed? By 1985, he thought he'd found a partial answer in what he called a person's Emotional Quotient (EQ), an obvious parallel to the long-standing measures of cognitive or rational abilities that we know as IQ, or Intelligence Quotient.

This was an interesting hypothesis, but it remained untested—until Bar-On developed an instrument which became known as the EQ-i, which stands for Emotional Quotient Inventory. He believed emotional intelligence was made up of a series of overlapping but distinctly different skills and attitudes which could be grouped under five general theme areas or "realms," then further subdivided into 15 components or "scales." This was essentially what came to be referred to as the Bar-On model of emotional intelligence, upon which the EQ-i was developed. Even when the EQ-i was in its infancy, Bar-On had a hunch that the skills it was designed to measure would eventually prove to be even more important than traditional cognitive skills when it came to successfully coping with life's demands.

While Bar-On was working toward the formulation of the EQ-i, we had been busy in our respective fields. Oddly enough, since we hadn't at that point met, both of us were gradually coming around to the same way of thinking. Steven had founded Multi-Health Systems (MHS), which publishes a wide selection of psychological tests and other materials. These tests performed (and continue to perform) an extremely valuable role. But, almost by definition, the majority of them dealt, one way or another, with the negative—the downside of human experience—in that they identified and assessed all sorts of difficulties, deficiencies, and problems.

Meanwhile, a movement known as positive psychology was gaining broad acceptance. Many practitioners began to suggest that in order to treat (for example) depression, a good first step would be to look for a skill or competency and build from there. An area in which someone was functioning well could serve as the basis for meaningful change, and point the way to an eventual cure.

At about this time, Steven was introduced to Reuven Bar-On, who was then attempting to interest North American publishers in his as-yet-unfinalized EQ-i. Steven was drawn to the concept at once, because Bar-On was looking at a number of clearly delineated skills that could with practice be improved—the flip side of what Steven was working on. The EQ-i offered promise and hope. If Bar-On was correct, almost everyone could benefit. MHS therefore began to collect data which would both fine-tune Bar-On's initial findings and make them more relevant to North American circumstances.

While these activities were under way, Howard had also been influenced by the positive psychology movement's emphasis on strengths that can be made stronger. (The Menninger Clinic—a renowned psychiatric facility located in Topeka, Kansas, which also operates a separate division that provides coaching to business executives—put this well: "You don't have to be sick to get better.") In his work as an organizational consultant, he'd been struck by the fact that many of the issues confronting the firms that sought his advice had nothing to do with accounting, strategic planning, or budget sheets. Rather, they were the results of faulty communication, of people's inability to understand how they and others functioned, and of a failure to see matters from someone else's perspective or grasp the impact of their own actions. He hadn't yet heard the term emotional intelligence; he was simply aware of his own observations—until the publication of Daniel Goleman's book helped to crystallize his thinking. Now there was a phrase to capture what he'd been dealing with.

Then, one day at his son's summer camp, Howard found himself listening to a stranger (who fortuitously turned out to be Steven) describe the preliminary research on emotional intelligence, and the existence of a valid scientific instrument that at long last both defined and measured emotional intelligence. All of which explains how the two of us got together, and why we've worked together ever since.

Since the early 1990s MHS, together with a worldwide network of researchers and practitioners, has administered the EQ-i and more recently the EQ-i 2.0 (translated into 45 languages) to well over one million people in 66 countries, building up a voluminous data bank and uncovering incontrovertible links between emotional intelligence and proven success in people's personal and working lives. Some of these remarkable stories, those of our "star performers," are detailed in Chapter 19. There you'll find instances of how the EQ-i has predicted and assisted in the success of real people in a wide variety of fields, from the military to professional hockey, from bankers to doctors to journalists to collection agents to teachers. Based on our findings, we know beyond doubt that EQ can be accurately determined and effectively improved upon on an individual basis. The purpose of this book is to show you how.

When Reuven Bar-On presented the model of the EQ-i at a meeting of the American Psychological Association in Toronto, Canada, in 1996, we were deluged with media attention. More than 100 North American newspapers reported on his findings, and, during that single week, we did dozens of radio and television interviews. Since then, the pace has quickened.

In 1997—the year MHS formally began to publish, distribute, and process the finalized EQ-i—Reuven Bar-On and Steven Stein were keynote speakers at the 50th anniversary celebration of Toronto's Jewish Vocational Services, a non-profit agency which offers community-based career counseling and psychological programs to the city's Jewish day schools. A smattering of free pamphlets, along with the usual cross-your-fingers-and-pray public service announcements, formed the bulk of the advance promotion, and organizers optimistically set up 350 chairs in a hotel ballroom. Who knew how many people might wander by out of idle curiosity, to hear about something as obscure as emotional intelligence?

The answer is: Quite a few. As it happened, the presentation was delayed for half an hour while hotel staff scrambled to open up a room divider and find more seating. The final tally showed that nearly 1,000 people—a cross-section ranging from mental health professionals to housewives to retirees—flocked to a basically unadvertised event. There are several reasons for this overwhelming response which, by the way, continued for a number of years in different countries around the world.

First, people are excited and relieved to receive confirmation of what they've instinctively known all along—that IQ needn't be taken quite so seriously as before, that other factors are at least as important when it comes to success in life. In fact, one can make the argument that in order for us to take advantage of our cognitive intelligence and flex it to the maximum, we first need good emotional intelligence. Why?

Because regardless of how brainy we may be, if we turn others off with abrasive behavior, are unaware of how we are presenting ourselves, or cave in under minimal stress, no one will stick around long enough to notice our high IQs.

Second, it's encouraging to discover that, thanks to the alternative or supplementary framework provided by the EQ-i, emotional intelligence can be reliably measured, and may eventually take its place alongside cognitive intelligence (which achieved its current status in part because there were tools that quantified it and made it real).

Third, it's heartening to learn that emotional intelligence cuts across the gender gap. Over and over again, we have found that men and women have remarkably similar overall scores on the EQ-i. This held true in a number of diverse countries and cultures worldwide. The only differences arose when it came to the 15 component scales. Women everywhere had higher scores in two of these categories—social responsibility and empathy—while men universally scored higher on stress tolerance. In addition, at least in North America, women came out slightly ahead on the interpersonal relationships scale, while men scored higher in self-regard. Suffice it to say that for every area of emotional intelligence in which women appear to enjoy a natural advantage, men have a counterbalancing strength elsewhere.

Our analysis of the newest datasets, based on more than 4,000 people tested with the EQ-i 2.0 throughout North America, stratified to match census data, once again confirms our earlier findings (with a few small modifications). As before, there were no overall differences in EQ between men and women. However, women scored higher in the interpersonal relationship realm than men. There were some small, but statistically significant, differences in the subscales as well, with males scoring higher in independence, problem solving, and stress tolerance. Women, on the other hand, scored higher in emotional self-awareness, emotional expression, and empathy.

Fourth, it's equally heartening to discover that emotional intelligence transcends race. Particularly in the United States, heated controversy has long surrounded the discrepancies (which arise for a number of complex and, themselves, arguable reasons) that have been found among the average IQ scores for groups of Caucasians, African-Americans, and Asian-Americans. Many readers may remember the furor that arose in 1994 over the publication of *The Bell Curve* by Richard Herrnstein and Charles Murray,[2] who chose to tackle this thorny question head-on. As a result of this furor, the findings and interpretations they reported were investigated by a special task force appointed by the American Psychological Association. And the acrimonious, though largely inconclusive, debate hasn't completely died down in the intervening years.

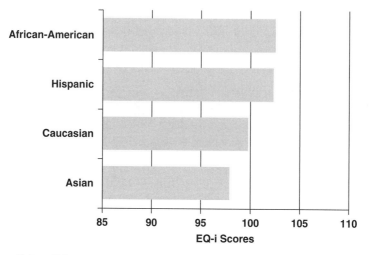

Figure I-1:   EQ Variance Across Ethnicities

This is one reason we attempted to compile the world's first data analysis of racial differences (if they existed at all) when it came to the components of emotional intelligence. Our first study was based on approximately 1,000 people located throughout North America who had completed the EQ-i. We compared the results obtained by members of the three races mentioned earlier, as well as those obtained by Hispanic-Americans. The average overall scores varied by less than 5 percent—a difference so small it might have arisen by chance. Nor were there any significant differences among average scores for each of the EQ-i's five realms. In short, there seem to be no emotional advantages or disadvantages whatsoever based on race. Thus members of any ethnic group can confidently take and benefit from the EQ-i, and EQ itself remains a measure that can be applied in good conscience throughout a range of multicultural settings.

These results were replicated in our 2010 study with the new EQ-i 2.0. This time we included a sample almost four times larger (3,888 people) from throughout North America in the testing. The results, as seen in Figure I-2 below, parallel what we found 17 years ago.

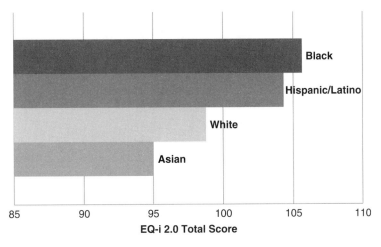

Figure I-2: EQ-i 2.0 Total Score

The last, and perhaps most important, point is that people are buoyed by the knowledge that—as you shall see in the following chapter—EQ is not permanently fixed. Age, gender, or ethnic backgrounds do not deter you from enhancing your EQ. The skills defined and measured by each of the EQ-i's component scales can be improved no matter how old you are, and the stronger your skills, the greater your chances for success. The stronger your emotional intelligence, the more likely you are to be successful as a worker, a parent, a manager, an adult child to your own parents, a partner to your significant other, or a candidate for a workplace position. It's never too late to make a change for the better. And if you really want to make that change in your life, you can.

Furthermore, the process can be started in childhood, which is why a version of the EQ-i for youths was also developed. Like its adult counterpart, the youth version helps children and adolescents to become more aware of their emotions; to be more positive about themselves; to get along better with others; to be better problem solvers; to better cope with stress; to be less impulsive; and to enjoy life. Research on emotional intelligence has demonstrated that it is a preventative measure against bad behavior.

Increasing EQ in youths may help reduce the risk of extreme violence and help prevent some of the atrocities seen in our schools, such as the murders at Columbine High. Developing emotional intelligence at an early age gives individuals an edge well into adulthood.

The EQ Edge, 3rd Edition, includes definitions and works that have been adapted from the new and completely revised *EQ-i 2.0 Technical Manual* and the *MSCEIT Technical Manual*, as well as research findings generated by administering the EQ-i, EQ-i 2.0, and MSCEIT to a large and ever-increasing number of people around the world.

PART I | The EQ Explosion

Chapter 1 | Exploring Emotional Intelligence

Redefining Intelligence and Achievement

Do you remember your high-school valedictorian? How about the class brain, who got straight As and seemed destined to follow a path of uninterrupted triumph? Chances are, you don't know what happened to these youthful academic achievers, but you can probably name one or two classmates who went on to chalk up major (and maybe highly unexpected) success. Perhaps they created and now head companies of their own or became prominent and well-respected leaders in their communities. But who'd have thought it at the time? Back then, they were busy socializing, playing guitar in the basement, or tinkering with mysterious spare parts in the garage. Maybe they just squeaked through school with passing grades. Their stars shone brightly only when they went out into the real world.

It is scarcely a revelation that not everyone's talents fit the school system's rather restrictive model for measuring achievement. History is full of brilliant, successful men and women who failed miserably or underachieved in the classroom, and whose teachers and guidance counselors relegated them to life on the margin. But despite this convincing body of evidence, society has persisted in believing that success in school equals success in life—or, at the very least, in the workplace. Now that assumption is being overturned.

Most of us know in our bones that there's a world of difference between school smarts and street smarts—between braininess and general savvy. The first has its place, but the second, while more intangible, is much more interesting. It's the ability to tune in to the world, to read situations and connect with others while taking charge of your own life. Now, thanks to the EQ-i, undeniable evidence has shown a close link between this ability—which has relatively little to do with intellect per se—and long-term success.

What is success? Let's define it as the ability to set and achieve your personal and professional goals, whatever they may be.

That sounds simple, but of course it's not. An individual's definition of success will quite naturally ebb and flow over time. We want different things and pursue different goals simply because we age, accumulating experience and shouldering responsibilities. Youthful idealism makes room for mature reality and the need for compromise; different imperatives or ingredients assume different intensities, depending on the particular role we're attempting to fill—for example, that of worker, spouse, or parent. What is our main concern at any given moment? To advance our career, to enjoy a happy marital relationship, or to offer loving support and guidance to our children? Perhaps we're faced with a serious illness, beside which all else pales in comparison, and success becomes a matter of survival. So much for supposedly simple definitions. But the basic aim on which most of us would agree—to succeed on our own terms (or on terms acceptable to us) in a wide variety of situations—remains a constant.

That's more than can be said for society's ideas of success, which are changing as we speak. Driven by the hot pursuit of science and technology, 20th-century culture long emphasized cognitive intelligence as the cornerstone for progress—just as financial reward has long been considered the primary result of that intelligence. The trouble is that sometimes this equation hasn't worked out as planned, as seen in the question: if you're so smart, why aren't you rich? Only in recent years have we begun to appreciate the powerful links between emotional intelligence and a greater, more satisfying, and more well-rounded definition of success which embraces the workplace, marriage and personal relationships, social popularity, and spiritual and physical well-being.

If you stop to think about your friends and family members—in fact, about your co-workers and the people you encounter in all sorts of day-to-day settings—whom do you consider to be the most successful? Who seem to enjoy the fullest and happiest lives? Are they necessarily the most intellectually or analytically gifted of individuals?

More likely they have other characteristics, other skills, which underlie their capacity to achieve what they desire. The more emotional and social sense you have, the easier it is to go efficiently and productively about your life. After decades of working in the fields of psychology and psychiatry, we've concluded that it's at least as important to be emotionally and socially intelligent as it is to be cognitively or analytically intelligent.

What Are the Differences between IQ and EQ?

Simply put, IQ is a measure of an individual's intellectual, analytical, logical, and rational abilities. As such, it's concerned with verbal, spatial, visual, and mathematical skills. It gauges how readily we learn new things; focus on tasks and exercises; retain and recall objective information; engage in a reasoning process; manipulate numbers; think abstractly as well as analytically; and solve problems by the application of prior knowledge. If you have a high IQ—the average is 100—you're well equipped to pass all sorts of examinations with flying colors, and (not incidentally) to score well on IQ tests.

All that's fine, yet everyone knows people who could send an IQ test sky-high, but who can't quite make good in either their personal or working lives. They rub others the wrong way; success just doesn't seem to pan out. Much of the time, they can't figure out why.

The reason why is that they're sorely lacking in emotional intelligence, which has been defined in several different ways. Reuven Bar-On called it "an array of non-cognitive capabilities, competencies, and skills that influence one's ability to succeed in coping with environmental demands and pressures."[1] Peter Salovey and Jack Mayer, who created the term "emotional intelligence" (as it applies today), describe it as "the ability to perceive emotions, to access and generate emotions so as to assist thought, to understand emotions and emotional meanings, and to reflectively regulate emotions in ways that promote emotional and intellectual growth."[2] In developing the EQ-i 2.0, emotional intelligence has been defined as "a set of emotional and social skills that influence the way we perceive and express ourselves, develop and maintain social relationships, cope with challenges, and use emotional information in an effective and meaningful way."[3]

In other words, it's a set of skills that enables us to make our way in a complex world—the personal, social, and survival aspects of overall intelligence, and the elusive common sense and sensitivity that are essential to effective daily functioning. In everyday language emotional intelligence is what we commonly refer to as "street smarts," or that uncommon ability we label "common sense." It has to do with our capacity to objectively assess our strengths, as well as be open to viewing and challenging our limitations, mistaken assumptions, unacknowledged biases, and shortsighted/self-defeating beliefs. Emotional intelligence also encompasses our ability to read the political and social environment, and landscape them; to intuitively grasp what others want and need, what their strengths and weaknesses are; to remain unruffled by stress; and to be engaging and the kind of person others want to be around.

A Brief History of Emotional Intelligence

How did emotional intelligence evolve? Plainly, it evolved along with humankind; the need to cope, to adapt and to get along with others was crucial to the survival of the early hunter-gatherer societies. The human brain reflects this undeniable fact. Sophisticated mapping techniques have recently confirmed that many thought processes pass through the brain's emotional centers as they take the physiological journey that converts outside information into individual action or response.

On the one hand, then, emotional intelligence is as old as time. In the 1870s, Charles Darwin published the first modern book on the role of emotional expression in survival and adaptation.[4] However, to gain a practical perspective, we'll focus on the development in the 20th century of the concept of EQ. Back in the 1920s, the American psychologist Edward Thorndike talked about something he called "social intelligence."[5] Later, the importance of "emotional factors" was recognized by David Wechsler, one of the fathers of IQ testing. In 1940, in a rarely cited paper, Wechsler urged that the "non-intellective aspects of general intelligence" be included in any "complete" measurement.[6] This paper also discussed what he called "affective" and "conative" abilities—basically, emotional and social intelligence—which he thought would prove critical to an overall view. Unfortunately, these factors were not included in Wechsler's IQ tests, and little attention was paid to them at the time.

In 1948 another American researcher, R.W. Leeper,[7] promoted the idea of "emotional thought," which he believed contributed to "logical thought." But few psychologists or educators pursued this line of questioning until more than 30 years later. (One notable exception was Albert Ellis, who, in 1955, began to explore what would become known as Rational Emotive Behavior Therapy—a process that involved teaching people to examine their emotions in a logical, thoughtful way.[8]) Then, in 1983, Howard Gardner of Harvard University wrote about the possibility of "multiple intelligences," including what he called "intra-physic capacities"—in essence, an aptitude for introspection—and "personal intelligence."[9]

By this time Reuven Bar-On was active in the field and had contributed the phrase "emotional quotient" or EQ.[10] The term "emotional intelligence" was coined and formally defined by John (Jack) Mayer of the University of New Hampshire and Peter Salovey of Yale University in 1990.[11] They expanded on Professor Gardner's concept, settled on the definition of emotional intelligence cited earlier in this chapter, and—with their colleague David Caruso—have since developed an alternative test of emotional intelligence that, unlike the EQ-i (Emotional Quotient Inventory), is not self-reporting but ability-based. This test, called the MSCEIT (Mayer-Salovey-Caruso Emotional Intelligence Test) has generated a considerable amount of research over the past nine years.[12] We have worked with them in the development of this test in the hope that looking at the phenomenon of emotional intelligence from two different perspectives will shed even more light on this important capacity. Some of the findings are presented later on in this book.

What About Cognitive Intelligence?

During the past 100 years cognitive intelligence and the means by which it's measured—that is, IQ and IQ testing—have dominated society's view of human potential.

In 1905 the French psychologist Alfred Binet, together with his colleague, the psychiatrist Theodore Simon, developed the first formal intelligence test.[13] Binet had been asked by the Parisian school commission to come up with a way children could be categorized according to ability. The aim was somewhat less than benign: to weed out the "feeble-minded," those who would not benefit from a publicly funded system. Binet had long believed that intelligence was an interlocking process which involved judgment, problem solving, and reasoning. Now he could put his theories into practice. He and Simon completed and published an IQ test—administered, at first, to children—that enabled him to obtain performance standards for different age groups. These formed the basis of what became known as "mental ages." The results of a test would give the mental age of a person in relation to average levels of growth and intellectual development.

In 1910 the Binet-Simon test migrated to the United States, where the educator and psychologist Henry Goddard[14] founded his own school for the "feeble-minded" in New Jersey. Later the test was modified and standardized for a wider American population by Lewis Terman at Stanford University, began to be administered to both children and adults, and became known as the Stanford-Binet test.[15]

At this time, the ability to measure cognitive intelligence assumed new importance. Not only could it identify and sidetrack the "feeble-minded" who would benefit only marginally from education, it could pick out those who scored high and could be expected to put their learning to best effect. IQ soon took on a life of its own. It was generally agreed to be a major factor not only in school but in the workplace and in personal relationships. But soon, cracks began to appear, and IQ was under attack.

First came a number of lengthy debates centering on the influence of genetics and the environment, nature versus nurture. Stormy controversies arose over cultural and racial differences. Foes of IQ testing said, in effect, that people were being unfairly and arbitrarily labeled—a harkening back, in a way, to the bad old days of spotting the "feeble-minded." By the 1960s, more and more studies had begun to question the relative importance of cognitive and analytic factors as a measure of overall intelligence. But—given the absence of a solid alternative framework—IQ persisted as the norm, no matter how muddied the original concept had become with the passage of time.

Comparing IQ and EQ

Cognitive intelligence, to be clear, refers to the ability to concentrate and plan, to organize material, to use words and to understand, assimilate, and interpret facts. In essence, IQ is a measure of an individual's personal information bank—his memory, vocabulary, mathematical skills, and visual-motor coordination. Some of these skills obviously contribute to doing well in life. That is why EQ's detractors are barking up the wrong tree when they claim that anyone who promotes emotional intelligence is out to replace IQ, or to write off its importance altogether. The fact remains, however, that IQ does not and cannot predict success in life. As for IQ's relevance in the workplace, studies have shown that it can serve to predict between 1 and 20 percent (the average is 6 percent) of success in a given job.[16] EQ, on the other hand, has been found to be directly responsible for between 27 and 45 percent of job success, depending on which field was under study.

In the book *The Millionaire Mind* by best-selling author Thomas Stanley,[17] a survey was taken of 733 multi-millionaires throughout the United States. When asked to rate the factors (out of 30) most responsible for their success, the top five were:

- Being honest with all people
- Being well disciplined
- Getting along with people
- Having a supportive spouse
- Working harder than most people

All five are reflections of emotional intelligence.

Cognitive intelligence, or IQ, was 21st on the list and only endorsed by 20 percent of the millionaires. In fact, it went even lower when millionaire attorneys and physicians were taken out of the analysis. SAT scores, highly related to IQ, were on average 1190, higher than the norm, but not high enough for acceptance to a top-rated college. What about grade point averages? They came in at 2.92 on a 4.0 scale. Again, nothing to make mom and dad especially proud.

Another major difference between cognitive and emotional intelligence is that IQ is pretty much set. It tends to peak when a person is 17, remain constant throughout adulthood, and wane during old age. EQ, however, is not fixed. A 1997 study of almost 4,000 people in Canada and the United States (see Figure 1-1) concluded that EQ rises steadily from an average of 95.3 (when you're in your late teens) to an average of 102.7 (where it remains throughout your 40s). Once you're past 50, it tapers off a bit, to an average of 101.5—not exactly a precipitous decline. The same pattern, you'll be pleased to know, holds true for both men and women.

We recently repeated this study during the revision process and development of the EQ-i 2.0. As seen in Figure 1-2, the data, collected in 2010, roughly parallels the findings from 13 years earlier. Our data this time around was based on 4,000 U.S. and Canadian citizens matched to the government census on gender, region, race, ethnicity, and social class. You'll notice that

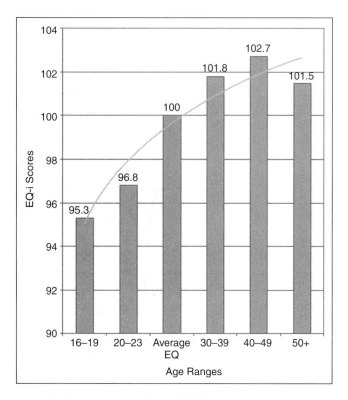

Figure 1-1:   EQ Over the Age Span (1997)

Reprinted with permission of Multi-Health Systems, Inc., Toronto, Canada. www.mhs.com

there have been some shifts in scores of the population over the 13-year period. Most important is that the slight shift downward has now moved up to the 70-year-olds (as opposed to the 50-years-plus cohort).

None of this ought to come as a surprise: we get older but wiser. We live and learn, and one of the things we learn is to balance emotion and reason. But these lessons are often submerged, worn away by sometimes conflicting duties and harsh realities. Take heart. To paraphrase Dr. Benjamin Spock, you feel more than you think you do. Better yet, you can do more about your feelings and behaviors whenever you wish, because emotional intelligence is so specific. That is, you can work on particular challenges as they arise in any of the EQ-i's 15 component scales; you needn't tackle everything

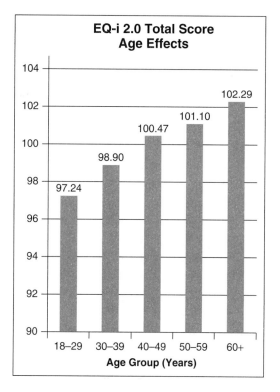

Figure 1-2: EQ Over the Age Span (2010)

Reprinted with permission of Multi-Health Systems, Inc., Toronto, Canada. www.mhs.com

at once. (By the way, the very real possibility of lifelong improvement as opposed to inevitable calcification or decline argues for the very important contributions that can be made by older people in the workplace. A shrewd employer would do well to anchor his or her staff with mature individuals. As might be expected, we've found that these elders add much-needed stability, but—more surprisingly—they also tend to prove more adept than their junior counterparts at problem solving and frequently have a firmer grip on reality.)

So much for a few of the major differences between IQ and EQ. But one or two misconceptions remain. For example, some people persist in confusing EQ with other psycho-social concepts that have made their way into other tests and surveys of human potential. To understand what makes EQ distinct, and to appreciate why the EQ-i 2.0 is a superior measuring tool, let's look at some of the things that EQ *is not*.

First of all, it isn't aptitude, which concerns a person's ability to perform well in a particular technical skill or activity or discipline. It isn't achievement, which concerns specific sorts of performance—as, for that matter, does a school report card. It isn't vocational interest, which centers on a person's natural inclination toward or predilection for a particular field of work: vocational testing might show that you have an interest in work which involves looking after the emotional needs of others, such as psychology, social work, ministry, or counseling; however, your aptitude might indicate that that you have excellent manual skills, which give you the capacity to perform well in jobs such as surgery, masonry, woodworking, or construction. Vocational interests and skills frequently do not coincide.

Nor is EQ personality—the unique set of traits that help form a person's characteristic, enduring, and dependable ways of thinking, feeling, and behaving. Imagine someone's personality as the way he or she meets and greets the world, or as the capsule answer to the question: what is he or she like? A reply might be, well, he's shy and thoughtful, a real straight-shooter. Or, she's kind of soft-spoken, but she's got a great sense of humor once you get to know her.

Personality is the concept most often confused with emotional intelligence, but it differs in two important ways. First, like IQ, the traits which comprise our personalities are fixed. If we're by inclination honest, introverted, or loyal, we're unlikely to strike off in some new and unexpected direction. Psychologists call these traits "static," and term an individual's personality, as a whole, "strategic"—another way of saying that it operates over the long haul. This enables personality tests to divide people into "types": the adventurer, the nurturer, the sensitive individual, and so forth. As a result, people can be rather too neatly pigeonholed: witness the so-called Type A personality (hard-driving and prone to anger) versus Type B (relaxed and less ambitious). The trouble with these arbitrary divisions is that the possibility of change for the better gets lost in the shuffle. People tend to feel they're stuck with the hand they were dealt by fate.

Emotional intelligence, however, is made up of short-term, tactical, "dynamic" skills which can be brought into play as the situation warrants. Thus the individual building blocks of emotional intelligence—and its overall structure—can be improved by means of training, coaching, and experience.

What Are the Building Blocks of EQ?

A full description of the development and refinement of the EQ-i 2.0 appears in Appendix A at the back of this book.

Reuven Bar-On originally developed a model that captured emotional intelligence by dividing it into five general areas or realms, and 15 subsections or scales. Based on updated research and the latest theories on emotional intelligence, the MHS team has created the new EQ-i 2.0, with some revisions. Chapters 3 through 17 will describe these realms and scales.

The Self-Perception Realm concerns your ability to know and manage yourself. It embraces Emotional Self-Awareness—the ability to recognize

Figure 1-3: Model of Emotional Intelligence

Reproduced with permission of Multi-Health Systems, Inc. (2011), Toronto, Canada. www.mhs.com

how you're feeling and why you're feeling that way, and the impact your emotions have on the thoughts and actions of yourself and others; Self-Regard—the ability to recognize your strengths and weaknesses and to feel good about yourself despite your weaknesses; and Self-Actualization—the ability to persistently try to improve yourself and pursue meaningful goals that lead to a richer life.

The Self-Expression Realm deals with the way you face the world. It includes Emotional Expression—the ability to express your feelings both in words and non-verbally; Assertiveness—the ability to clearly express your thoughts and beliefs, stand your ground, and defend a position in a constructive way; and Independence—the ability to be self-directed and self-controlled, to stand on your own two feet.

The Interpersonal Realm concerns your "people skills"—your ability to interact and get along with others. It is composed of three scales. Interpersonal Relationships refers to the ability to forge and maintain relationships that are mutually beneficial and marked by give-and-take and a sense of trust and compassion. Empathy is the ability to recognize, understand, and appreciate what others may be feeling and thinking. It is the ability to view the world through another person's eyes. Social Responsibility is the ability to be a cooperative and contributing member of your social group and to society at large.

The Decision-Making Realm involves your ability to use your emotions in the best way to help you solve problems and make optimal choices. Its three scales are Impulse Control—the ability to resist or delay a temptation to act rashly; Reality Testing—the ability to see things as they actually are, rather than the way you wish or fear they might be; and Problem Solving—the ability to find solutions to problems where emotions are involved using the right emotion at an optimum value.

The Stress-Management Realm concerns your ability to be flexible, tolerate stress, and control impulses. Its three scales are Flexibility—the ability to adjust your feelings, thoughts, and actions to changing, challenging, or unfamiliar conditions; Stress Tolerance—the ability to remain calm and focused, to constructively withstand adverse events and conflicting emotions without caving in; and Optimism—the ability to maintain a realistically positive attitude, particularly in the face of adversity.

There is also an independent indicator of your Happiness. Happiness is the ability to feel satisfied with life, to enjoy yourself and others, and to experience zest and enthusiasm in a range of activities.

Table 1-1

The EQ-i 2.0 Scales and What They Assess

EQ-i 2.0 Scales	The EI competency assessed by each scale
Self-Perception	
Emotional Self-Awareness	*Ability to be aware of and understand one's feelings and their impact*
Self-Regard	*Ability to respect and accept one's strengths and weaknesses*
Self-Actualization	*Ability to improve oneself and pursue meaningful objectives*
Self-Expression	
Emotional Expression	*Ability to express one's feelings verbally and non-verbally*
Independence	*Ability to be self-directed and free of emotional dependency on others*
Assertiveness	*Ability to express feelings, beliefs, and thoughts in a nondestructive way*
Interpersonal	
Interpersonal Relationships	*Ability to develop and maintain mutually satisfying relationships*
Empathy	*Ability to recognize, understand, and appreciate the feelings of others*
Social Responsibility	*Ability to contribute to society, one's social group, and to the welfare of others*
Decision Making	
Impulse Control	*Ability to resist or delay an impulse, drive, or temptation to act*
Reality Testing	*Ability to remain objective by seeing things as they really are*
Problem Solving	*Ability to solve problems where emotions are involved using emotions*

(continued)

Table 1-1

The EQ-i 2.0 Scales and What They Assess *(continued)*

EQ-i 2.0 Scales	The EI competency assessed by each scale
Stress-Management	
Flexibility	*Ability to adapt one's feeling, thinking, and behavior to change*
Stress Tolerance	*Ability to effectively cope with stressful or difficult situations*
Optimism	*Ability to be remain hopeful and resilient, despite setbacks*
Additional Scale	
Happiness	*Ability to feel satisfied with oneself, others, and life in general*

Definitions presented with permission of Multi-Health Systems. Slightly modified from *Emotional Quotient Inventory 2.0 Manual (2010)*, Multi-Health Systems, Inc., Toronto, Canada. www.mhs.com

This Book and the EQ-i 2.0

The EQ-i 2.0 is composed of 133 items, and is self-reporting. You fill it out, responding to how often each item applies to you, with one of five possible answers ranging from "never/rarely" to "always/almost always." Each of the 16 scales is individually scored, as is each of the five realms. Finally, a total score is obtained. Rather like an IQ test, this ranges up or down from 100—as do scores in each of the realms and scales.

The EQ-i 2.0 has been designed to contain a great many nuances and shadings. It is not a test that spits out a measure of one's emotional intelligence. Rather, it must be administered and interpreted by a trained professional skilled in understanding these nuances and the interrelationships between the scores of the 16 components which constitute emotional intelligence. In addition, they must be able to give feedback to the person being tested to confirm or question the accuracy of the test results. The results give information at three different levels: how one is doing as a whole, compared with the population at large; how one is doing in the five realms; and how one is doing in the 16 scales. This specificity yields far more pertinent readings than many IQ tests, which provide only a single, cumulative figure.

If you're interested in the EQ-i 2.0, we've explained in Appendix 1 how you can have it administered by a qualified professional in your area. For the moment, the aim of this book is to enable you to enhance your emotional intelligence on your own, whether or not you choose to take the EQ-i 2.0 itself. For additional information you can visit www.mhs.com and select "emotional intelligence."

Can I Really Enhance My EQ?

We know that emotional intelligence can be enhanced because we've seen it happen over and over again as we've worked with corporate CEOs and other executives, school teachers, military personnel, counselors and consultants, mental health professionals, and husbands and wives. Adopting proven methods found in cognitive and behavioral therapy, as well as from psychodynamic theory, we have trained many of these individuals to increase their emotional intelligence in easily understandable and proven ways.

Crucial to this is the issue of success, as defined earlier in the book. As we collected the EQ scores for hundreds of thousands of very different people, certain trends began to emerge. Those who are successful in their marriages have a particular profile that is more effectual than those who haven't been able to make their marriages work. People who are more successful in dealing with health problems score higher in various scales of the EQ-i 2.0 than those who do not. And, of course, those who succeed in all manner of different professions tend to excel in certain scales as well. So far, researchers at MHS have been able to use this ever-growing database to develop profiles for navy pilots, high-tech workers, lawyers, journalists, sales professionals, and a myriad other job descriptions.

How did we do so? Let's say that John Smith, a senior manager at a given company, feels he could be more successful, more efficient in his duties. Or, perhaps, his superiors feel he could be, and have urged him to upgrade his skills. First, we take a look at his job description. What does he do; what roles does he perform? The answers to these questions allow us to figure out which of the 16 scales are most germane to his position. But chances are that his position is not unique—so we move on to construct an EQ profile of his most successful peers within that firm, and in other comparable firms. Next, John himself takes the EQ-i 2.0, following which his results are scored and interpreted. We then submit a detailed report outlining his relative strengths and weaknesses. These are compared to his successful (and, in some cases, less successful) peers. If asked, we might go on to focus training on those attributes most crucial to his job, and on which he needs the most help. Eventually, his low or mediocre scores will improve, and his profile will begin to more accurately mirror that of stellar performers. He'll have developed new abilities or been able to bolster latent ones, so that he functions more like the successful senior executive he wishes to be.

Or perhaps John Smith, while functioning perfectly well at work, might be experiencing difficulties with his personal life. If so, we examine his EQ-i 2.0 results and compare them to the profiles of men of his age and position who enjoy a more successful marital relationship. Different flash points or trouble spots, and different shortcomings, may well emerge. Although every role a person seeks to fill—that of worker, spouse, parent, or what-have-you—requires the exercise of all of emotional intelligence's 16 scales, their relative weight or intensity within the mix will vary. Assessing John Smith now in another context—as a member of a group of married men—we can focus training on those abilities that enable husbands to get along better with their wives. His chances of achieving success in this role will be greatly enhanced if he knows what skills successful spouses possess.

In addition, there'll be an inevitable spillover or cross-pollination from role to role. Insight is gained, and can be brought to bear across the board. If John learns to communicate more openly and effectively with his wife, he's apt to take those lessons with him to the office, with beneficial results for all concerned.

In this way, the EQ-i 2.0 goes beyond a mere 100-based score for rating someone in relation to the population as a whole. It's a far more precise and subtle instrument that can capture and measure those skills directly related to attaining success in countless group categories, occupations, or personal situations. We have developed profiles for working mothers, single parents of both sexes, and middle-aged persons coping with and caring for an aging or incapacitated parent of their own. The list goes on, and is potentially endless, because emotional intelligence remains of importance across the socioeconomic spectrum.

At first glance, no two people could be more dissimilar than the CEO of a major corporation and a person rendered homeless by bad times. But both could agree on the definition of success offered earlier, and both can train themselves to develop the qualities they need to succeed in their respective environments. The CEO is looking for a way to better negotiate the snakes-and-ladders business world. The homeless person is looking for a way to effectively utilize health and social services and, with effort, eventually to re-enter the mainstream. This is not a flippant parallel. Successful homeless people have the skills that allow them to successfully access a safe bed in a hostel, survive on the mean streets, and willingly work toward a resolution of the problems that beset them. Success on their own terms is just as much an issue for them as it is for the CEO.

Does It Matter Whether You're Emotionally Smart or Dumb?

If emotional intelligence redefines what it means to be smart, then Reuven Bar-On was correct when he remarked that "it levels out the playing field for success. It helps account for those cases where some high-IQ individuals falter in life, while others with only modest IQ can do exceptionally well."[18]

Unfortunately, these and other statements have led to a rash of misinterpretation and ill-considered attacks on the very concept of emotional intelligence. We are not concerned with rebuttal, but one or two points should be made.

For some folk, the very presence of the dreaded E-word—"emotion"—sends them running in the opposite direction. In the course of our seminars and public presentations, we're often confronted by disbelievers who make the obligatory crack about "hugging one another," or "women's style" taking over the workplace, if not the entire world. Often they settle down and start to both listen and learn. These individuals are almost always male. Men are far more apt to denigrate the importance of emotional intelligence—perhaps because of a lingering suspicion that they're more emotionally challenged. Soon, however, what the doubter had previously dismissed as intangible or airy-fairy will become solid and clear, and we'll often win a grudging convert.

Another favorite ploy is to dismiss EQ as a crutch, a magic wand, or a cure-all. It is none of these things. As we've stated, no one suggests that EQ will entirely displace or supplant IQ. Rather, the two are complementary; they can peacefully and productively co-exist. For one thing, you must have a certain baseline IQ to understand what EQ can do for you, and to put in the time and effort required to enhance your skills. Thus, IQ is a necessary foundation, without which you can't hope to flex your EQ. EQ is certainly not meant to prop up or excuse the real or imagined shortcomings of the intellectually disadvantaged. Developing an understanding of emotional intelligence doesn't mean launching emotional affirmative action.

We aren't denying that some people are more cognitively intelligent than others. This type of intelligence may take them further faster, if they choose certain paths in life. To be frank, there are areas where you don't need a whole lot of emotional intelligence on the job. A successful hit man, for example, would do well to subdue his capacity for empathy while going about his business.

More seriously, skeptics protest that, while emotional intelligence may have its place, "nice" people don't necessarily achieve scientific or medical breakthroughs, write timeless works of literature, or compose landmark music. It doesn't matter whether Shakespeare was emotionally intelligent; his work endures. Even if he were an awful person, he was still a genius, and we still have *King Lear*. True enough—but once again, the skeptics have missed the point. First, EQ isn't about being "nice" to everyone in every circumstance, as we shall see. And second, even a genius can use a bit of help. This is why we say the higher your IQ, the more important your EQ. After all, what else is going to define the differences between those who possess high IQs? What else will give them the edge they need to perform even better?

When a skeptic cites the lone inventor who makes an earth-shaking discovery or the "great man" who single-handedly alters the course of history—often for the worse—we have an answer ready. Think how much more these people could have achieved had they been able to exercise more suitable emotional skills! The real tragedy occurs when someone is intellectually well-endowed but, because of emotional stumbling blocks, is incapable of making the sorts of contributions to society—and to his or her own life—that might otherwise result from those superior mental powers. You might be as sharp as a tack, but if you can't convey what you know to other people, you're in trouble. As creative and skillful as you might be, if you're unaware of how you relate to others, if you behave disdainfully or angrily or impulsively, no one will stick around long enough to admire your skill and creativity. Metaphorically, IQ allows you to enter the elevator, but it is EQ that fuels your elevator's upward trajectory.

Too often, intellectually gifted individuals paint themselves into a small—although admittedly brilliant—corner. Their minds, in a way, are closed and inward-looking. Nor are they necessarily all that content with what they see, despite their gifts. Hence that old cliché, the misunderstood genius. Few of us are geniuses but, no matter where you are on the intellectual spectrum, EQ can galvanize you and enable you to take advantage of your full potential.

The Importance of Emotional Intelligence in the Business World

In his book *The Highwaymen*,[19] which profiles leading players in the fields of communications and information technology, Ken Auletta quotes the investment banker Felix Rohatyn (who was then involved in the attempted takeover of Paramount Communications by Viacom International) as follows: "Most deals are 50 percent emotion and 50 percent economics." Rohatyn was talking about the personalities involved, the shifting dynamics of the protracted negotiations, which were being conducted for the highest possible stakes. But the same could be said of the vast majority of business transactions, so shouldn't they be approached from a position of strength?

If you still believe that emotional intelligence is somehow flighty, a fuzzy shortcut to some ill-conceived nirvana, some more real-world examples may change your mind. An industry survey asked 195 business owners in British Columbia which, out of 187 possible choices, they felt were the most important and desirable qualities when it came to hiring new staff.[20] The results were clear, by a landslide. The quality most prized was "common sense." But what exactly does common sense entail? This same survey spoke to the question: some of the business owners called it "being responsive to customers, dealing with them effectively, and talking and writing in a relevant way." In other words, the core skills associated with several of the scales of emotional intelligence.

In the June 21, 1999, *Fortune* cover article, "Why CEOs Fail," authors Ram Charan and Geoffrey Colvin demonstrate that unsuccessful CEOs put strategy before people. Successful CEOs shine—not in the arena of planning or finances—but in the area of emotional intelligence. They show integrity, people acumen, assertiveness, effective communication, and trust-building behavior.

In the late 1990s the CEO of a major corporation, a man who had been groomed for this position for a number of years, was fired after being at the helm for a short time. Why? He was an excellent accountant, a first-rate strategist. However, he lacked people skills. His arrogance alienated workers, his method of dismissing a top-ranking executive was an embarrassment to the board, and his strategies—particularly for a company that sees itself as people-friendly—appeared ruthless and greedy.

Writing in *Fast Company* (June 1999), Paul Weiand, CEO of a leadership development program in Pennsylvania, emphasizes that strong leadership begins with self-awareness: knowing who you are and what your values are. He accentuates the importance of communication, authenticity, and the capacity for non-defensive listening; nothing to do with strategic planning or budgetary knowledge—but everything to do with emotional intelligence. Weiand's emphasis on self-awareness is echoed by Peter Drucker, the seminal thinker on management, who, in his book *Management Challenges for the 21st Century*, stresses that self-awareness and the capacity to build mutually satisfying relationships provide the backbone of strong management.

An article in the business section of *The Globe and Mail*, a leading Canadian national newspaper, stated that any new CEO "has 90 days to make a mark on the company." A number of executives and industry analysts were quoted in support of this notion. According to them, an incoming CEO, having first obtained boardroom backing, should hit the road and hold face-to-face, town-hall-style meetings; explain his or her vision and seek the advice of employees at every level; state the company's new goals and find out what stands in the way of their implementation; get a three-ring binder and take lots of notes; deliver bad news quickly and in person, thus putting a cap on lingering doubts; ensure needed political support by cultivating contacts with the appropriate level of government; and be available to and open with the media.

As you can see, not one of these activities involves the evaluation of assets and liabilities, the development of strategic planning exercises, the analysis of financial statements, or an all-consuming focus on the bottom line. Rather, each one depends on—indeed, constitutes—emotional intelligence: listening to and understanding people's concerns, fostering meaningful dialogue, building trust, and establishing personal relationships with all the parties involved.

Another illustration of emotional intelligence's real-world applicability comes from an interview we conducted with a senior police officer in a major American city. We wanted to talk about the impending retirement of the chief, who'd succeeded in uniting a fragmented and demoralized force. We asked how he'd gone about the task, expecting to hear the usual testimony as to how bright he was, how he'd increased his budget allocation, how he exemplified the nuts and bolts of police procedure as we dimly understood it. Rather, we learned that, although the departing chief wasn't the smartest man around, he commanded intense loyalty from everyone, because he talked straight to everyone regardless of rank. He made it clear that he expected and welcomed straight talk in return. He was genuinely interested in his staff, worked well under internal, political, and personal pressure, and was universally respected and admired. We took lots of notes, but they boiled down to the fact that the chief's success in the demanding world of law enforcement was explicitly connected to his emotional intelligence, even though he might not have recognized the term or admitted the connection.

Finally, here's a real-life example that is not the result of research—it's from your own world. Take a moment to think about the worst mentor or boss you have ever worked for—the person who brought dread into your heart at the thought of returning to work every Monday morning. The person who made you—or almost made you—quit your job. Jot down half a dozen characteristics that made this person so unbearable to work with.

Now, think of the best boss or mentor you ever had—someone whom you learned from, and who was a pleasure to work alongside. On the same piece of paper, write down a list of six or seven attributes of that person.

Were the ogre's qualities related to his inability to develop or fulfill the mission of that company, strategize successfully, understand and make use of financial information, be familiar with policies, procedures, and legal regulations? Was that boss/mentor whom you would "take a bullet for" held in such esteem by you because he did know how to carry out a SWOT analysis, prioritize objectives, outguess the stock market, or create and follow policies and procedures so magnificently? We bet not. We bet that most—if not all—of the qualities of the boss/mentor you dreaded did not reflect limitations in his IQ, but rather shortcomings in his EQ. As for the boss/mentor you might "take a bullet for," chances are your commitment to him was also not on the basis of his IQ, but on his EQ. For proof, just read down both lists—the limitations and strengths of the qualities you wrote function as your own research that emphasizes how EQ can outshine IQ in the workplace and beyond.

No matter what corner of the world you call your own, it's in your own best interests to open your mind to new possibilities and new ways to change. Those changes will not come easily; there's no such thing as a quick fix. Old habits, old modes of behavior are like old clothes—comfortable, broken-in, reassuring, and predictable. Building unfamiliar skills requires awareness, dedication, and practice on your part. As well, any change involves an element of risk—there's no guarantee of success. Nor, even when you achieve a higher level of emotional intelligence, will you deal with each and every situation in the best possible way. But you will possess a new level of knowledge that will enable you to chart new ways to behave in response to the conditions you encounter. You won't always perform at the top of your game, but you'll be better prepared, better trained. Based on our knowledge and experience, we believe that by reading and putting into practice the materials in this book, you can and will gain new insights into yourself and others which will enable you to change for the better and achieve greater success in your life.

Chapter 2

The Airport and the ABCDEs

Before we begin to examine and work with the 16 scales of emotional intelligence as defined by the EQ-i 2.0, let's look at a couple of examples that show EQ in action.

Flight Canceled

The scene is a typical big-city airport. More than 100 passengers are awaiting their call to board Flight 107, which is already running half an hour behind schedule. Finally, the ticket agent—let's call her Sally—announces the flight has been canceled due to mechanical difficulties. She thanks the passengers for their patience and asks them to step forward to discuss alternative arrangements. Collective anger sweeps the line of frustrated travelers, whose best-laid plans have suddenly been thrown into disarray.

John's heart sinks. He'd been planning an evening's worth of hard work upon reaching his destination. He has to prepare for an important presentation the following morning, and Flight 107 is the last direct connection of the day. This is disaster in capital letters.

The man immediately in front of him in line—let's call him Sam—is in a rage. When he reaches the ticket counter, he appears to be out of control, cursing loudly and threatening legal action against the airline. He is at pains to let everyone within earshot know how important he is. "Do you know who I am?" he cries. "I'm the director of sales for Diversified Widgets International!" (Because this is a true story, we've disguised the true name of the well-known Fortune 500 company.) "I've got to close a deal that's been in the works for six months. You have no idea how much it'll cost me to miss this flight. And you're going to pay for it! You and your damn fool airline! I'll never fly with you again! You're incompetent and I'm going to report you, and I'll see that you're demoted if it's the last thing I do!" With that, he turns on his heel and stalks away, muttering further imprecations over his shoulder.

The only person who can possibly help Sam reach his destination is Sally, the long-suffering ticket agent whom he proceeds to insult, intimidate, and alienate. But in Sam's mind, Sally is merely a convenient target, a handy outlet for his ungovernable anger. He'd been on the boil ever since the flight was first posted as departing late, dreaming up all sorts of worst-case scenarios. When one materialized, he let loose.

Sam is unaccustomed to paying attention to his internal state. He has absolutely no idea how angry he is, even though the people around him can see that he's ready to explode. He's incapable of recognizing his feelings, let alone controlling them. His anger makes it impossible for him to think clearly or to act in his own best interests. Instead, he has alienated Sally, the only person who can help him make his flight.

Is this an isolated incident? The chances are overwhelming that Sam habitually lashes out at everyone in much this same way, placing in jeopardy both his career and personal life.

How could this encounter have been handled differently? John's position is no less difficult than Sam's. He's traveling for the not entirely welcome purpose of meeting at nine o'clock the next morning with the top managers from his largest account. They want him to justify the cost of his services, because they've received a lower competing bid. If he's not on time—which by the looks of things he won't be—they may interpret his absence as a sign that he no longer values their business. If he loses their business, his annual bonus and perhaps his job will soon be under scrutiny. John had planned on making the final changes to his presentation software in the privacy of his hotel room that evening. Now he has no hotel at all, and tomorrow's early flight won't get him there in time. This scenario could easily be a recipe for panic.

But John knows he must somehow keep his cool. Even as the displeasure and agitation of his fellow travelers grows, and Sam is busy yelling at Sally the ticket agent, John begins to reflect on other, equally dire situations he has experienced. He'd come out of those in one piece, and he takes comfort in that fact, even though he can't see how this one can be salvaged. Simultaneously, though, he also begins to react instinctively to Sam's ongoing rant. "I can't believe that guy," he says to himself. "He's dumping on the only person who can save him. I can understand his being angry. We're all angry. But that's not the way to get what he wants, and it's not going to get me what I need."

John spends a minute or so analyzing his predicament, always aware of how he's feeling. He tells himself to remain calm. There has to be a solution, if only he keeps his head. He can't quite stem his anxiety, but he pays attention to and understands the depressing and uncomfortable thoughts that creep in from the edges of his consciousness.

When he reaches the ticket counter, he's prepared. "It must be hard for you to have to deal with people like that," he says to Sally.

"You have no idea," she replies—but her half-smile shows that she thinks he just might.

John smiles back. "The airline's got problems and people think it's your fault? It doesn't make sense to blame you. Really, I feel bad for what you have to put up with."

By this time, Sally is regaining both a wider smile and her confidence. "It comes with the job," she says. "Now, how can I help you?"

John briefly explains his plight, and manages to convey how appreciative he'd be if there were anything she could do. He says he'd be willing to take a camel if it could get him to his presentation on time.

Sally manages a laugh, and turns to her keyboard. After what seems like an eternity, she comes up with a route which will take John 1,000 miles out of his way—but that, with a change of plane, will get him to his hotel room by midnight. He thanks her profusely and adds that he'll be writing a letter of commendation to the airline. After all, he stresses, people love to complain when things go wrong, but seldom take the time to acknowledge when someone helps them out.

The result? John gets to his destination, a little bit jet-lagged but more or less prepared, because he puts his time aboard the alternative flights to good use. Sam, however, is hung out to dry, forced to scramble in order to find a hotel near the airport, where he broods on the fact that he won't make his appointment and shouts at the person who delivers his room service order.

Why do we like to tell this story? Because the two men's experiences cover almost every component of emotional intelligence, from self-awareness and empathy to impulse control and optimism. Note that their respective success and failure had virtually nothing to do with IQ or rank or position. John's adventures had a happy ending in large part because he made good use of his people skills, whereas Sam failed because he had no people skills to speak of. Bear this scenario in mind—we will return to it from time to time as we work our way through the following chapters.

The ABCDEs

Next, let's take a look at one of the fundamental frameworks that underpin many of the vignettes and exercises we'll encounter throughout this book. It's known as ABCDE—a system for altering your perceptions, attitudes, and behavior that was pioneered by the late Dr. Albert Ellis, internationally recognized as the father of Rational Emotive Behavior Theory and Therapy. Ellis's great contribution to 20th-century psychology was his insistence that you can modify and change your feelings by means of logical and deductive reasoning, instead of allowing your feelings to get the better of you.

To illustrate how it works, let's look at another scenario, this one involving young love.

Bobby and Brenda had been dating ever since her family moved into the neighborhood a year or so earlier. Three months ago, however, Brenda left to attend college in another state. They'd stayed in touch by phone and e-mail, but had enjoyed only one brief visit, when she'd flown back for her sister's birthday. So Bobby was eagerly awaiting her return for Christmas. Imagine his surprise when he looked out the window on December 20 and saw her car parked in the driveway of her house. "Gee, she's home already," he thought. "I'm surprised she didn't stop by." He sat and waited for the phone to ring, but to no avail.

Later that evening, at the dinner table, Bobby's father couldn't help but notice his unaccustomed silence.

"You seem a bit preoccupied," he said. "It's like you're not even here."

"I'm kind of upset," Bobby sighed. "Brenda's been home for hours and she hasn't called. I'm really worried that she's lost interest in me. She's probably found herself another guy—someone at the college. I don't feel all that much like eating. I'm gonna go to my room." With those words, he stood up and slouched off.

How can we understand Bobby's sudden downward spiral? At first glance the answer seems obvious: Bobby was upset simply because Brenda didn't call him. Ellis would label Brenda's failure to call the activating event (A) and Bobby's reaction the consequence (C). In this scenario the consequence was twofold: Bobby felt demoralized, sad, and pessimistic, and withdrew by rising from the table and seeking refuge in his room. A—Brenda's not calling—appears to lead directly to C.

However, this reading of what transpired leaves out a crucial, often overlooked, intermediate step: beliefs (B)—in this case, Bobby's beliefs, triggered by the sight of Brenda's parked car (A). These morose and unsubstantiated beliefs, or self-talk, that filled Bobby's mind were what actually caused his depression and withdrawal (C).

The critical lesson is that if A leads to B and B to C, Bobby can change the consequences by identifying and defusing his self-defeating beliefs and replacing them with different, more adaptive and realistic beliefs.

And what works for Bobby can work for you.

Before we explain the ABCDE chart, which will help you identify and defuse your beliefs, we need to define what we mean by beliefs. Beliefs are shorthand for the silent self-talk we engage in throughout the day. Our internal dialogue is ongoing and continuous, but we are usually unaware of it. It is the "boy, it's cold outside" we mutter inside our heads when we step out into a chilly fall day; the "I hope the light stays green" that runs through our mind as we approach a traffic light; the "damn, I hate when that happens" we murmur internally when we try to fit the wrong key into a lock.

Some of your undermining self-talk may be caused by "dated tapes": the automatic replay of frequent and harsh statements made to you when you were a child. Often these take the form of "Can't you do anything right?" or "You'll never get ahead." Identifying these dated tapes can help defuse their power.

Central to the completion of the ABCDE chart is the ability to tune in to this inner dialogue, this belief system that is responsible for our feelings and behavior. With this in mind, follow the easily learned, research-backed steps detailed next. Through them you can bolster your emotional intelligence by changing the beliefs that undermine it and supplanting them with beliefs that enhance it. The exercises in Chapters 3 through 17 will often refer you back to this chapter. For these exercises to have the most impact, you should know how to create and complete the ABCDE chart. Buy an ordinary spiral-bound notebook and complete the steps on the following pages.

We recognize that some people are turned off by written exercises—it may remind them too much of all the burdensome and boring homework they had to do in high school or college. When asked to attend to their "silent talk"—their B when facing this A of exercises—often they report having such silent talk as: "I hate writing things down and making charts . . . this is too much like homework . . . it's too hard . . . I am going to fail . . . you'll just prove that I can't change . . . I can never change."

If you experience some of these beliefs, the following ABCDE chart and exercises will show you how you can change these self-sabotaging thoughts.

If you look at other areas of your life, you will probably find that you take to similar exercises without experiencing them as "work" or "too boring" or "too hard," or "proof of how much of a failure I am." If one of your hobbies is golf, skiing, quilting, cooking, or wine tasting, you are probably more proficient now than you were when you started.

Why? Because you worked at it, took lessons, learned from videos, books, seminars, or professional teachers. What you are embarking on with this book is the same: step-by-step exercises which will facilitate your increasing awareness of how to strengthen those skills that enhance your emotional intelligence and amplify your abilities to be more successful in your professional and personal life.

So, purchase the notebook and get going.

1. Draw the five columns, as shown in Table 2-1 below.

Table 2-1

A	B	C	D	E

2. Think of an upsetting situation you experienced over the past week. In the C (consequence) column, write down what your unpleasant feelings were and what behaviors accompanied them. Bobby's responses are illustrated in Table 2-2.

Table 2-2

A	B	C	D	E
		I feel sad, worried, upset, pessimistic. I have become withdrawn.		

3. Write down the incident—the activating event—that seemed to trigger this upsetting situation in column A, as Bobby has done in Table 2-3.

Table 2-3

A	B	C	D	E
Seeing Brenda's car in the driveway; realizing she was home but hadn't called.		I feel sad, worried, upset, pessimistic. I have become withdrawn.		

4. The key aspect of the ABCDE approach is to now capture your Bs: that almost imperceptible, easily overlooked self-talk triggered by the activating event. See if you can pin down what went on in your mind right after the activating event. Bobby homed in on his self-talk and discovered the beliefs in column B of Table 2-4 on the next page.

Table 2-4

A	B	C	D	E
Seeing Brenda's car in the driveway; realizing she was home but hadn't called.	Brenda should have called! She's probably lost interest in me. I bet she found someone else. I knew this would happen. Nothing ever works out for me. I'll never find anyone like her again. I can't stand this feeling.	I feel sad, worried, upset, pessimistic. I have become withdrawn.		

5. Your next task is to actively debate, dispute, and discard (D) these maladaptive, self-defeating beliefs that give rise to your Cs. Submit every element of your internal monologue to rigorous examination by asking yourself the following key questions and writing down your answers in column D, as Bobby did (see Table 2-5).

   - *Where's the proof?* List the objective, verifiable evidence that supports each belief, or the lack thereof. Bobby had no objective proof that Brenda had lost interest in him. Had they been fighting recently? No. Had she been calling him less frequently? No. When she did call, had she seemed less loving? No.

   - *Are there alternative, more logical explanations to explain the activating event?* Bobby wrote down every conceivable alternative explanation for why Brenda might not have called him: she was tired after the long drive and fell asleep; she and her parents had gone out to visit her sister; she had just arrived home moments before and was busy talking to her folks; her parents had demanded that she spend some time with them; she still had the flu she had mentioned to him a few days before; she wanted to unpack and freshen up before coming over to see him.

   - *If someone asked me for advice about this scenario, what might I say that could help alter his/her perspective?* For Bobby, it was helpful to imagine how he might respond if his good friend Jake came to him after seeing his girlfriend Kathy's car in her driveway, and voiced concern that she no longer loved him and had probably found another boyfriend. Bobby found himself thinking: "Hold on, Jake, you and Kathy have been going together for a long time. You have a good relationship and she's very up front about any concerns she has. I think you are overreacting. There's no evidence at all, from what you've told me, that she no longer wants to be with you. And, Jake, I think you're making things worse for yourself just sitting around fretting. Why don't you call her; maybe you'll find out she's not home or she's asleep or she was just about to call you. Do something! Don't just sit there."

   - *Have I ever been in a similar situation before, held a similar belief, only to find out that it was wrong?* Bobby remembered that he often "catastrophizes" in the early stages of relationships with a new girlfriend. When Carmine—the girl he had dated two years ago—was 15 or 20 minutes late meeting him, he always overreacted. And it

Table 2-5

A	B	C	D	E
Seeing Brenda's car in the drive way; realizing she was home but hadn't called.	Brenda should have called! She's probably lost interest in me. I bet she found someone else. I knew this would happen. Nothing ever works out for me. I'll never find anyone like her again. I can't stand this feeling.	I feel sad, worried, upset, pessimistic. I have become withdrawn.	We haven't been arguing more frequently. She hasn't been calling me less frequently. She hasn't been any less loving. She was tired after her trip and fell asleep. She went to visit her sister. Her parents are monopolizing her time. She still has the flu. She's unpacking, freshening up before coming over.	

(continued)

Table 2-5 *(continued)*

A	B	C	D	E
			I'm overreacting; we have a good relationship. She's up-front about concerns. I should call her! I need to stop being so insecure. Remember Carmine? I tend to catastrophize. She hasn't lost interest; she would tell me. I need to work on my lack of confidence.	

never turned out that she had lost interest in him. It was just another example of her lack of attention to detail. In fact, it was he who ultimately broke up with her.

- *If so, did I learn anything from that outcome, and can I apply that knowledge to this situation?* Bobby realized, "I tend to think the worst when it comes to new girlfriends. I imagine the worst possible outcome—they've lost interest and are seeing someone else. That belief turns out to be a reflection of my own lack of confidence."

6. Finally, in column E, write down the effects of filling in column D—how debating, disputing, and discarding have shifted your understanding and beliefs about the activating event and, consequently, your feelings and behaviors.

The power of the ABCDE approach is that defusing illogical, maladaptive beliefs allows more rational and adaptive beliefs to emerge, and shifts your Cs to more effective, adaptive feelings and behaviors.

Changing Hot Feelings to Cool Feelings

Another method of addressing your self-defeating belief system is by identifying and moving away from "hot" feelings to "cool" feelings. Hot feelings have a spiraling effect on mood and thoughts, while cool feelings tend to have a less intense effect. Although cool feelings may still be unpleasant to some degree, they are less incapacitating.

Cool feelings are responses to adverse situations such as job loss or trouble in a marriage that are less harmful and far healthier than hot feelings, and far easier to deal with. Table 2-6 demonstrates the differences between hot, maladaptive feelings and their cool, adaptive counterparts.

Only by replacing unhealthy emotions with less volatile substitutes can we manage our feelings better and address our real problems in the outside world. Just as, in our scenario, Bobby has no hope of turning around his state of mind until he recognizes and comes to terms with his depressed mood and irritable behavior.

The Major Musts and the Absolute Shoulds

Many factors conspire to produce unwarranted "hot feelings," but the prime offenders are Major Musts and Absolute Shoulds. Each can be broken down

Table 2-6

Hot feelings	Cool feelings
Rage, fury, and anger	Annoyance and irritation
Despondency, despair, depression, and pessimism	Sadness
Severe guilt, intense remorse	Regret
Self-worthlessness, self-hate	Self-disappointment
Severe hurt	Mild bruising
Anxiety, fear, and panic	Concern

into what we demand of ourselves and others, and what we expect of the world at large.

Here are Major Musts in action:

I must _____ (in order for me to feel okay).

You (he/she/they) must _____ (in order for me to feel okay).

The world and my living conditions must _____ (in order for me to feel okay).

. . . and the Absolute Shoulds:

I absolutely should _____ (in order for me to feel okay).

You (he/she/they) absolutely should _____ (in order for me to feel okay).

The world and my living conditions absolutely should _____ (in order for me to feel okay).

These demands make no sense. There's no law stating that any of us must behave in certain ways or attain certain goals. Nor must others behave in accordance with our wishes. As for the world at large, it's notoriously unfair. These sweeping and unrealistic expectations, when they aren't fulfilled, lead straight to a full plate of red-hot feelings.

In our scenario, the idea that Brenda must or should call Bobby the second she comes home is irrational. There may be all sorts of valid reasons why she doesn't call, but, at any rate, why must she call? Bobby would certainly prefer that she did so, but Brenda might well prefer that he call her to see whether she's arrived.

If Bobby were able to replace his musts and shoulds with far more appropriate "prefers," which give everybody room for negotiation and compromise, he'd be well on the way to cooler, more sensible feelings.

As you might imagine, all these musts and shoulds lead inescapably to even more irrational and erroneous conclusions. These conclusions are what we call "hot links" to hot emotions, because they inevitably make matters worse. Fortunately, they too can be cooled off by means of very simple techniques. The five main conclusions—or "thinking errors"—and their preferred substitutes are as follows:

"This is awful." Instead of wallowing in despair and telling yourself "This is 100 percent, irredeemably awful," try using moderating or mitigating terms that will serve to tone down the sense of catastrophe. Whatever's bugging you may be inconvenient, a real hassle, a pain in the neck, or anything else you choose to call it. It probably isn't the end of the world.

"I can't stand it." Instead of falling into this trap, remind yourself that you have in fact stood—and will continue to stand—all manner of difficult situations. They're a part of life, and life has a habit of going on.

Condemnation and damnation. Heaping ashes on your own head or consigning other people to horrible fates can only lead to anger and fury. That anger points two ways, and is equally wounding. Blaming yourself for everything that goes wrong or viewing what has happened as well-merited punishment for your sins and shortcomings, real or imagined, is not going to make your situation any better. As for blaming others, it may enlarge your vocabulary, but it does little good to get you out of any hole you have dug for yourself. Remind yourself that blame is not constructive; look for ways to resolve the problem instead.

"I'm worthless." If this were true, there'd be no point in you or anybody else doing anything to aid a lost cause. We all carry enough of a load at the best of times, without saying things like "I'm no good—a complete and utter screw-up. That's why I always fail. I don't deserve good things." Thoughts and expressions of self-worthlessness lead straight to depression and despair. Remind yourself that, even if you have made a mistake or an error in judgment, you have more good qualities than bad,

you often do things right, you can learn from your mistakes, and you are still a good person who deserves good things.

Always and never. Statements along the lines of "Everyone always dumps on me; they never give me a hand" or "I [or things in general] will never get better, never change," are plainly self-defeating and invite feelings of hopelessness and helplessness. Put your feelings into perspective: there is always hope for change, and while some people may sometimes dump on you, many people do, in fact, give you a hand.

Tune in to What Your Body Is Telling You

A skeptic might say: why not wallow in the worst and get it over with, perhaps achieving some sort of catharsis? Not so long ago, this was the popular wisdom in certain circles. Letting it all hang out was considered preferable to suppressing strong emotions; venting one's anger or despair was deemed healthier than bottling it up.

There's a degree of truth in that point of view, but psychological truths often come with more subtle shadings than popular catch-phrases would have us believe. More recent research indicates that, paradoxically, "venting" magnifies angry feelings, rather than relieving them.

The time to detect and weed out your irrational beliefs is when your emotions are running hot—when you're upset, anxious, irate, defensive, depressed, or stressed out. Because feelings and bodily responses are so closely linked that when you are uncertain as to what you are feeling—other than it *is* unpleasant—you can begin to obtain a more accurate fix on that feeling by becoming aware of how your body is behaving. Several examples appear in Table 2-7.

Focusing on our bodies' manifestations of these and many other feelings allows us to classify those feelings as belonging to one of the four basic emotional families: Anxiety, Anger, Depression, or Contentment. Contentment presents no problem. As for the rest, identifying and labeling them afford us a degree of control. We can begin to talk ourselves out of them, detecting and disputing the irrational beliefs that set them in motion and achieving new, more desirable effects.

Table 2-7

Feelings	Physical signs
Anger	Hands-on-hips posture, pounding heart, sweating, and rapid breathing
Rage	Clenched fists
Fury	Cold-focused stare, loud and rapid speech
Depression	Fatigue
Despair	Weighed-down posture
Despondency	Slouching, staring into space, a slow, hesitant voice, frequent sighing
Anxiety	Restlessness, pounding heart, rapid breathing
Fear	Tenseness
Panic	Aching muscles and headaches, tension in neck and shoulders

A Happy Ending

Filling in the chart helped Bobby master the art of ABCDE instead of succumbing to gloom, as demonstrated by his new, improved self-talk: "Wow, I'm feeling down. And no wonder! Look at what I've been saying to myself. This is no way to behave. Who says that Brenda has to do anything, let alone phone me the minute she gets back? Okay, she didn't phone. There are all sorts of logical explanations. What isn't logical is my dreaming up some guy she's thrown me over for. That's nonsense—there's no evidence of that at all. She's always been open and up front with me. And how do I thank her? By going off on this weird tangent and sitting in my room. I'm going to do something about it. In fact, I'm going to call her now and welcome her home."

As you can see, Bobby's ability to identify and overcome his irrational beliefs enabled him to move from hot to cool emotions, discover alternative and more plausible reasons for Brenda's actions, admit to and confront his feelings of rejection, conquer them, and behave in a logical and positive manner. And even if, despite his efforts, the events should prove to be a worst-case scenario—that is, if Brenda actually wants to dump him, and is waiting to tell him so—he'll still be better prepared to deal with that reality in a truthful and honest way.

(By the way, when Bobby called Brenda, he found out that, tired from the long drive home, she was indeed asleep. He left a message for her to call him when she got up. Two hours later, the doorbell rang, and Brenda slid into his arms and whispered how much she had missed him.)

PART II | The Self-Perception Realm

This realm of emotional intelligence concerns what we generally refer to as the "inner self."[1] It determines how in touch with your feelings you are, how good you feel about yourself and about what you're doing in life. Success in this area means that you are aware of your feelings, feel strong, and have confidence in pursuing your life goals.

Chapter 3

Emotional Self-Awareness

"He who knows the universe and does not know himself knows nothing."

—JEAN DE LA FONTAINE, 1679

DEFINITION:
Emotional self-awareness is the ability to recognize your feelings, differentiate between them, know why you are feeling these feelings, and recognize the impact your feelings have on others around you.[2]

Consider Sam, the enraged passenger on Flight 107. He was completely unaware of how enraged he was and particularly oblivious to the impact that rage and its accompanying behavior were having on the ticket agent. Certainly, he was unaware how his feelings and behavior were undermining the success of his getting on the next flight.

Consider another example: Art returned home one evening after learning that his bonus—on which he had been counting—had not come through. He stomped into the family room and blasted his 16-year-old daughter, Sandra:

"Stop watching TV! That's all you seem to do. If you put in as much time studying as you do watching TV, your marks would be a hell of a lot better!"

"Gee, Dad," Sandra responded, startled, "that's not fair. I don't watch that much—"

"Don't tell me I'm not fair," roared her father. "TV is a privilege, not a right. Now get out of here, wash up, and get ready for dinner."

Art's wife, Martha, drawn to the family room by the commotion, questioned: "What's all the noise about?"

"The kid does nothing but watch TV," Art fumed.

"Whoa, Art, why are you so angry?" Martha exclaimed.

Art exploded: "I am not angry, I'm simply irritated by her laziness—and don't contradict me in front of her!"

"Art, I'm not contradicting you, I'm just trying to understand why you're so upset."

"I said don't criticize me in front of the children. Can't we have a peaceful dinner?"

As a result of this exchange, Sandra stopped watching the television and went upstairs, but would not come down for dinner. Art, fuming, and Martha, hurt and bewildered, ate in silence.

Was TV the culprit? No. Was Sandra watching way too much television? Maybe, but that's not the issue either. Most importantly, Art was unaware of the impact that the disappointment of not getting his bonus had on him. He did not have the capacity to take his emotional temperature and recognize the feelings of anger, bitterness, and disappointment that swirled within him. Nor was he aware of how these feelings had pushed him to take out his anger and bitterness inappropriately on Sandra and Martha.

How might Art have responded if he had had a stronger ability to be self-aware? First, he would have recognized his internal turmoil, perhaps by noticing the tension in his neck, the way he uncharacteristically swore to himself about the traffic on the drive home or the force with which he slammed his car door. By asking himself what had occurred that day that could have upset him, he would also have been conscious of how his anger related to the disappointing precipitant of not receiving his bonus. He would have recognized that these feelings of anger and bitterness put him at risk for behaving with uncharacteristic anger toward his family.

As a result of his self-awareness, Art might have entered his home and stated, "Guys, I'm upset and angry. Sandra, turn the TV off, it's too noisy for the state I'm in and, boy, am I in a bad mood. But it has nothing to do with you guys. I'm upset because of something at work. I think it will take me an hour or so to calm down. So forgive me if I sound angry; I probably need a bit of space, no demands, and a lot of tender loving care."

In this scenario, Art knows that he feels angry, recognizes why he is in this state, and is aware that he is at risk of behaving angrily toward his family. He communicates this to them immediately, and offers suggestions about what they can do to help him calm down. This kind of communication, blended with his real attempts not to behave too irritably, will allow his family to support him in his attempts to settle down.

Know Thyself

Emotional self-awareness is the foundation on which most of the other elements of emotional intelligence are built, the necessary first step toward exploring and coming to understand yourself, and toward change. Obviously, what you don't recognize, you can't manage. If you aren't aware of what you're doing, why you're doing it, and the way it's affecting others, you can't change. If, in your own blinkered view, there's nothing wrong, then there's no need or reason to change. That's why self-awareness is key and basic. Mastering this one overarching skill will empower you to work toward improvement in all of emotional intelligence's other areas. Without it, though you might sincerely try to address problems one by one, you'd end up going round in circles. You'd get no feedback; you'd be unable to monitor your progress, and your chances of achieving your goals would be severely impeded.

Individuals with a strong sense of self-awareness recognize when they feel out of sorts, irritable, sad, or seductive, and perceive how these feelings alter their behavior in a way that may alienate others. Usually, they can also figure out what incident precipitated their feelings. The capacity to know what they are feeling and how they are behaving allows them a degree of control over their potentially alienating behavior.

The Boss as Despot

What happens when self-awareness is lacking? Here's an example of how things go off the rails with a vengeance.

Everyone in the office seemed to realize what was going on except the one person who most needed to know—the boss himself. What his subordinates had come to expect, and what they hated the most about him, was the way he played the bully. His normal speaking voice was a dull roar. He'd order his staff around, assuming that it was his role and his right to do so. On the rare occasions when someone dared to ask what had made him so upset, his stock response was a knee-jerk denial: "What the hell do you mean? I'm not angry." This high-decibel self-defense seemed quite absurd to any dispassionate observer, but it was offered with complete sincerity by the boss, who quite literally didn't recognize how he was feeling or realize how he was behaving.

This scenario is extreme, but scarcely unique. Anger is perhaps the prime offender in the emotional spectrum. It skews our judgment, making us oblivious to our surroundings and to ourselves. Its extreme physiological manifestations make it even harder for us to escape its grip long enough to register what's happening, let alone correct our behavior. Angry people are quite often unaware that they're angry. They're dimly aware that something's happening, but they don't know what it is. Obviously their actions are having an effect on them and on those around them, but they can't grasp the extent of the negative impact.

This also holds true—to varying degrees—with respect to any other emotion or behavior. We're often the last to see ourselves or our moods with any degree of clarity. And yet being aware of any emotion is the first step toward controlling it.

Out-of-control emotions always work against us. If you're angry and sarcastic and belittling, and don't even know it, two things are bound to follow. First—physiologically speaking—you are at risk of driving up your blood pressure or developing an ulcer. Second, you'll turn people off without understanding why. They'll flee from you, or at the very least view you in a highly negative light. No matter how strong your other abilities—the knowledge you possess or the skills you've acquired—you won't get a chance to demonstrate them. Key relationships will sour before they can be forged. You'll weaken your capacity for empathy and impair your ability to deal sensitively and effectively with others in all sorts of situations.

Once upon a time in the workplace, the boss-as-despot model was accepted, even desired. Generations of managers have yelled their way up the ladder; their tactics were considered essential to a company's profits. Such bosses had no compunctions about riding their staff hard in order to get the job done. Unfortunately, those whose style centers on pushing people around succeed primarily in pushing people—including the cream of the corporation—out the door.

Thirty years ago, that approach may have worked well enough. The economy was more traditional; employees tended to hang on to what they had, remaining loyal to a firm through thick and thin. Today, the majority of talented individuals simply won't put up with it. They know that it constitutes an unhealthy and stressful work environment. They also know that if they're good at what they do, they can find a more congenial place to exercise their skills, even if it means taking a salary cut. Shareholders also have come to realize that in the long term a bully boss does little to enhance the value of a company's stock. The cost of recruiting and training an endless cycle of replacement employees eventually takes its toll on the bottom line. Even more important, the poor morale engendered by a tyrant at the top leads to dwindling productivity. Truly competent leaders know better than to scream or muscle their way to success.

In fact, one of us (Steven) was exposed to a more recent example. While carrying out a leadership exercise with a group, which included a number of former employees of Enron, I received a bit of a surprise. One of the participants, a senior executive who was a survivor of the Enron demise, looked at the charts we created where participants described the characteristics of the best boss and worst boss they ever worked for. He said it was interesting how many of those characteristics were valued by the senior team at Enron.

Thinking he was referring to the "good boss charts," I asked him which ones? He walked over to the "bad boss charts" and selected the characteristics below. These are the characteristics the senior team at Enron valued in a leader during the two years before it imploded:

Explosive

High ego

Always being right

Results driven

Ability to minimize ethical issues

Rigidity

No emotional control

Having serious attitude

It's clear to see how these characteristics can be viewed as indicative of leadership. They help establish one's dominance in the group. By being explosive—or scary as some people describe it—you create an environment of fear. When people are fearful, most of them, especially the weaker ones, will not challenge you. So you are basically using negative emotions to enhance and maintain a dominant leadership role.

Many of the characteristics cited above help define leadership in a traditional, patriarchal way. By focusing on one's ego, always demanding to be right, and being rigid—like many of yesterday's leaders, who preferred to go down with the ship rather than change course—the trappings of the leader become more important than the success of the group (or company) as a whole.

Today's leaders, that is in successful organizations we've looked at, operate in the best interest of the team, the organization, and society as a whole. We're finding emotional skills, such as emotional self-awareness and social responsibility, better measures of leader success than any specific technical or cognitive intelligence skill. While leaders need to have a certain level of cognitive intelligence and critical thinking (knowing when to be strategic and when to be tactical) they also need emotional intelligence in order to be successful today.

Addressing the "Boss as Despot"

Is there anything an employee can do when faced with a boss as despot? Yes, there are a number of EQ-based steps that can increase the chance of successfully addressing this issue. First, do a reality check. Ask close associates how *they* view him/her. If the consistent feedback is that he/she is a tyrant, then your view is accurate.

In the rare circumstance that no one else shares your view of him/her—as tyrannical—then it is wise to use your skills of self-awareness and self-reflection to wonder if there is something unique about the relationship that you have developed with him or her that may account for his/her reacting in such a belittling way to you. Is there something about your behavior, attitude, verbal or non-verbal communication that rankles him/her?

To deal with the more common situation where you and your colleagues view the boss as a despot, ask yourself if you can live with this behavior without becoming overly stressed or its interfering with your productivity. If not, consider addressing this issue with him/her.

Ask to speak with him/her privately and specify that you would need 20 to 30 minutes. You do not want to meet and begin to discuss this difficulty only to be interrupted and told that there are only five or 10 minutes allocated for the meeting.

You begin the meeting by communicating the following: that you are very invested in doing your job well; very invested in having he/she benefit from your good work; you are committed to being a successful support to him/her in his/her getting work done; and to that end you believe that he/she would want honest, clear feedback from you that would make his/her job run smoothly and would also help motivate other of his/her direct reports.

Articulating these governing principles will help set the stage for him/her to understand that what you are speaking about is not whining, complaining, or being negative. It is in the service of facilitating him/her and the whole team, including you, to work more effectively and successfully.

Then, you tell him/her of your concerns: "I notice that you are often angry with me in a belittling and sarcastic way. This interferes with our relationship and with my being as successful as I want to be in supporting you, helping you look good, and getting my job done well."

If he/she seems interested in what you are saying, reflects on it, and says that he/she was unaware but will attempt to change that behavior—all is good.

But what about the opposite scenario? What if he/she responds by bellowing, "I'm not angry, I'm never angry! You're just too sensitive!" And then smacks the table with his/her fist to emphasize that point.

At this juncture you use the information that is emerging right then and there in the relationship: "You may not feel angry, but you come across angrily; like right now. Your voice changed; you're yelling; you pounded the table with your fist; and you seemed to have dismissed my comment about your appearing angry without much reflection. Actually, you have sort of gone on the defensive, turned the tables, and pointed out that it's not you who's angry, it's me who's hypersensitive.

"Now, this is difficult for me to talk about, but I am dedicated to making this relationship as good as it can be so I can do my job really well, and, as your direct report, do whatever I can to make your job go smoothly and make you successful. I think we can agree that that's a win-win for both of us. And that's why I'm discussing this with you: I want a win-win for both of us. And I'm assuming that you want that too." Then listen carefully to his/her reply. If he/she becomes more defensive, denies, and dismisses his/her behavior even more forcefully, then this is important information for you to consider. It may mean that he/she is limited in his/her capacity for self-awareness, for acknowledging any shortcomings in his/her behavior, and in his/her flexibility to change.

If this is so, then you might want to consider speaking to some of your colleagues to see if any of them are interested in having a similar discussion with him/her—given the outcome of your discussion. If not, there are only three options open to you: tolerate it, look elsewhere for a job, or consider speaking with his/her superior, not alone but with one or two or your colleagues who share a similar perspective of his/her despotic behavior.

Self-Awareness Gone Missing in Action

Sixty-year-old Rick, the entrepreneurial founder and current CEO of Xecutive Xtreme Sportz, an extreme sports company focusing on high-income middle-aged athletes involved in activities like heli-skiing, mountain climbing, and Ironman competition, had recently hired Luke as the COO.

Wanting to show the importance of "keeping in touch" with front-line sales people, Rick invited Luke to accompany him to one of the Xecutive Xtreme Sportz megastores.

Once inside, an attractive salesperson in her mid-20 s approached them.

"Hi, I'm Brenda," she said with a smile. "May I help you?"

"This store must have a policy of only hiring women who are helpful and beautiful!" Rick responded suggestively, adding, "Don't they, Luke?" Luke nodded half-heartedly, quickly stating, "We're looking for skis that are quite adaptable in extreme skiing conditions, in very powdery snow."

"Great," Brenda said, looking at Luke. "We've got a fabulous selection. What size are you looking for?"

"He needs 185s," Rick interjected, and, gazing momentarily at her breasts, asked, "What size are you?"

At this point, Luke, perplexed and uncomfortable with the lascivious undertones to Rick's comments, attempted to refocus on their task of assessing how this front-line employee deals with potential niche customers who are considering making an expensive purchase.

"Do many folks who come here just window-shop when it comes to these high-end skis? Or do they actually make the purchase?" he asked. "As a salesperson, how can you possibly make a difference in helping individuals commit to buy such a high-end item?"

Before Brenda had an opportunity to reply, Rick turned to Luke and jokingly interjected, "You are one serious dude, Luke!" Luke replied: "I guess." Then he grew silent.

Later, outside of the megastore, Rick joked to Luke that he seemed a little "buttoned-down," adding, "I guess it's just the accountant in you!"

Rick had little capacity for self-awareness. He was oblivious to how inappropriate his flirtatious and suggestive behavior was, especially when directed to a woman young enough to be his daughter. He was also unaware of the embarrassment he caused both Luke and Brenda. At a deeper level, Rick was also oblivious to the competitive feelings he had towards his youthful-looking, 42-year-old, recently hired COO, and his need to bolster his own sense of potency and vitality as he approached the age of retirement through his inappropriate come-ons to Brenda. The problem was not Luke's behavior; it was Rick's.

Become Aware of Others' Reactions to Your Behavior

Another seemingly simple vignette illustrates how a little self-awareness can have significant effects. A colleague reported the following story:

"You know, in my new administrative position, I end up going to a lot of meetings. Sometimes the meetings run back to back. To make a good impression I usually dash from one meeting to another, so I'll arrive only a few minutes late. But when I began to pay attention to the reactions of others to my entrance, I discovered something quite interesting: they seemed uneasy, uncomfortable, even. I recognized that, somehow, by rushing in I was not presenting myself in a good light.

"So I began to take a look at how I entered the room. Because I was rushing, I usually came in out of breath, perspiring and, no doubt, sending a message that I was flustered and disorganized.

"Now I make a conscious effort to slow down to a relaxed but serious gait about 10 paces before I reach the door (which gives me just enough time to catch my breath). I walk in confidently, apologize for being late, and sit down, casually pulling out my notes and maintaining a composed and orga- nized manner. And I have noticed that the others no longer look awkward or uneasy. In fact, they seem to have regained their sense of esteem for me."

This man's self-awareness did not involve a complex understanding of his inner workings, but rather an awareness that, when he rushed, he entered the room in a manner that could be interpreted as disorganized and flustered and that, as a result, others tended to take him less than seriously. By becoming aware of this reaction, he could consciously change his actions. Now, when he walked into the room in a confident manner, the group responded by viewing him as someone of significance. His simple insight led to a small change in behavior that carried notable consequences.

Know Your "Ouch Points"

The goal of emotional self-awareness isn't to analyze our emotions to death, unduly suppress them, or do away with them altogether. We all behave in inappropriate ways some of the time. Nor will we ever be rid of unpleasant feelings; they're entirely natural after disappointment, criticism, or loss. But we must strive to be conscious of what we feel and why we feel the way we do, so that we aren't driven blindly by internal forces or pushed into self-defeating behavior by default, for want of the requisite information.

Being emotionally self-aware also has a preventative benefit. Remember the ABCDE technique described in the previous chapter, and the role played by irrational and debilitating self-talk? If we learn to interpret correctly the events that stimulate this self-talk, we can, with practice, learn to alter what we tell ourselves when we see the activating event coming.

Let's say that you are aware of your "ouch points"—those deep-seated sore spots that others unknowingly prod. If you know you're about to face a job performance evaluation, which is bound to entail at least some degree of criticism, you can brace and prepare yourself by remaining on the lookout for irrational beliefs. Say, for example, that in times past your self-talk has been instinctively defensive, along the lines of "Who does she (the evaluator) think she is? This is absolutely useless. She ought to be dealing with my strengths, not tearing me down." Knowing what blind alleys you've strayed into before, you can work to reprogram your interior monologue. You can also be alert to tangible signals that your anger is rising: body signs such as shoulder tension and a raised voice. Knowledge is power—and self-knowledge is premium power that leads to successful emotional management.

An effective method of dealing with such self-talk is to follow the ABCDE method by utilizing the "Four Ds": disputing, debating, differentiating, and discarding, as detailed in Chapter 2.

Using the "Four Ds" method can shift inaccurate and maladaptive self-talk to a more realistic inner monologue that brings with it a positive attitude and more productive behavior. This is captured in a continuation of the previous vignette. Here, you might respond to your initial reaction of, "Who does she think she is? She ought to be dealing with my strengths, not tearing me down!"—with the following thinking:

"Wait a minute! What's this about 'tearing me down?' Where's the evidence that she wants to tear me down? Is that her style? Are there other explanations? After all, I report to her, so of course she wants to point how I can better myself. If I do better, she looks better. I realize I do have some difficulty hearing negative feedback, but I can learn from her, and use that feedback to my advantage.

"So my response of feeling torn down does not mean that her intent is to tear me down. There is a difference. It is more likely that she wishes to be helpful. I must remember to differentiate my response from the other person's intent, particularly when it comes to negative feedback."

Exercises

Emotional self-awareness is crucial for success, whatever our role. Why? Because if we cannot recognize how we are feeling, if we cannot take our "emotional temperature," we are at risk of behaving in demeaning, angry, belittling, and belligerent ways that will turn others off. Consequently, they will flee from us, avoid us, and view us in a highly negative light. So, regardless of our role—be it as boss, potential partner, or employee—and no matter how strong our other abilities, the knowledge we possess, or the skills we have acquired, we will never have a chance to demonstrate them if others run in the opposite direction when they see us coming.

Self-awareness is a critical foundation of emotional intelligence because what we are unaware of we cannot change, and self-awareness is the first step in modifying our otherwise alienating behaviors. To do so, we must be conscious of what we are feeling and the impact these feelings have on others. Otherwise, we will be unsuccessful in building key relationships. Additionally, without self-awareness, we will fail to notice when we are feeling stress, we will weaken whatever capacity for empathy we may have, and we will be compromised in our ability to offer sensitively delivered verbal communications to others.

Self-Assessment

Note: Use the notebook you used in the previous chapter for the purpose of answering these questions and recording your progress while carrying out the exercises that appear throughout the book.

These exercises are designed to help you survey your "internal landscape," gaining insight into and information about your feelings. You can identify feelings in three ways: directly; by spotting the bodily sensations that accompany them; and by homing in on the thoughts that may illuminate them.

1. On a page in your notebook, write down the first emotion in the list below:

   Anger

   Happiness

   Fear

   Anxiety

   Sadness

   Underneath it, briefly describe a situation or interaction that occurred over the past several days that elicited that feeling. Next, divide the remainder of the page into three vertical columns. In the first column make a list of the circumstances that seemed to trigger that feeling; in the second, list the bodily sensations that accompanied it; and in the third, list your internal dialogue or self-talk associated with it.

2. Repeat this exercise with each of the other feelings on the list, allocating a new page for each feeling.

3. Review the list of feelings and rank the intensity of each on a scale of one to 10. Note which feeling you tend to experience most intensely. That feeling probably indicates your "ouch point"—which, when probed, may interfere with strong interpersonal relationships, clearheaded reality testing, and effective problem solving.

4. For each of the five situations you recorded, was the outcome reasonably good, somewhat neutral, or something you regret and believe or wish you could have handled better? If it was neutral or unsatisfactory, write down ways in which your feeling might have interfered with your behavior and prevented you from achieving a more desirable end result.

5. List some of the emotions that you're generally more aware of than others. For example, do you usually notice the negative side of the equation (when you are angry or sad), or do good times and happy experiences make an equally strong impression?

6. For these emotions, make a list of specific situations that usually set them off.

7. Next, make a list of the people in your life who are most likely to trigger these feelings.

8. There is often a strong relationship between thoughts and feelings, because what we tell ourselves about an event will influence the way we feel about it. To see how this works, write down two or three occasions when you experienced a particularly strong emotion. Then write down the emotions involved, and list the thoughts that triggered them.

9. Now make a list of the bodily sensations that were associated with each of these feelings. Note how closely the feeling, its associated bodily symptom, and the thoughts that set it off correspond to the links between feelings, bodily sensations and thoughts you observed in Self-Assessment, Exercise 1.

Self-Assignments

These techniques will help you hone your capacity to get in touch with feelings as they occur.

1. Over the next week, record the strongest emotion you experience each day. Beside each emotion, write down your accompanying bodily sensations and thoughts. In a final column, write down how you became aware of that feeling. That is, did you recognize the emotion as it occurred, become aware of it through bodily sensations, or become aware of it through thoughts?

2. As you do this, pay attention to shifts in your feelings. When you notice a change, try to zero in on the particular emotion, and record it in your notebook.

3. If you have difficulty keeping track of shifting feelings, try to focus instead on bodily sensations and physical manifestations—clenched fists, a hands-on-hips posture, a whining voice, irregular breathing, or a tightened jaw. Move from your identification of these physical states to the emotions they may represent.

4. Next, be aware of your thoughts, and note whether they're consistent with the emotion that your body language suggests that you're feeling.

5. Read a book or watch television or a movie—but make sure what you read or watch is very dramatic (a suspense or mystery story), very

frightening (good old-fashioned horror), very funny, or very romantic. Be aware of how you feel as the plot carries you along. Notice when you hope or fear something is about to happen—and how your feelings change when that something occurs. When the credits roll, use your notebook to record your feelings, bodily changes, and thoughts. Which were you aware of first? Could you lock on to a feeling directly, or did you have to work your way back to it using thoughts and physical cues?

6. Whenever you have the opportunity, use your notebook to record bodily changes such as perspiring, clenching your fists, talking more slowly than usual, or walking rapidly, and note also how you're thinking and feeling at the time. Note how altering your behavior (unclenching your fists or slowing your pace) can actually shift your feelings from, for example, aggression to calmness and relaxation.

7. If people remark on your appearance, saying that you look angry, upset, or sad, don't dismiss their comments out of hand. From their exterior vantage point, they may have a clearer picture of what's going on in your head, because of the signals you're unconsciously sending. Reflect and consider their remarks. Could they be right? What *are* you feelings? What *is* your behavior signaling?

    If the individual who made this remark is someone whom you know well and feel relatively close to, you might enquire: "What do you notice that signals I might be angry (or upset or sad)?" Reflect and consider their remark. Could they be right? What *are* you feeling? What *is* your behavior signaling?

    If the individual who made this comment is a close friend, you might also ask: "How are you picking up on that? In what way am I signaling it?" Next, reflect and consider on the feedback he/she gives you. It could be useful information for you to use to become more aware of what you're feeling and how that impacts on your behavior and others around you.

8. When you walk by a mirror, catch a glimpse of your facial expression. What might a person who saw that expression assume you were feeling? Does it, in fact, reflect what you're feeling at the time?

* * *

As you become more skilled at these exercises and assignments, try to be as open to the messages from your internal world as you are to events in the external world of family, loved ones, friends, and co-workers. That way, with the aid of your notebook entries, you'll become more and more aware of how external situations are translated into feelings that can be understood and managed for the better.

Also, learn how to use meditation or relaxation exercises (described in Chapter 16)—they will help you to better focus your mind on your internal feelings.

Self-Regard

Chapter 4

"No one can make you feel inferior without your consent."

—ELEANOR ROOSEVELT, *THIS IS MY STORY*, 1937

DEFINITION:

Self-regard is the ability to respect and accept yourself—essentially liking the way you are. To have healthy self-regard is to appreciate your perceived positive aspects and possibilities, as well as to accept your negative aspects and limitations and still feel good about yourself. It's knowing your strengths and weaknesses, and liking yourself, "warts and all." This conceptual component of emotional intelligence is associated with general feelings of security, inner strength, self-assuredness, self-confidence, and self-adequacy. Because individuals with healthy self-regard know their strengths and weaknesses and feel good about themselves, they have no trouble openly and appropriately acknowledging when they have made mistakes, are wrong, or don't know all the answers. Feeling sure of oneself is dependent upon self-respect and self-esteem, which are based on a fairly well-developed sense of identity. People with good self-regard feel fulfilled and satisfied with themselves. At the opposite end of the continuum are feelings of personal inadequacy and inferiority.[1]

For example, Marcie was frequently concerned that she didn't make a good enough impression on others in meetings: "I don't think I was dressed up enough" or "Maybe I talked too much and hogged the conversation." An objective observer would disagree with both, but Marcie set the bar for her everyday social interactions so high that it was impossible for her to live up to her expectations of herself. She was unable to recognize her strengths—that she was both quite presentable in attire and engaging in interactions.

Ishmail, on the other hand, could not forgive himself for any perceived failures: "I got an 85 on the exam. It should have been a 95. What is the matter with me? I lost 10 marks on stupid mistakes. Geez, I'm dumb." Ishmail's self-talk reflects the severe criticism he rains upon himself for not being perfect, and his lack of tolerance of making any mistakes. He cannot accept his "warts."

Self-Regard Is Not Self-Esteem

You want to like and think highly of yourself, but what's really important is to know the pluses *and* minuses involved. Self-esteem, as we know, has become a buzz-phrase in both the classroom and the workplace, not to mention a multi-billion-dollar industry. There are a whole host of books, audio and video recordings, software, and Internet sites devoted solely to increasing it. Some of them, alas, are way off target.

We certainly aren't minimizing the idea of feeling good about yourself. The problem is that an undue emphasis on self-esteem leads to blindly pumping yourself up. Telling yourself how great you are may or may not be a valid part of an approach to repairing a damaged ego, but it's not an end in itself. This is why educators and psychologists have recently begun to reexamine the three-decades-old inculcation of self-esteem in young children that was supposed to serve as a sort of inoculation against aggressive tendencies and other emotional difficulties.

Low self-esteem may indeed be dysfunctional, but artificially high self-esteem may be almost as problematic. The child who learns the "I am special" mantra without simultaneously building necessary life skills is done a tremendous disservice. Ladling out lavish and indiscriminate praise without making sure that you're helping the child actually achieve something that merits approval can lead to devastation when the world fails to continue to pat him or her on the back for success that wasn't earned. Real self-esteem is built up gradually, layer by layer, through taking justifiable pride in real accomplishment, not through a third party's weaving a cocoon of unrealistic positivity.

As for the idea that self-esteem necessarily puts a damper on aggression and other disorders, we'd point out that Dr. Robert Hare, the world's foremost expert on psychopaths, has assessed a large number of serial killers and other violent repeat offenders who languish in prisons around the globe.[2] Many claim to enjoy extremely high self-esteem (an example of what Hare terms their "grandiose" behavior) and picture themselves as absolutely wonderful human beings. Their mothers love them; their girlfriends worship them. Plainly, you can have far too much of a good thing.

Like Yourself, Warts and All

Of course, you don't want to fixate on weaknesses, either, which is every bit as unbalanced as denying shortcomings (out of fear that they somehow cancel out your strengths, no matter how demonstrable those may be). Nor do you want to either blow your strengths out of all proportion or fall into the trap of fearing that they'll never be strong enough. The idea is to like yourself as a total—and sometimes contradictory—package.

Besides, self-esteem is all too often built on shaky ground. Let's think back to the airport scene described in Chapter 2, and Sam's verbal assault on the ticket agent. His opening gambit was to tell her how important he was. What were the odds that this would advance his cause—that is, to get aboard a plane? Did he really believe that she'd be impressed or intimidated by his boasting? The only result of his self-puffery was to turn her off. Among his other problems, Sam has an inflated sense of his own worth. Informing people how rich and famous and powerful you are, especially in the middle of a crisis during which you need to enlist their support, is bound to work against you.

Sam's behavior also gave a very strong message that he cared not a bit about the ticket agent's predicament—a message that certainly alienated the agent and undercut any chance of his making that next flight. It made him appear a fool, and weak in the bargain. In fact, this behavior is often a sign of deep insecurities. Sam quite probably has inflated his own worth in numerous other circumstances. If, on the other hand, he had high self-regard, he'd also have the wit to behave politely and further his ends, as did John, the next passenger in line. In sum, then, self-regard means that you feel comfortable enough about yourself that you don't have to go around attempting (and usually failing) to bowl people over with fancy titles or the other trappings of oversized egos. If you've really got it, you don't need to flaunt it.

Don't Bite Off More Than You Can Chew

Consider the thousands of would-be entrepreneurs who set wildly unrealistic goals, declaring that they're going to be "the next Bill Gates." By this, they mean not only that they'll do it their way but that they'll do it all themselves. They inevitably fail, because they don't acknowledge their blind spots and shortcomings, those areas where others could give them a hand. If they do get a business up and running, they very often can't delegate or collaborate effectively, because they are, at root, insecure.

In fact, they haven't been paying attention to what made Bill Gates so successful. He's perhaps the world's richest self-made billionaire. He arouses strong and not always positive reactions, but no one denies that he built a uniquely successful company from scratch, at the same time serving as a pioneer in the transition to personal computers. His enormous contribution to the information and communication age may not fully be appreciated for many years to come, but he may yet be ranked along with Henry Ford as a 20th-century business icon.

Surely someone as intelligent and accomplished as Gates must be extremely self-absorbed, conceited, and full of himself. Anyone who could make that much money that quickly would be entirely justified in thinking that he or she is exceptional. Gates's ego must be boundless, as big as the moon.

On the contrary. Gates, like most truly successful people, isn't like that at all. Those who know him reveal that he always flies economy class, instead of business or executive—in part because he doesn't feel the need to advertise who, and how great, he is. Besides, as he sees it, he's pretty skinny and doesn't need the wider seat that you get up front.

Mike Sax, a personal acquaintance of Gates, once told a trade newspaper that Gates "can appear cocky sometimes. But he doesn't have too much ego to acknowledge that there are people who know more about specific topics than he does. He's smart enough to surround himself with people who know about technology, business, and marketing." We suspect that Gates, if he took the EQ-i, would score rather high when it came to self-regard.

Much importance—perhaps too much—is attached to the necessity of projecting an air of all-encompassing confidence in the workplace. But there's a fine line involved. People who act like know-it-alls are more likely headed for a rough landing. By thinking that they've got a handle on every-thing, they over-extend themselves. The more they venture into unfamiliar areas, the more vulnerable they become. It's knowing what you don't know, finding out who knows it, and capitalizing on that knowledge that separates the successes from the could-have-beens, should-have-beens, and almosts.

In the business world we often see leaders who fail because of difficul-ties with their self-regard, whose self-regard is shaky—that is, who cannot tolerate having any "warts," and certainly cannot tolerate having their warts visible publicly. They cover up their fragile self-regard by never admitting when they are wrong, by blaming others for their own mistakes, and over emphasizing their "strengths" in order to make sure that nobody inadver-tently notices their warts. They present as know-it-alls who need to surround themselves with "yes men," who cannot tolerate any suggestion of criticism, who never allow that they are responsible for an error but rather deal with a mistake by finding someone else to blame.

Exercises

What makes self-regard important for life success? In our research, we have found that many people who are satisfied with their life and accomplishments score high in self-regard. Once again, we don't mean they inflate their self-worth. Rather, they are accurate at gauging and appreciating their strengths and weaknesses. One way we validate this is with an instrument called the EQ-i 2.0 360. This compares a person with how others who know him or her well—managers, peers, subordinates, spouse—would complete the same ratings on that person.

The better you are at knowing and capitalizing on your strengths, the more confident you will be in your short- and long-term interactions. Getting a handle on your strengths helps you build them even more. Suppose you discover that you are pretty good at math. Manipulating numbers comes easily to you and you enjoy solving mathematical problems. By doing more work in this area, practicing with harder and harder problems, you get even better at it. Many people who are highly proficient in math really enjoy working with numbers. They also have an accurate sense of what kinds of problems they are good at. The same holds true with your emotional skills. Knowing your strengths and working to develop them even more can really help you excel.

On the other hand, we've often seen people fail at some things because they thought they could do everything. They overestimate their capabilities. Really successful people know what they're not good at. They decide whether to work at improving themselves in those areas or to surround themselves with others who can compensate for their weaknesses. Think of some of the most happily married people you know. While they may have similar interests and tastes, do they have complementary skills? Is one partner more cool and collected under stress, one better at managing household finances? Does one better discipline the children and is one more socially extroverted with friends? An important key to success is being aware of your limitations and knowing how you will deal with them. And this requires a degree of self-awareness.

Self-Assessment

1. How much do you like yourself?
2. What are your greatest strengths? (For example, loyalty, a sense of humor, good negotiating skills, friendliness, or honesty.)
3. What are your greatest weaknesses? (For example, bad temper, procrastination, or the inability to manage money.)
4. What do you consider your single greatest strength?
5. How has this helped you in life?
6. How could you improve on this strength even more?
7. How can you use it to help you achieve more of your goals at work, at home, or in contact with others?
8. What do you consider your most serious weakness?
9. How has this hurt you in the past?
10. Have you tried to do anything about it? If so, with what results?
11. How would improving yourself in this area help you at work, at home, or in contact with others?

12. What one thing would you most like to change about yourself?
13. How could you begin to effect change in this area?

Self-Assignments

1. Look at your answer to Self-Assessment Question 1. Then, set a goal as to how you would like to feel about yourself. Write it down in your notebook. Write down the benefits of feeling good about yourself (you'll have more confidence, other people will respect you more, etc.).

2. Now look back at your answer to Self-Assessment Question 4, and write your greatest strength at the top of a fresh page in your notebook. Each evening, over the course of a week, record how this strength has helped you in various situations during the day. Note what you can do to fine-tune or improve this strength even more. Set up a course of action for developing this skill.

Table 4-1

Weakness	Goal	Strategy
Can't connect on a personal level with co-workers.	Get to know each of them better.	Socialize outside working hours. Ask about each person's family. Ask about their personal interests and share yours with them.
Impatience with daughter.	Develop more patience.	Determine in what situations impatience emerges. Analyze why these situations might stir impatience. Consider your reaction to being treated impatiently by your own parents. Involve your daughter in a discussion about how she views your impatience. Find out her thoughts on how you and she might do things differently in order to help your impatience.

3. Have conversations with people you are close to. Ask them what they see as your personal strengths. Find out why they chose those areas and what it is about you that they think makes you strong in those areas. Also ask about your weaknesses. How could they see you improve in these areas? Self-regard is largely an "awareness" skill. Looking at yourself more objectively and honestly is a major step in any self-improvement.

4. Following the example in Table 4-1, draw a chart in your notebook for as many weaknesses as you choose. Identify the shortcoming, set a goal, and imagine a course of action that will enable you to attain it.

Chapter 5

Self-Actualization

"Whereas the average individuals often have not the slightest idea of what they are, of what they want, of what their own opinions are, self-actualizing individuals have superior awareness of their own impulses, desires, opinions, and subjective reactions in general."

—ABRAHAM MASLOW

DEFINITION:

Self-actualization is the ability to realize your potential capacities. This component of emotional intelligence is manifested by your becoming involved in pursuits that lead to a meaningful, rich, and full life. Striving to actualize your potential involves developing enjoyable and meaningful activities and can mean a lifelong effort and an enthusiastic commitment to long-term goals. Self-actualization is an ongoing, dynamic process of striving toward the maximum development of your abilities and talents, of persistently trying to do your best and to improve yourself in general. Excitement about your interests energizes and motivates you to continue these interests. Self-actualization is affiliated with feelings of self-satisfaction.[1] Individuals with healthy self-actualization are pleased with their place on life's highway with respect to their personal, occupational, and financial destinations.

Bob and Dan were old friends who grew up together in the same neighborhood. They went to high school and college together and, after graduation, both were hired for sales positions, but by two different companies. Bob sold hydraulic pumps, while Dan sold farm machinery. After eight years, both were still with the same firms, but that's where the similarities end.

Dan worked between 60 and 70 hours a week. On average, he managed to make his quota each year, although sometimes he fell slightly behind. He spent his working days—which usually began at seven in the morning and went on until eight at night—telephoning prospects and customers, reviewing sales reports, developing budgets, and learning about new product lines. He seldom left the office except to call on clients, and frequently ate lunch at his desk, claiming that he was too busy to go to restaurants. His weekends were spent recovering from this grueling schedule. He lived and breathed his job, with the result that his wife accused him of being a workaholic.

Bob's lifestyle was planets apart. His work week was, by comparison, short—on average, no more than 40 hours. His topics of conversation reflected his varied interests: his most recent golf game or ski vacation, what he and his family had done the previous weekend, his retirement investments, his fitness program, the many charitable causes he supported, his photography class, his jazz collection, and the latest standings of several sports teams. Did his career suffer as a result of these activities? Not at all. Interestingly enough, he usually exceeded his quota by a comfortable margin.

Does this mean that selling farm machinery is harder than selling hydraulic pumps? Should Dan consider (as he, in fact, did) changing companies? No to the first question, and a qualified no to the second. Dan's narrow and driven lifestyle and mediocre on-the-job performance wouldn't necessarily take a turn for the better if he switched firms. More likely, he'd take his troubles with him. Over and over again, administering the EQ-i 2.0 has shown that the most successful salespeople tend to score high in self-actualization. This makes sense. If you're genuinely interested and involved in a wide variety of activities, you're obviously going to be able to connect with a wide variety of clients. You'll function far more effectively and be apt to achieve more in your chosen field.

Set Action-Oriented Goals

We admit that self-actualization sounds a bit like psychological jargon, but the concept is really quite integral to individual well-being. Abraham

Maslow was the first to coin the term, in the 1940s, as part of his "hierarchy of needs" theory. He believed that there are five basic needs that must be satisfied if we're to survive and then go on to live happy and fully realized lives.

First, we must attend to our basic physiological needs: air to breathe, water to drink, food to eat, and a tolerable temperature. Then we must achieve safety, so that we aren't in pain or peril. Next comes love—the need to belong, to be wanted and cared about by friends, relatives, and family. Fourth is esteem—the need to achieve self-respect, to take pride in our accomplishments and know that they're recognized by others. Then comes self-actualization, which Maslow defines this way: "One must do what he or she can do."

Based on this framework, we developed something we call The Life Map (shown in Figure 5-1) to help you chart your own course of self-actualization. Self-actualization involves being satisfied with where you are on life's highway—satisfied with all your achievements, at work, at play, and in relationships. The idea is to strive for a healthy balance between the many activities that make up your life. For example, how much time do you spend in Relationship County? How quickly do you speed through Family Bliss Borough to reach Traveltown, Fitness Junction, or Retirement City? How often do you want to put your feet up in Relax Village? Your own personal life map would reflect other interests: Cottage Cove or Tennis-at-Tina's Center. And what about the quality of the time spent at each location? Each should be important and meaningful in itself. Take a moment now to see what you accomplish as you move along the pathways of your life. What goals would you like to reach in each area, in return for the time and effort you devote to them? How many hours per week or month are you willing to commit to those goals?

Each of us has goals, which are as individual as we are. Perhaps they're simple and straightforward: losing those last 10 pounds, quitting smoking, getting a better paying job, graduating from university. Or they may be more nebulous: getting into shape, making a fortune, meeting the perfect mate. Many people—despite repeated tumbles off the wagon in question—continue to make New Year's resolutions. How often do we keep these wonderful promises to ourselves? For most of us, the unfortunate answer is: not very often.

How do we go about setting goals that are in fact meaningful and attainable? A good first step is to know the difference between results-oriented goals and activity-oriented goals, as described by Shane Murphy,[2] a sports

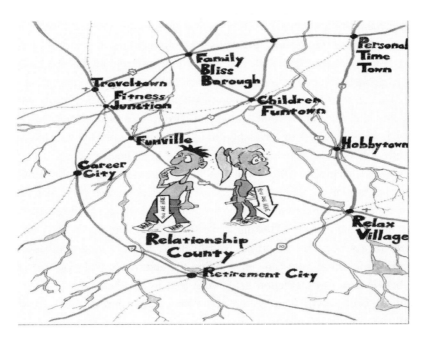

Figure 5-1:   The Life Map

© 2005 Reprinted with permission of Multi-Health Systems, Inc., Toronto, Canada. www.mhs.com

psychologist who has worked with many Olympic athletes in the United States.

Even if results-oriented goals appear to be sensible and specific, they all too often set us up for failure because the anticipated results will occur too far down the line. They're a destination, and what we should be focused on is the journey. What happens when we don't reach our end point quickly enough? We feel badly, and start to slide back into the bad old ways. Do you want to lose 10 pounds? That's fair enough—but it depends on how you go about it. Do you want to make some extravagant sum of money in the next five years or improve your love life or buy a bigger house or move to some other part of the country? Results-oriented goals like these can become little more than a wish list, composed of things we'd get around to if only we had the time. Meanwhile, day by day, precious little progress is made toward them.

To make real progress, you need action-oriented goals—the specific, manageable steps that lead to the desired result. Let's tackle those pesky 10 pounds. The best way to take them off—and keep them off—is to eat and exercise sensibly, breaking each day down into a number of chances to make small changes for the better. Action goals should always be stated in positive terms—rewards, not denials. So, instead of telling yourself to eat less, you'd rephrase the commandment as "eat more fruits and vegetables." It's usually easier to augment behavior than to forever think in terms of cutting back.

You can modify your action plan as often as you wish, considering and, if necessary, rejecting specific techniques. If one doesn't work, it's no great loss. Something else—or a variation of the same technique—will enable you to succeed. The idea is to set a large number of small goals that can plausibly be reached. That way, you grow accustomed to success; you can congratulate yourself as you go along. Then, if you fail to reach some particular goal, you'll be far less likely to throw up your hands. Instead, you'll learn from the failure, and carry on. Sticking to the so-called bottom line at any cost, or "keeping your eyes on the prize," isn't likely to gain you long-term success. If you spend all of your time envisioning the end result, you won't be able to buckle down to the action goals you need to get there. Also, you'll be stymied, because you won't be apt to try new approaches and seek creative new solutions to the quest.

Do What You Love

Career counselors often bemoan the fact that too many people who are seeking a direction in life begin (and quite often continue) an interview by dwelling on how much money they can make in a given field. They may know or sense they're good at something totally different, but they shun their natural inclination because it won't pay off. They may hate working with computers all day; they can barely sit still for an hour at a time. But that's where, in their minds, the future is. "The" future becomes—out of economic necessity—their future also. As a result, they may learn about computers, and become more or less employable. They may also become extremely unhappy, and not nearly as successful as someone who's legitimately drawn to the wonders of technology.

Career success is very seldom based on career duress—what a person believes he or she has to do in order to make a living. That's not a very shining prize. It may get you a paycheck, but it won't get you where you want (and ought) to go. We don't suppose that Bill Gates set out with the specific goal of becoming the world's richest self-made business magnate. He set out to gratify his personal passion for computers, and pursued that passion with vigor. Everything else flowed from this well-founded decision.

Or take Michael Dell, the founder of Dell Computers, whose family urged him to become a physician. Dell actually enrolled in a pre-med course at the University of Texas, but spent most of his time selling the computers he'd cobbled together while studiously neglecting his classes. As we know, he then very wisely followed his true inclination, his true calling in life. Thanks to Dell's innovative marketing techniques, his firm grew into the world's largest computer manufacturer (as of 2001, ranked number one in global market share), worth—at time of writing—about $61.1 billion in revenue (fiscal year 2009).

A more recent darling of the high-tech world, Mark Zuckerberg, founder of Facebook, was featured in the popular movie *The Social Network*. Among other things, Zuckerberg is renowned as the world's youngest billionaire (estimated to be worth $6.9 billion by *Forbes* magazine). While there is some debate around the accuracy of the movie's depiction of events, there is consensus in the observation that he was not driven to success by money. As depicted in the film, he resisted commercializing the Facebook site for a long period of time. As a teenager he developed a computer program called Synapse that sorted music into the listening habits of users. When AOL and Microsoft offered to purchase the site, he turned them down.

Zuckerberg was most excited about the potential of a social network. He was driven by the possibilities of getting more and more people to open up about themselves and network with others online. In 2005, the MTV network wanted to buy Facebook for $75 million. After he turned them down Yahoo! offered him a billion dollars in 2006. Imagine—a billion dollars! He is among the few people in the world to have ever turned down a billion-dollar offer.

In an interview with *The New Yorker* magazine,[3] Zuckerberg was asked about the deal. To the amazement of Terry Semel, the CEO of Yahoo! at the time, Zuckerberg responded, "It's not about the price. This is my baby, and I want to keep running it, I want to keep growing it." Semel was shocked.

Next, for something completely different, consider Jerry Seinfeld, who did much to redefine television comedy and wound up with all the tangible evidence of success—multi-million-dollar contracts and a garage full of Porsches. Did he have these things in mind when he was a struggling young man? Perhaps—but they must have seemed awfully remote. Friends have written accounts of Seinfeld's life that describe a down-to-earth personality rooted in solid values. He loved doing comedy and worked hard at it for many years on the stand-up circuit, often in front of blasé or downright hostile audiences. He perfected his routines, carefully studied other performers, and kept a minutely detailed notebook of his experiences and observations.[4] Like Gates, Dell, and Zuckerberg, Seinfeld owes his success to a combination of factors. All four men had a lot of skill and a bit of luck, managed to be in the right place at the right time, and—most important—did what they truly loved to do and knew in their bones they were good at. That's why all four far exceeded any long-term goals they might have set in the early stages of their careers.

Oh, and just to be fair to all of the women who have asked us why we have only used male examples in earlier editions of this book, we'd like to add Oprah Winfrey to this list.

Let Your Internal Light Shine

Self-actualization can combine with emotional self-awareness where our ability to track our immediate, short-term feelings can help signal something larger in our life. Think of it as an internal light we all carry within us. Some of us are aware of our light and what makes it glow brighter, while others ignore their internal light, chasing life goals that have been defined for them by others, whether a "good" job, money, or a certain lifestyle. They often work hard enough to accomplish the goal successfully, but end up unhappy, to everyone else's surprise.

Roger always wanted to be a musician. He loved writing, arranging, and performing music and earned money through high school by playing local gigs with a band he put together. His parents always saw him as a dentist. As far as they were concerned, dentistry was the only career option for Roger. Fortunately, Roger was a good student. He had no real interest in spending his life working in people's mouths but felt he had to appease the wishes of his overbearing parents. He was accepted into dentistry school and forced himself to work through the courses, most of which bored him greatly. Weekends he dedicated to his music, continuing to play various bars and clubs with his own band. Roger had difficulty even imagining himself spending his days practicing dentistry. When he graduated, rather than opening his own office, he worked part-time in various other dentists' offices. His focus continued to be on his music.

Roger's internal light glowed when it came to pursuing his interest in music. It dimmed throughout his days of practicing dentistry. However, he managed both to keep his parents happy and follow his light. Not everyone can follow two paths as intensively as Roger and make them work. He currently practices dentistry only two days a week. But his light glows brightly—the rest of his time he spends on his music.

Live Life to the Fullest

Setting goals ought to be a lifelong experience. The need doesn't diminish as we age. Consider Susan, who seemed to have everything going for her—a loving husband, three grown kids who excelled at university, and a job she greatly enjoyed. The problem was that, in her 40s, she found herself a "parent" again—this time caring for her own parents.

Except for their weekly shopping excursion, Susan's mother and father seldom left the house she'd grown up in. They sat in front of the television, waiting for news items that would substantiate their long-held beliefs. They were intolerant of immigrants, people of color, liberal policies, strange new technologies, international terrorists, uppity youths, overeducated academics, or anything else that deviated from their view of the world.

Susan's parents were in good health; they weren't incapacitated physically or mentally. But they conjured up all sorts of imaginary ailments. Susan wound up driving them from specialist to specialist, even though they had a car and two valid licenses of their own.

Time and again, Susan had attempted to interest them in all sorts of activities—volunteer work, meeting new people, trying something new. The more she tried, the more they protested that what they needed was her. In their late 60s, their lives had effectively ground to a halt.

Susan's elderly neighbor Beth, on the other hand, presented a vastly different story. She was in her 80s and had lost her husband several years before. She mourned his passing and then, supported by a wide circle of friends, went on to deal with the rest of her life. She'd been a nurse, and strongly believed in fitness and health-consciousness. Even losing the vision in one eye didn't slow her down. She belonged to the local YWCA and swam lengths every morning. Then she'd socialize with other women of her age and outlook. She took care to walk every day, and once a year would join her friends for a week-long camping trip.

To keep her mind as active as her body, Beth read widely, borrowing books from the public library. She avidly signed up for a wide range of seniors' courses at a nearby university campus, taking anything that appealed to her. She always tried to support worthwhile charities—not only with donations, but by going out and spending time at fundraising events. When she traveled, she made a point of staying at a branch of the Elderhostel network. This introduced her to many new friends from across the country and overseas, with whom she kept in touch. After some hesitation, she bought herself a second-hand computer and found to her delight that the Internet wasn't nearly as intimidating as some people claimed. In fact, it brought the whole world into her home—a prospect she welcomed with curiosity, rather than rejecting with dismay.

In sum, who do you think was miles ahead in terms of self-actualization? Obviously, Beth was living a much more desirable existence than Susan's parents, who'd given up on every front. Whatever our age, we can choose to think and feel young. It all depends on how much effort we're willing to expend.

That caution applies to Susan herself. Her life reflects a serious imbalance that's already begun to catch up with her, and will only get worse. She loves her parents and wants to help them, but the time and energy she's expending on their care is out of all proportion to the end results. She must take immediate steps to provide them with different and healthier ways of meeting their needs, so that she can get on with her own life, her own needs. Only then will she be able—like Beth—to live her life to the fullest.

Strike a Balance

Living life to the fullest means, in daily practice, two things. First, self-actualization is the ability to love your work, to really get into whatever it is you do. If you fit this definition, you're very privileged. You're going to perform as well as possible all the time, because work becomes a pleasure, something you'd engage in even if the financial rewards weren't there.

In our dealings with hockey players and other professional athletes, we've seen young men who are pretty much in it for the money. They tend to be the sloggers, the enforcers, the also-rans. They last a couple of seasons, and go back where they came from. But we've also seen the likes of Wayne Gretzky (the world's most famous hockey player), who earned (and continues to earn) more money than all these characters put together. Why? Because Gretzky loves the game of hockey. It is both a constant joy and a constant challenge to his remarkable skills—which is why he transcended it during his playing career. He earned every penny that came his way—because no one ever had to dangle a fat salary in front of him to compel him to go the extra mile.

But work isn't the only game in town. That's why real self-actualization involves the need to be well-rounded, to strike a balance in everything you do. Today's employers are increasingly recognizing this fact. They don't want people who habitually burn the midnight oil in panic mode; they want people who can shut the office door, go home and pursue personal interests and hobbies. Remember, then, that self-actualization means being where you want to be, in work and in all the varied aspects of your personal life.

Exercises

What does self-actualization have to do with your success in life? Quite a lot. The most successful and happy people are those in tune with the things that excite them. They tend to have goals or areas of interest that they pursue with vigor. Identifying what activities you want to spend your time on and who you want to spend time with is the first step. The next step is to work those areas into your busy, ongoing life and make them priorities.

Self-Assessment

1. How many hours per week do you spend at work? With family? With friends? Alone?
2. Self-actualization involves maximizing your time in each of these areas. How satisfied (on a scale of **Very** to **Not at All**) are you with the quality of the time you spend at work? With family? With friends? Alone?
3. In which of these areas would you most like to improve the quality of your time?
4. What do you like best about being at work? With family? With friends? Alone?
5. What do you like least about being at work? With family? With friends? Alone?
6. What are your long-term goals in each of these areas?
7. What are your short-term (two- to six-month) goals in each of these areas? What actions will help you attain these goals?
8. What are your hobbies and interests?
9. Which would you like to pursue more actively?

10. What new areas would you like to explore?
11. Are your interests wide and varied, or do you prefer to focus on a smaller number of favorite fields? People who succeed in self-actualization tend to fall into one of two distinct categories. Those in the first group find one or two activities or hobbies that interest them passionately and pursue these with zeal and commitment. Those in the second group are no less passionate, but they have more diverse interests and love to investigate anything that catches their fancy. They may eventually settle on a couple of primary choices, but they remain open to almost any possibility. Neither approach is preferable—it's all a matter of personal choice.

Self-Assignments

1. Write down two ways you can improve your time in each of these areas: at work, with family, with friends, alone.
2. Keep track of each pleasant event or activity that occurs in each part of your life. How long did this activity last? How did you maximize your enjoyment?
3. The Internet is a marvelous way to broaden your experience. Begin by searching for a topic that appeals to you and see how many sites are devoted to it. Then move on through other, related topics. As you may already know, this is potentially rewarding but inevitably time-consuming, so be prepared. Your search will turn up any number of books that pertain to your topic of choice. A mega-bookstore in any large city, or a virtual store on the Web, is bound to carry all sorts of titles. Scan the aisles, on foot or in cyberspace, and see which ones you'd like to investigate more deeply.

PART III | The Self-Expression Realm

Chapter 6

Emotional Expression

"Self-expression must pass into communication for its fulfillment."

—PEARL S. BUCK

DEFINITION:
Emotional expression involves openly expressing feelings both verbally and non-verbally. In our interactions with others, whether or not we are aware of it, we constantly give out messages at an emotional level. These messages can be conveyed through the words we use and their meaning, the tone and volume of our speech, the expression on our face, or our body language. Others register these emotional messages that we send out; they also register their responses to them, both consciously and unconsciously. People who exhibit effective emotional expression are open and congruent in the emotional messages they send to others.[1]

Jane had made many sales presentations before. She knew her product inside out, was well trained, and had lots of sales experience. This was a big opportunity for her. If she landed this sale she would close her biggest client account. It would also be one of the biggest accounts for her company.

She had gotten some help from the graphics department in preparing her presentation. The senior accountant helped her fine-tune her numbers. She was well aware of the competition and what they offered. She was confident she had the best product at the best price. All she needed was a smooth presentation to win the business.

Everything started out simply enough. There were five people in the board room representing different interests from the prospective client's company. PowerPoint was ready, she had everyone's attention. Throughout her presentation, perhaps due to her excitement, Jane had a smirk on her face. It was almost as though she was laughing at a private joke. Her voice also increased in pitch and she spoke faster when she talked about the areas where she knew she had the competition beat.

While the decision-makers thought she was quite thorough, covering all the points they wanted to hear, they couldn't stop talking about her demeanor. What did she think was so funny? Or was she looking down on them? Did she not think this was a serious bid? Unfortunately, this puzzlement dominated their conversation during their review of her presentation. In the end, they felt that her competitor, while not quoting the best price, was more serious in wanting to work with them and would take their concerns into account over the long haul. They valued a partner they felt would be attuned to their needs and would adapt to meet them. Jane, in their opinion, would be too rigid and over-focused on selling her products and their benefits, as opposed to developing a partnership that would see both parties getting their needs met.

We often overlook the importance of how we come across to others. In fact, in a series of studies reported by Albert Mehrabian,[2] when it comes to the information people take in, he concluded that people retain 7 percent of the words spoken, 38 percent tone of voice, and 55 percent body language.

Now this might seem hard to believe, but here's an example we can use to drive the point home. You may be old enough to remember, or maybe your history class covered, the events surrounding the election of John F. Kennedy as president of the United States. The campaign between the candidates—John F. Kennedy and Richard Nixon—was intense, with Nixon and the Republicans slightly ahead before they debated each other. The climax of the election was the first-ever televised presidential candidate debate.

The event was widely covered on both radio and television. It drew one of the largest media audiences at that time. During the evening debate, both candidates spoke about the issues in some detail, at least by television standards. When radio listeners were polled after the debate about who had won, the majority of them thought Nixon had bested Kennedy. But the story among television viewers was different, with them polling almost two-to-one in favor of Kennedy as the "victor" of the debate.

What accounts for this difference? A big part of it was physical appearance: Nixon had pasty skin and a five o'clock shadow, he sweated and looked somewhat sickly and even haggard, and appeared glowering and angry at times. Kennedy, by contrast, appeared relaxed, vigorous, and fit. Also, while Nixon focused on debating Kennedy himself, Kennedy spoke directly to the American viewers through the camera lens.

Many years ago, when one of us (Steven) was an undergraduate student in psychology, there was a lot of interest in the study of physical attractiveness and the effect it has on how you are treated by others. Three psychologists pioneered the research in this area—Drs. Ellen Berscheid, Elaine Walster, and Karen Dion.[3]

The research has consistently shown that teachers who receive student essays with an identification picture on the essay rate the same essay significantly higher when the attached picture is of a good-looking male or female student, as compared to identical essays whose photograph is of a plain-looking male or female student. In fact, a major review of the published scientific research in this area carried out by psychologist Dr. Vicki Ritts and her colleagues at Southern Illinois University has confirmed that physically attractive students are usually judged more favorably by teachers in a number of dimensions, including intelligence, academic potential, grades, and social skills.[4]

The subconscious impact of seeing a good-looking student positively affects the grade given by the teacher, while a photograph of a plain-looking student subconsciously influences the marks given in a negative direction. In both of these situations, the teacher is unaware that how he/she feels about the student's looks has influenced what should be an objective rational grading process.

You might wonder, does being treated differently because of the way you look influence the way you behave toward others? Well, many years ago one of us (Steven) completed his psychology undergraduate thesis by looking at this very question. Working with Dr. Karen Dion as supervisor, he helped complete and publish a landmark study demonstrating that attractiveness was an important factor in how persuasive fifth- and sixth-grade children were with their peers.[5]

The way we come across to others greatly influences their opinion of us. Of course there are many people who don't seem to care what others think of them. We all know of people who may be eccentric, asocial, or just disinterested in others. On the clinical side, we know about people in the autistic spectrum—suffering from Asperger's disorder, specifically—who are fairly oblivious about how they come across to others.

Recently, at MHS, working with psychologists Dr. Sam Goldstein and Dr. Jack Naglieri, we carried out the largest-ever test validation on comparison groups of children and adolescents with autism spectrum disorder and matched controls. More than 2,500 ratings were collected and thoroughly analyzed. Among the key areas of dysfunction identified, two significant areas differentiated the autistic group from others: their difficulties in social communication and social emotional reciprocity. Specifically, in interactions with others, those with autism showed little emotion, had difficulty keeping a conversation going, rarely shared their enjoyment with others, failed to show an interest in others, didn't start conversations, nor did they look people in the eyes when talking to them.

Interestingly, we've seen many "normal" people in the corporate world share some of these characteristics, although maybe not in as extreme a way as our clinical samples. Think about people you may work with. Are there some who are more interested in staring at their computer screen than looking at you when you speak to them? Do you interact with people who seem to have little interest in you? Are there others who just don't seem to share any enjoyment or happiness?

How Self-Awareness Plays Out in the Public Eye

In the autumn of 1982, before manufacturers placed a sealant barrier on the tops of medicine bottles, poison was slipped into a number of Tylenol containers, resulting in a number of deaths. In a television interview, a spokesperson from Johnson & Johnson not only condemned the poisoning of the medicines, but talked emotionally—with tears in his eyes—about the tragedy of the deaths. He then explained that Johnson & Johnson were recalling all Tylenol medications, and would see to it that a safety barrier was put over each vial.

The spokesperson was quite open about his sadness and pain. His words, tone, and the tears in his eyes spoke to the authenticity of his emotions. The public, identifying with such genuine feelings, and his steps to ensure that such a tragedy would never happen again, continued to support Tylenol as an important medication, and did not abandon the company. While at the time of these deaths, the market share of Tylenol dropped from 35 percent to 10 percent, it rebounded over the next year, ultimately becoming the most popular pain medication in the United States.

Watching the interview, it was clear how the spokesperson was aware of and expressed his emotions. The congruity between his behavior and his feelings verified the genuineness of his emotional state. Johnson & Johnson's action of recalling all Tylenol medications, thus putting public safety before corporate profits, was congruent with their spokesperson's televised message.

Now, consider how Tony Hayward, the CEO of BP, responded to the explosion of the Deepwater Horizon oil rig, which occurred on April 20, 2010, resulting in the deaths of 11 people on the rig, and the massive leak of up to 100,000 barrels of oil per day from the ocean floor. Although Mr. Hayward initially talked of taking full responsibility for this disaster, his behavior, of which he seemed completely unaware, showed him instead as a self-absorbed dilettante, unconcerned about the economic, ecological, and human costs of this widespread pollution, and more perturbed by the inconvenience this event caused to his own life.

Quotes attributed to him, such as "We made a few little mistakes early on,"[6] as his summation of this massive spill; his telling a cameraman to "Get out of there";[7] and his public statement that "We're sorry for the massive disruption it's caused to their lives," but then adding, "There's no one who wants this thing over more than I do...I'd like my life back!"[8] added to the popular view of him as self-preoccupied and unmoved by the damage caused to others.

That he also took time off from overseeing this disaster to attend a yacht race, in which a boat he co-owned participated, while the Gulf oil spill continued, only highlighted him as an elitist gadfly, more concerned about his own entertainment and pleasures than about the very real economic and ecological damages caused by the spill on his watch.

In the end, Hayward lost his job as CEO, in part because he was either oblivious to, or unconcerned about, the image he presented to the public. He came across as a business leader who was more like Nero fiddling while

Rome burned than a man with the ethics, responsibility, and genuine concern for the welfare of others, as was the spokesperson of Johnson & Johnson.

Expression of Authentic and Congruent Emotions

The sight of the Johnson & Johnson spokesperson talking about, and showing his concern and upset over, the Tylenol tragedy had a powerful impact on television viewers, as did his immediate recall of all Tylenol products. This example doesn't directly speak to the importance of self-awareness of emotions, but does illustrate the dramatic impact of authentic and congruent emotional messages—his words and his tearfulness—on the public.

Expression of Non-Congruent Emotions

Can you recall a time when you were in the office with a colleague or boss who told you that he/she was interested and concerned about the problem you were describing, while simultaneously glancing at his/her BlackBerry or iPhone throughout the meeting? What was the impact on you? How self-aware did you think he/she was? Probably you felt angry that your co-worker was treating you as if you and your concerns were unimportant. Actions speak louder than words, particularly when there's a lack of congruity between them, and you likely ended up feeling dismissed, rather than treated respectfully.

The importance of congruity in expressing emotions that are in sync with your words is captured in the vignette of the CEO who stated at a town hall meeting of employees: "From now on, this organization will embrace empathy, and the consideration of all our clients—be they internal or external. Any employee at any level who fails to behave in an empathic manner will automatically be fired, period."

Exercises

1. How self-aware are you? Rank yourself on a scale of 1 (a little) to 10 (almost all the time).
2. Think about and write down a vignette of an interaction between you and someone else in your workplace that did not go as well as you intended. Focusing on this one situation, reflect on what you were saying; what meaning might the words you chose have conveyed; and what

was conveyed by the tone of your voice, the pace of your talking, and your facial expression or other body language? After reflecting on these questions, consider whether how you expressed yourself had a bearing on why things did not go well.

3. Ask a trusted friend/colleague/significant other what your attitude is when expressing yourself, particularly on a subject or situation that you find quite meaningful. Your attitude consists of the tone of your voice, the pacing of your words, your tendency to interrupt or to not listen, and your attention to the verbal and non-verbal feedback you are constantly being given by others to your own verbal and non-verbal expressions.

4. Choose a TV drama, sitcom, or reality show, and focus on one character. What is he/she expressing emotionally through his/her verbal and non-verbal communication? Is there a congruency between his/her words and his/her non-verbal communication? What feedback is he/she receiving about his/her emotional expression from those who are exposed to it? How aware is the character of this feedback? Is he/she successful at attaining his/her goals? If not, why not? What might he/she do in order to more effectively attain his/her goals?

5. Choose another TV program and, this time, mute the sound and focus only on the non-verbal emotions that are being expressed by one of the characters. Ask yourself the same questions that were posed in Question 4.

6. How do the examples in Questions 3, 4, and 5 resonate with you? Can you identify with some of the issues that you have uncovered? If so, write down one or two vignettes where you have been successful in expressing yourself emotionally. Next, contrast that with another situation where you have been unsuccessful in expressing yourself emotionally. What might you have done differently concerning emotional expression in the example where things did not go well for you?

Chapter 7

Independence

"It is the mark of an educated man to be able to entertain a thought without accepting it."

—ARISTOTLE

DEFINITION:

Independence is the ability to be self-directed and self-controlled in your thinking and actions and to be free of emotional dependency. Independent people are self-reliant in planning and making important decisions. They can stand on their own two feet. They may, however, seek and consider other people's opinions before making the right decision for themselves in the end; consulting others is not necessarily a sign of dependency. Independent people are able to function autonomously—they avoid clinging to others in order to satisfy their emotional needs.[1] The ability to be independent rests on one's degree of self-confidence and inner strength, and the desire to meet expectations and obligations without becoming a slave to them.

Sam was a friendly enough person. He was in his second year of college and had a large circle of acquaintances. He missed classes and constantly relied on others for their notes, but managed to scrape by. He would become a close enough friend with someone for as long as he could use him or her to help him get through whatever course they were in together. He couldn't even study alone. Somehow, he was able to manipulate others well enough to get notes, help with assignments, and assistance on essays. He even had people walk him through material he had to learn for tests and exams.

Sam is a perfect example of a leech or mooch. He was completely dependent on others to get him through his academics. When he was in high school, his parents, along with an endless string of tutors, got him through his assignments. No one had ever taught Sam study skills, or had ever allowed him to be responsible for his own performance. Now he was terrified of being left on his own for even the simplest assignment.

How will Sam survive in the real world of work, should he even be responsible enough to get his own job? What can be done to help Sam become more independent and responsible for his own behavior? It will be difficult for someone like Sam to change until his back is up against the wall.

The Buck Stops with You

Let's redefine independence as the ability to stand on your own two feet (which is why it's tied to assertiveness), and to acknowledge that the buck stops with you. It means taking charge of your own life, being your own person, and seeking your own direction. People who crave acceptance at any cost and are scared stiff of giving the slightest offense have grave difficulty exercising independence. You must be prepared to adopt a course of action, having first justified it in your own mind, then deal with the possibility that other people will disagree with you. So be it. You must also respect their need for independence, and give them the same amount of rope.

Obviously, independent action involves a degree of risk, and sometimes you'll do or say the wrong thing. Learn from these situations, forgive yourself for them and don't let them hinder you in the future. Usually, although you may not believe it at the time, you really don't have all that much to lose. Weigh the alternatives carefully, looking at the benefits of each possible response. Then consider the downside—the very worst that could happen—should you follow through with each of your choices. To your surprise, you may find that in relatively few cases will the world come crashing to a halt if you aren't 100 percent correct.

That's the point—no one is right 100 percent of the time. If a baseball player safely hits three pitches out of 10, he's a hero. Some of history's most successful and honored men and women made huge, seemingly irreparable mistakes somewhere along the line, or went up countless blind alleys in pursuit of a goal. Thomas Edison once confessed that he'd devised 3,000 different conceptual models in connection with the electric light. Only one panned out, but it made up for all the rest of them. Think of the world leaders and prominent personalities who've rebounded from apparent failure (and in some cases downright disgrace) to achieve great things. Making mistakes is profoundly human, as everyone knows. Very few people will remember your missteps along the way. Instead, they'll applaud your achievements.

Be Decisive

Shelly sailed through high school and college, gaining high marks in every subject. Still, she always seemed in need of reassurance, and never expressed confidence in her abilities. She socialized only with a small circle of friends. She was attractive and fashionable, but on close inspection her style was always a matter of following the crowd, rather than making a statement of her own taste.

With her undergraduate degree in hand, Shelly applied to and was accepted at a prestigious law school. But before the course began, she found herself growing increasingly disenchanted with the idea of higher education. She therefore decided to work for a year, hoping this would help her determine a direction in life. Having put her finances in order, she could then decide whether to go back to college and pursue law or find a new career. Meanwhile, she got a job as a customer service representative with a mail-order company.

Two months later, Shelly knew more about the firm's products than some of her co-workers who'd been there for years. She had an easy manner and was well equipped to deal with customers' questions and complaints. But Shelly also had a problem: she was terminally indecisive. She was entirely aware of the firm's policies regarding returns and warranty service, but after obtaining all the facts she needed she was unable to move on a complaint until she checked with someone else. Often she checked with everyone in sight, which created tension throughout the office. Her co-workers felt that she didn't trust their viewpoints, and responded by gradually becoming less willing to help her out.

Part of this sorry state of affairs was Shelly's lack of confidence. Another part was her need to protect herself from blame, in case she made the wrong decision. As a result, she wound up with a long list of impatient customers who complained to her supervisor, who then had to investigate each claim. Whenever her superior would confront her, Shelly would go instantly on the defensive. Privately, she confided to her friends that the job was beneath her. Her refrain was constant: she'd been accepted by a prestigious law school, and all her co-workers were glorified clerks who had no right to criticize or question her.

Shelly's behavior is an example of how high IQ can backfire if EQ isn't up to par. The ability to be independent is a skill that affects both our personal life decisions and our value to an employer. The less supervision an employee requires, the more productive he or she is.

Pursue New Interests

Independence is also linked to self-regard: when you feel better about yourself, others respect you more. Making decisions and acting upon them, then following through to deal with the consequences, are important to success. The more you practice, the better you become, and the more your confidence will rise.

Sheila, an attractive though somewhat shy 16-year-old, had many acquaintances but few close friends, and attended a high school that—like so many others—was awash in cliques. There were groups and subgroups devoted primarily to sports or to the latest fashion trends. Others excelled at putting everyone else down. Still others were dubbed losers by all concerned.

Sheila floated around betwixt and between. Her social life, to be frank, was going nowhere. No one really disliked her, but no one felt warm enough toward her to invite her into their particular set. As well, just like Shelly the service rep, she hated to make decisions. By Thursday night, she'd be in a state of high anxiety about her weekend plans. She wasn't on anyone's party list and didn't know how to get herself included.

Although Sheila might be considered shy or introverted, all she needed was an emotional kick start. She had no difficulty carrying on a conversation once it got under way. She had a good sense of humor, and showed real concern for her friends. But she always seemed to be a follower, never taking the initiative. Even her friends recognized this.

There was a pleading, almost desperate quality to her phone calls, which is why all the plan-making frequently came to nothing. She'd wind up home alone because she was reluctant to go anywhere without someone to hold her hand.

One day, her mother gently but persistently began to confront her on the issue. She urged Sheila to stop waiting for the phone to ring and to stop insisting that one of her friends accompany her wherever she went. Instead, her mother said, she ought to do things on her own—at first, without telling anyone, so as to lessen her anxiety. So Sheila started off, simply enough, with a solo trip to the shopping mall. She found it strangely liberating to be lost in the crowd, with no need to pay attention to what her friends might think. After a couple of visits, she realized that she was starting to notice things—new fashions, interesting people—that her friends had somehow managed to overlook. These were duly reported to her friends, who began to wonder what they were missing.

From this promising beginning, Sheila followed a series of gradual steps, going to movies, museums and galleries, farmers' markets, book shops, and used-clothing stores. To Sheila's surprise, her new activities were of interest to her friends, who started calling her more often. They wanted to know where she was going and what she was doing. She'd tell them, and ask if they'd like to come along. Were they interested? Of course—because step by step, she was becoming a more independent and therefore more interesting person.

Remember, though, that true independence doesn't mean ignoring everyone else and charging off in your own direction. Never turning to others for help is just as bad as always doing so. If you have to prove your independence by making it a point of pride to reject sensible advice, you're in trouble. The idea is to be smart enough to consult a wide variety of sources, and selective enough to weigh the results and reach a decision that you find satisfactory.

Making Your Work Decisions Work

As division head in marketing, Alex seemed to have a strong capacity for solving problems independently. He understood the difficulties, could develop and implement solutions, and keep track of the outcomes. He had a very strong and close working relationship with Sally, the VP to whom he reported and, after five years in this position, knew how Sally wanted problems identified and solved, and the solutions implemented. Although he turned to Sally frequently for direction during his first two years, by his third year he seemed to be functioning quite independently.

When Sally was promoted to senior VP of another division, Alex was a shoe-in for the vacated VP's role. And he acquired it easily. However, once in this position, he seemed quite uncertain about decision making—especially when it came to roadblocks and obstacles to the division's goals. He waffled. He could not take a stand or be decisive. He turned to others seemingly for input, yet on closer examination it seemed that what he really wanted was for others to make decisions for him. Despite mentoring on how to prioritize problems and a course on problem solving, Alex became increasingly uncertain and self-doubting. Ultimately, he resigned.

What happened? What went wrong was that Alex's supervisors did not look closely enough at his ability to function independently. They minimized the reality that it took him two years to become comfortable in his role and stop turning to Sally for direction. They also overlooked the subtle signs that even during his third, fourth, and fifth years on the job he was still implicitly and covertly highly dependent on Sally. That is, he was good at his job not because he was truly independent—although he seemed so on the surface—but because he "memorized" Sally's way of problem solving for his particular role. The steps of brainstorming, solution seeking and implementation were not authentically his, but Sally's. He mimicked her approach, step by step. It was not truly his own. It was not based on pondering the issues, selecting what he thought was the best solution or flexibly implementing it. It was simply a memorized template that he inflexibly followed.

Once into his new position of VP, with its new challenges, different obstacles, unfamiliar solutions, and increased routes of implementation—and without Sally to give him a template—Alex's underlying dependency emerged in full force. Unable to stand on his own two feet, worried about making errors, insecure about his own abilities, Alex became increasingly anxious and paralyzed. The mentoring courses he was offered missed the point: they did not acknowledge or help him deal with his underlying dependency.

This vignette illustrates how some people look as if they are independent, as long as they have someone on the sidelines who allows them to feel secure, but once really on their own, knowing that the buck stops with them and that it is up to them to make the final decision, these individuals' true colors—their underlying and powerful dependency—emerge. This vignette also speaks to the importance of senior management paying attention to and scanning for clues as to whether an individual is truly independent, or only looks that way under special situations. If Alex's senior executives had paid more attention to the amount of time it took him to settle into his marketing position, the very close—perhaps too close—relationship he had with Sally, and had explored whether his seemingly independent style was more a reflection of his memorizing and inflexibly applying Sally's ways of doing things, they might not have been so quick to promote Alex to a position that called for the independence he did not truly have.

Exercises

The capacity to be independent—to be self-directed and self-controlled in your thinking and actions—is another vital component of success. At its core, independence reflects a pervasive sense of autonomy: the ability to pursue your own thinking and go after your own self-determined goals. If you cannot define what you want, cannot figure out how to get there, or cannot be definitive, you will be hampered in your pursuit of success. People who lack independence tend to be clingy and needy. They chronically seek protection and support from others, which undermines their ability to determine what they want and to be confident enough to pursue it.

Self-Assessment

1. Over the next week, record any occasion when you turned to someone else to help you make a decision. Then assess whether you were asking for input (useful information that would be of value to you in making up your own mind) or for that person to take over and make the decision for you.
2. Based on your responses, where do you think you fall on the dependence–independence continuum?
3. During this same time period, how often did a friend, co-worker, or significant other indicate that you were turning to him or her a bit too often and really ought to stand on your own two feet?
4. Based on the frequency of this reaction, do you think you're closer to dependence or independence?

5. Is there a degree of consistency between your answers to questions 2 and 4? If so, it should give you a fair idea of your capacity for independence. If there's a marked discrepancy, try to understand why, in order to bring the two assessments closer together.

6. If you've found yourself behaving dependently, how did you feel about your decision? How did you feel about yourself, and about how the other person might regard you? If you felt bad to some degree, make a list of the costs of dependent behavior.

Self-Assignments

Remind yourself how to set up the ABCDE chart by looking back at Chapter 2.

The urge to turn constantly to others for help stems in part from counter-productive self-talk. Dependent people are driven by fear—fear of making a mistake and having to live with the outcome, fear of ridicule or disapproval, fear that they will feel even more terrible and worthless than before. But the so-called solution of turning constantly to others can only amplify esteem-eroding feelings of incompetence, indecisiveness, and neediness.

1. At the end of each day, record in your notebook any dependent scenarios, and describe the self-talk that interfered with and undermined your attempts to take matters into your own hands. Typically, your self-talk might sound like this: "What if I make the wrong decision? I'll look foolish and be humiliated. I won't be able to live with the embarrassment."

2. If your self-talk is mired in these harmful belief systems, write down arguments against it—using the dispute-and-debate technique described in earlier chapters.

3. Be aware that at times, this self-talk stems from childhood, and takes the form of what are known as "dated tapes." This refers to what our parents might have said or done when it came to decision-making. Themes such as "father knows best," or "here, let me do that for you, I know all about it," or "I haven't got all day to wait for you to make up your mind," still carry power in our adult lives. Remind yourself that that was then and this is now. This can be difficult if your parents criticized you for making a child's inevitable errors, instead of having the capacity to encourage you in authentic decisions. Did their attitude convey that only their decisions were correct? Do you think that they were over-protective?

When you feel that you are having trouble making an independent decision, ask yourself if your reluctance to decide can be traced back to your "dated tapes," and dispute and debate those echoes of the past.

4. Over the next week, restrain from turning automatically to others, and take a chance at making your own decision. If it's correct, great. If not, accept the consequences (which won't be as earth-shaking as you fear), and use your disputing and debating skills to guard against self-recriminating self-talk.

5. At times, the obstacles to independent behavior are rooted in low self-regard, which makes it difficult to tolerate mistakes and fuels even more harmful self-talk. If so, exercises aimed at increasing your capacity for independence should be paired with others designed to strengthen self-regard, as described in the next chapter.

Chapter 8 | Assertiveness

"The more arguments you win, the fewer friends you'll have."

—ANONYMOUS BUT TOTALLY ACCURATE PROVERB

DEFINITION:
Assertiveness comprises three basic components: (1) the ability to express feelings (for example, to accept and express anger, warmth, and sexual feelings); (2) the ability to express beliefs and thoughts openly (being able to voice opinions, disagree, and take a definite stand, even if it is emotionally difficult to do so and even if you have something to lose by doing so); and (3) the ability to stand up for personal rights (not allowing others to bother you or take advantage of you). Assertive people are not over-controlled or shy—they are able to express their feelings and beliefs (often directly) and they do so without being aggressive or abusive.[1]

Juanita was a brilliant young marketing assistant at a large advertising agency. She had excelled in all her subjects throughout high school and college, always placing in the top 10 percent of her class. She had a keen eye for details and a quick wit. She was devastated, however, when after her first year at a prominent New York City ad agency she was not among the few who were fast-tracked for promotions. Although she worked hard and her work was of high quality, others always saw her as being behind the scenes.

Not being very extroverted, Juanita preferred to get the job done in a neat, quiet, and efficient way. She held modesty as a virtue and would never brag about her accomplishments. In meetings, she listened carefully, but did not actively contribute to discussions. Even when great ideas came to her, she withheld them for later, when she could quietly think them through and then enter them into her computer. But she noticed that the people who did speak up at these meetings, whether their comments and ideas were well grounded or not, were the ones who were quickly moving up in the company. Finally, when she realized that her introversion was holding her back, she decided to enroll in an assertiveness-training seminar.

Juanita learned to rehearse the assertiveness skills she needed to present her views to a group. The first issue was her anxiety. She learned to take several slow breaths, which allowed her to focus. She visualized scenarios, so she could practice entering into conversations. She rehearsed different approaches, and prepared, as much as possible, ways to deal with any opposition to her views.

A few weeks after the seminar finished, Juanita sat in on a strategy meeting to decide whether a TV-commercial script under review for one of their largest clients was suitably focused on the client's key message to consumers. Juanita knew right away that the message wasn't geared to the young audience the client was aiming at.

Waiting for an appropriate break in the discussion, Juanita intervened: "Can we just step back a bit? If you don't mind, I just want to mention something that the client stressed at our first development meeting. They wanted a campaign that spoke directly to youth. This piece goes over the heads of our key audience."

She went on to offer two specific examples of how they were missing their objective. There were some people with objections to her perspective, but taking their criticisms into account, and presenting her well-thought-out case with just the right combination of reason and emotion, she convinced the team she was right. She then went on to spell out what elements the new campaign should have to meet the client's needs.

Speaking out in a work-group setting was not easy for Juanita. Not doing so before had hindered her ability to be recognized for her work. Now, after a year and a half at her job, she was finally being noticed. She started getting the recognition she deserved, and soon got the promotion she desired. Her new assertiveness played a big role in Juanita's increased success at her job. Moreover, she was better able to deal with group situations in other areas of her life.

What Is Meant by Assertiveness?

Assertiveness is much misunderstood. That's ironic, because assertiveness involves the ability to communicate clearly, specifically, and unambiguously, while at the same time being sensitive to the needs of others and their responses in a particular encounter.

One very interesting study we released back in 1999 garnered a fair degree of media attention. We'd found, based on the administration of the EQ-i to 4,000 people, that Americans scored significantly higher in emotional intelligence than did Canadians in several areas, notably reality testing, happiness, optimism, and assertiveness. By this last factor, we meant that the Canadians surveyed were more reticent, more apt to take the overly polite way out, less able to express what they wanted and why. But the commentary was startling. When we were interviewed on radio and TV talk shows, many of the hosts and most of the callers took us to task for suggesting that Canadians ought to be "more like" our neighbors to the south. The last thing in the world they wanted, they said (at considerable length), was to be as loud and pushy as they perceived Americans to be.

Well, that's not what we mean by assertiveness. According to our findings, Canadians do tend to be more passive and—a key word—*indirect* in their dealings with others. Americans are more to the point, more no-nonsense. But the distinction was one of degree, not kind. In fact, there's no single way of being assertive. Within the definition of assertiveness, there is latitude for interpretation. Everyone has his or her own style. You can be humorous or serious, concise or eloquent. We aren't all the same, and the idea isn't to use the concept of emotional intelligence as a whole to turn Americans and Canadians or anybody else into clones.

The ability to act with a proper degree of assertiveness breaks down three ways. First, you must have sufficient self-awareness to be able to recognize feelings before you express them. Second, you must have sufficient impulse control and emotional expression to express disapproval and even anger (if a degree of anger is called for) without letting it escalate into fury, and to express a range of desires in the appropriate way, with the appropriate intensity. Third and last, you must stand up for your own rights, your own causes and deeply held beliefs. This means being able to disagree with others without resorting to emotional sabotage or subterfuge, and being able to walk a fine line, defending your wishes while, at the same time, respecting another person's point of view and being sensitive to their needs.

This often results in a constructive compromise—what's known as a "win-win" situation. Because the bonds of a relationship are strengthened when both parties show consideration, both are far more likely to walk away from the encounter with their needs at least partially fulfilled.

By the way, as part of our work on the new EQ-i 2.0 we reexamined the differences in emotional intelligence between Americans and Canadians. This time, based on testing over 6,000 people in 2010, we found there have been changes since our original data collection in 1997. Canadians are now pretty much equivalent to their American neighbors. There were a few minor distinctions. Americans have slightly higher impulse control than Canadians, but Canadians are a bit more flexible. Canadians also seem to be a tad higher in stress management.

Assertiveness Is Not Aggression

A very common mistake is to confuse assertive behavior with aggressive conduct. Indeed, this is why some people shy away from the very idea of assertiveness. To them, it equals aggression; they fear that they'll hurt others, or that they won't seem likeable. Not so—assertiveness is characterized by a clear statement of one's beliefs and/or feelings, accompanied by a consideration of the thoughts and feelings of others. Without this consideration, certainly, assertiveness becomes aggression, as can be seen in the examples provided below.

Allen wants to strengthen his working relationship with Marvin, a new co-worker. He is aware that Marvin knows few people in the city, having relocated just three weeks ago. He'd like to invite Marvin over for dinner, but he realizes that Rita, his wife, may not be prepared to accommodate a guest at such short notice. So he phones home:

> Allen: Rita, I'm just having a beer with Marvin, a guy who's just started working with us. He's only been in the city for a couple of weeks, and knows next to no one. I thought it

would be nice if I had him over for dinner. How would tonight be?

Rita: What is it . . . five o'clock? You're really not giving me very much notice. Why not have him over some other time?

Allen: I guess I could invite him another time. But he seems at a loose end tonight. Look, I recognize that it's kind of late, but we have some steaks in the freezer, and I could pick up salad and dessert on the way home. And we could certainly hang around here for another hour, maybe shoot a game of pool before leaving. I could hold off coming home until, say, seven or even eight. That would give you two or three hours to unwind and get ready. What do you say?

Rita: Well . . . three hours should be enough. And all I'd have to do is set the table and defrost the steaks.

Allen: Great! See you around eight.

This simple example provides an excellent illustration of assertiveness. Allen is clear about his wishes: to have Marvin over for dinner. He explains the short notice—Marvin is new in town and at a loose end. He recognizes that Rita needs time to relax, ought not to have additional work, and would want to offer a level of hospitality about which she can feel proud. He considerately addresses each of her concerns by offering to pitch in with salad and dessert and giving her additional time to get ready at a reasonable pace.

But let's rewind this scenario to see what would happen if Allen behaved aggressively rather than assertively. While assertive people clearly articulate and defend their wishes or thoughts, they are also considerate of the other person's position and sensitive to the other person's feelings. The latter point separates assertiveness from aggression. Aggressive people do not respect anyone else's viewpoint, nor are they considerate of the other person's needs or feelings. They force their views or desires to be accepted through bullying, intimidation, and manipulation. Aggression leaves no room for compromise. Rather, it is one-sided—an unremitting expression of what the aggressive person wants and a simultaneous attempt to force others to acquiesce.

Sometimes aggression is easy to spot—the perpetrator just bulldozes ahead. But sometimes, aggressors are strangely indirect in expressing their wishes, as if they need to get the lay of the land before coming out and saying what they mean. Often this leaves the other person feeling that aggressors have a hidden agenda. We know they're being rude, unpleasant, and domineering, but we aren't sure exactly what they're after.

In either case, aggressive people offer little or nothing in return for the satisfaction of their agenda, hidden or otherwise. Over time, others react with mistrust and anger. They seek to retaliate by undermining the aggressor or by looking for ways to pay him or her back. Or, more commonly, they simply tune out and avoid any further interactions. As a result, aggressive people end up feeling isolated, alienated, without anyone in their corner and devoid of meaningful social support—all of which fuels their aggression or drives them toward even more aberrant behavior.

If Allen were to behave aggressively, the interchange with Rita might unfold very differently:

Allen: Hi, honey, how was your day?

Rita: Not too bad.

Allen: Well, I just thought I'd give you a call and see how things are going, see how you're doing.

Rita: Oh, that's awfully nice.

Allen: Look, I've got this new co-worker and I thought it would be a good idea to have him over for dinner tonight. He's just been in the city for a couple of weeks and doesn't know anyone, and it would really help me solidify my relationship with him.

Rita: Gee, hon, it's a bit short notice.

Allen: Ah, don't worry about it. Your day's been pretty smooth, and we've got steaks in the freezer.

Rita: Yeah, but I'd like to get the house in order and make myself a little presentable, Allen.

Allen: You're always presentable. And don't worry about the house; it's fine the way it is. You always get too wound up about the floor being so clean you can eat off it. Just relax.

Rita: Allen, I don't really think you're being fair.

Allen: Of course I'm being fair. What do you mean, I'm not being fair? You're not being fair. I've been busting my ass all day working, like I do every day. You've had an easy day. You're presentable, the house is fine—you just worry too much. All you have to do is thaw out the steaks. I'll handle the barbecue. If you think that's so unfair, why don't you go out and get a job and I'll stay home and clean up the house and make myself presentable?

Allen eventually got his way through bullying, but with a complete disregard for Rita's feelings. He maneuvered Rita into a general comment that he could use to bolster his own position—the idea that she had a pretty good day. Then he made a unilateral demand that he bring Marvin over for dinner, while simultaneously dismissing and belittling all of Rita's concerns. Finally, he attacked her self-esteem and played on any guilt she might feel about her role as homemaker, while positioning himself as the long-suffering breadwinner. Although he won the battle, Allen will probably lose the war because his ongoing, relentless bullying and dismissal of his wife's needs will ultimately demoralize and alienate Rita, and weaken any sense of collaboration in their relationship.

Using Assertiveness at Work

Aggression is a very common and corrosive dynamic in the workplace. Consider the following interaction between Daniel, the vice-president, and Marla, who is one of two recently appointed department heads who report directly to him.

Daniel: Marla, I just got this e-mail from my senior VP that he needs that info you and I have been talking about by tomorrow, Friday, not Monday. That means you're going to have to crunch those numbers tonight so we can have it ready for him.

Marla: Tonight! It's my 10th anniversary! We've planned for weeks to go out for dinner and a play, and I just...

> Daniel: Marla, you're not listening. This has to be done. I need it done. Too bad about your anniversary. Sometimes life is not fair.
>
> Marla: But isn't there another…
>
> Daniel: Don't tell me there's another way. There's no other way. Has to be done for tomorrow. That means you do it this evening.
>
> Marla: But—
>
> Daniel: Don't "but" me! How long have you been here? Two months? I've been here five years and let me remind you of something else: I'm the boss, you're the subordinate. What I say goes. Cancel your plans, celebrate some other time, and get those figures done tonight. Am I clear?

Marla did as she was commanded. But being so talked down to, silenced, not heard, and threatened, left a bitter taste with her. Although on the surface she continued to seemingly respect Daniel's demands, she found herself frequently withholding important information from him, not going the extra mile for him, and in the long run playing a subtle role in ensuring that he didn't look good to his superiors. Daniel's aggressive behavior lost him an important support—Marla—in his dealings with his other department head, Steve. Marla had let Steve know of Daniel's demeaning behavior, and both sought to undermine Daniel in subtle yet important ways.

Let us see how this scenario might have played out had Daniel been assertive instead of aggressive:

> Daniel: Marla, I just got this e-mail from my senior VP that he needs that info you and I have been talking about by tomorrow, Friday, not Monday. That means you're going to have to crunch those numbers tonight so we can have it ready for him.
>
> Marla: Tonight! It's my 10th anniversary! We've planned for weeks to go out for dinner and a play, and I just…
>
> Daniel: Oh boy, I can see that this task is coming at a terrible time.
>
> Marla: Yes, we have been planning this for weeks and we're both looking forward to it.

Daniel: Well, we have to have this ready for Friday; Monday would be too late because the client with whom we're dealing needs it Monday. So, given all this, how do you think we can handle it?

Marla: Well, I don't know. Wait, you said you received an e-mail from your senior VP. Would it help if you talked to him just to clarify? Maybe there's a little bit of wiggle room and he might be okay for Monday, if the client can wait until Tuesday. Could you look into that?

Daniel: That's a good idea. Sure, I'll look into it, and if it works out, everyone's happy. But Marla, we need a backup plan to that, too. If it ends up that this has to be done for tomorrow—and it may—how are you going to deal with that? And with your husband, who's probably going to be equally disappointed?

Marla: I don't know . . . Well, our anniversary is actually on Sunday, but we were celebrating it tonight. I guess we could see if we could change our dinner reservations, but I think it would be impossible to get tickets to the play.

Daniel: If you can see about changing your dinner reservations, I can see about looking after the tickets. We always have tickets on hand for some of the more popular downtown plays. And if I can't get tickets for Saturday, I'll see about doing it for some other weekend soon.

Marla: Thanks for being so understanding. I know getting the work done is important for you. It's important for me, too.

In this scenario Daniel still stands his ground, but he is sensitive to Marla's disappointment, invites her to come up with alternative ways of solving her dilemma, accepts one of the ways, but realistically points out that this still may not work out and they're still left with having to get the job done. Marla is able to think about shifting the day of the celebration and Daniel helps by offering to look after the tickets.

This interchange left Marla feeling quite positive, even though she still may end up doing the work of having to crunch those figures on Thursday. The reason she feels good is that Daniel was clear about the importance of getting this work done, but he also listened to her, made her feel heard, understood, empathized with, and respected. He was not intimidating or demanding, but invited her to be part of the solution; and not once did he use the authority invested in his position to intimidate or belittle her.

Overcoming Passiveness and Passive-Aggressive Behavior

Assertiveness is often characterized as a mid-point along a line drawn between passiveness and aggression. Passive people have difficulty expressing themselves to others. They bottle things up and avoid dealing with uncomfortable situations; they wait for others to come to them, for things to be handed to them on a platter. (But, since they don't or can't communicate what they want, others aren't likely to provide it or aid them in obtaining it.) That is why they frequently miss out on any number of life's opportunities, and why others may take advantage of them. Often they feel like the proverbial doormat, always being stepped on. Some just lie back and take it; they don't really care about what's become the normal order of things.

Others, though, are what's known as passive-aggressive. They may seem to go along for the ride without complaint, but inside, they're seething with resentment about the fact or with suspicion that others constantly exploit their good nature. Instead of speaking out or confronting the issue in an honest way, they repress that anger. But only for a while. Then, usually when it's least called for, they lash out, at times subconsciously.

Passive aggression can manifest in a variety of ways. Sometimes it's as simple as not responding to requests or expectations, like the husband who agrees, in a voice that sounds like a speak-your-weight machine, to take out the garbage "after the next commercial." Of course, the garbage trucks come and go and the husband remains on inactive duty in front of the TV, having "gotten back" at his wife for her constant "nagging."

Passiveness and passive aggression are clearly long-standing patterns of behavior, and they're hard to break. In hopes of doing so, back in the mid-1950s, Dr. Albert Ellis developed his Rational Emotive Behavior Therapy, as described in Chapter 2. Several years ago, one of us (Steven) had the opportunity to participate in the Associate Fellowship Program that Ellis ran at his New York institute. One of the assignments included an exercise designed to help people overcome the passive or passive-aggressive form of assertiveness deficiency.

Each participant was asked to describe something that he or she was afraid to do in public—the only conditions being that the activity couldn't be illegal, unethical, or lead to any real harm or danger. In fact, most of the activities involved baseless fears—the idea that, if these things were done, other people would think the participant silly. The exercise demanded that each person carry out this very activity. One woman dreaded the idea of riding the subway and having people watch her. Her assignment was not only to board a train, but to shout out the name of each station as the train pulled in. At the end of the day she could easily have been hired as a conductor.

Another participant was a young man (we'll call him Stanley) who must have weighed at least 300 pounds and stood six-foot-five. He was a successful psychologist, but he too had a secret fear. To be precise, when he received food in a restaurant that was improperly cooked, he was incapable of reporting the problem to his waiter; he'd rather eat something raw or broiled past all recognition than ask to have it taken back. You can easily guess what his assignment was.

On Sunday afternoon, several of us accompanied Stanley to a nearby Chinese restaurant. The waiter stood about five feet tall, and weighed perhaps 125 pounds, but Stanley could scarcely bear to look at him. When the soup arrived, Stanley started wolfing it down, in the hope that he'd finish before the waiter returned. No such luck. Stanley was in obvious distress; his face was flushed and his hands were shaking. His anxiety, which we'd been on the verge of making fun of, was very real. At last, summoning up every ounce of courage he could muster, he asked in a voice barely louder than a whisper that the "too-cold" hot and sour soup be returned. Of course, the waiter politely whisked the bowl away, and Stanley's body instantly relaxed. He looked, and admitted that he felt, as if a tremendous weight had been lifted from his shoulders.

Stanley's experience demonstrates that it doesn't matter how big you are physically, or how much power you may wield in a given social interaction. The ability to assert yourself is a state of mind, as well as a skill that can be fine-tuned with practice.

Indirect Assertiveness

At times, the impact that speaking up might have on others who are present at the interaction requires that assertiveness be muted: Victoria, who had been invited to a dinner party at the home of people she did not know well, found herself seated next to a man named Charles, a well-spoken and generally delightful companion. He had a way with words, and entertained the table with stories of his travels around the country as sales manager for a software firm. But Charles also had a far less pleasant side to him, which became apparent when he launched into a series of jokes about blacks, Jews, and Asians.

Victoria was highly uncomfortable; she found racist humor crude and demeaning. But she was a guest in someone else's home, and the host seemed to be entering into the spirit of the conversation.

She considered ignoring Charles, in hopes that he would move on to something else, but it soon became clear that he wouldn't. If the two of them had been alone or if they'd been among strangers, she would have voiced her wishes quite clearly: "I don't like racist comments. Please stop." However, she was an invited guest at a dinner party, didn't know the hosts all that well, and did not wish to embarrass them or their other guests. Her strong sense of reality testing allowed her to read the political complexity in the situation.

She decided to voice her concerns, but in an indirect manner that would get her point across without causing unnecessary embarrassment or tension at the party.

"Charles," she joked, "do you know any good lawyer stories or salesman stories? I'd like to make them the butt of our jokes for a while." Everyone laughed, and Charles seemed to get the point: he came up with an innocuous and suitably self-deprecating joke about salesmen.

The party continued, and Victoria felt good about the stance she had taken. She knew she would have reproached herself later if she hadn't spoken out, and she was satisfied at having found a position midway between passive silence and clear assertiveness, which might have offended her hosts.

Much has been made lately of the virtues of standing your ground, of gaining self-respect by refusing to let others trample on your legitimate feelings. Fair enough—but often the way we express this new confidence kicks off another set of difficulties in our relationships. Making your own views known, or getting what you personally desire, forms only half the picture. Focusing on that component alone is aggressive. Bearing in mind the wishes of others while attempting to get your own wants met by legitimate means is assertive.

The Benefits of Assertiveness

There's very little to be gained from being passive. Passive people fail to voice their wishes at all—or, if they try, they take refuge in an unclear and ambiguous manner. They tend to back down, cave in, and acquiesce to someone else's position. As a result, they feel constantly unhappy and defeated.

Passive-aggressive behavior does no good, either. It's like the stack of oily rags in the furnace room that sooner or later flares up in seemingly spontaneous combustion. People who behave in this way seem to be pushovers, but they're prone to brooding and tend to nurture long-delayed revenge. Then they suddenly explode in ways that—because they've been bottling up their unhappiness for so long—are even more out of proportion and unrelated to the events at hand.

Aggression dead-ends; it never succeeds for long. For one thing, the aggressive and anger-driven personality is under non-stop self-inflicted stress. This is a very unpleasant state of mind and body; it's terribly draining to be forever argumentative and looking for a fight. As well, you never know when someone bigger, louder, and pushier than you will come on the scene. Worse yet, you never know when your aggressive ways will catch up with you in deadly earnest. Several recent reviews have confirmed the significant role that hostility, anger, and aggressiveness play in predicting coronary heart disease (heart attacks) even when compared against stress, cholesterol levels, nutrition, exercise, and other factors.[2]

Assertiveness, however, is full of benefits. It's really quite liberating, as many formerly passive personalities have found. It opens up many new possibilities and does indeed "win friends and influence people," bringing you into closer and more honest contact with those you meet. This is one of the key distinctions between assertiveness and aggression. When you're assertive, even in an unpleasant or uneasy situation, the other person feels respected and accepted, not put down. Behave aggressively, and he or she reacts defensively and angrily, tries to make an end run around you by achieving some unrelated effect or walks away laden with unpleasant thoughts and feelings directed toward you. Being assertive means that you must constantly bear other people and their reactions in mind. Eye contact, body language, tone of voice, and choice of words are all important, along with a degree of tact that, if mastered, could get you into the diplomatic service in no time flat.

Exercises

Success means achieving what you set out to attain. Assertive people are positioned to achieve their goals in part because they tell others what they want, what they believe in, or how they feel in a clear, unambiguous way, while considering and respecting other positions. And they stand their ground when others offer resistance. This combination of clearly articulating what they want and where they stand, while being respectful of the needs of others increases the probability that they will obtain their wishes.

Success eludes passive people because they are often not clear in their own minds about what they want, and they certainly have difficulty expressing their wishes or needs clearly and unambiguously to others. So how can others give them what they want or aid them in obtaining it? Passive people also cave in, change their minds, or take back their requests at the slightest sign of resistance.

Aggressive people have trouble achieving their goals because—although they might be clear about what they want or where they stand—they put forth their wishes and beliefs in ways that are disrespectful, inconsiderate, or belittling of others. As a result, those around aggressive people perceive them as destructive, self-centered, self-serving, or angry, and either avoid them or agree to go along with them under pressure, but ultimately withdraw support or sabotage them.

If you can learn to recognize what you want, what you believe in, or how you feel, and put this forth without beating around the bush, there is no reason why others will not give you what you want, or help you obtain it.

Self-Assessment

Throughout these exercises bear in mind the continuum: passive . . . assertive . . . aggressive.

1. Shoshanna, 14, enters the family room where her older sister, Lisa, has been watching television for the past three hours. Shoshanna wants to watch her favorite program, which starts in five minutes.

So she:

a) knowing that Lisa always hogs the TV set when she has it, decides to go upstairs to her room and listen to CDs instead.

b) states emphatically, "You're always watching TV. I never get a chance to watch it. You're unfair. I want to watch. It's my turn now. Get out of here or I'm going to tell Dad."

c) says, "Lisa, I know you want to continue watching TV, but my program is coming up in five minutes and I'd like to watch it. It's over in an hour, then you can go back to watching TV again. Remember when I did the same for you two days ago?"

Before you look at the answers below, can you determine which of the above responses is assertive, which is aggressive, and which is passive?

Response a) is passive: Shoshanna withdraws. Response b) is aggressive: Shoshanna is coming on too strong, speaking too harshly, and threatening without any consideration for Lisa. Response c) is assertive: Shoshanna clearly lets Lisa know what she wants, considers Lisa's needs by stating she will watch for only an hour, and points out her own previous consideration.

2. In your notebook, write down a situation that took place in the past week in which you behaved passively. Under that vignette write down the thoughts that went through your mind that interfered with your behaving assertively. Looking back, what were you concerned might happen if you behaved assertively? How did you expect the other person might react?

3. Write down a situation in the past week where you behaved too aggressively. In a column, write down the thoughts and feelings you experienced at that time. How did the other person react?

4. Write down a scenario in which you behaved assertively in the past week. What were the thoughts and feelings that accompanied your being assertive? How did the other person react?

Self-Assignments

Remind yourself how to set up the ABCDE chart by looking back at Chapter 2.

As you can see from these exercises, we often behave in unassertive and passive ways because of the silent self-talk that goes on in our heads. Commonly, self-talk has to do with fearful expectations that others might become angry with us, belittle us, or mock us. Some of us also have another family of self-talk that makes us fear that assertiveness will hurt, damage, or humiliate others.

For those of us who respond aggressively instead of assertively, our self-talk usually has to do with the idea or feeling that we are being put down, disrespected, or dominated by the other person.

Note: It may be that readers might think that all these exercises are too much work. We believe that, indeed, it takes some effort—or work—just like developing any skill takes effort. Earlier, in Chapter 2, we pointed out the similarities between practicing these exercises to gain a new skill—assertiveness, for example—to practicing a new golf stroke to, say, correct a hook. The benefit of the effort required is that it enhances the skill: practice your golf stroke and you'll be delighted at how straight you swing. Practice these exercises, and you will be similarly pleased with the enhanced success you'll achieve in your professional and personal life.

1. Go back to the scenarios you wrote down earlier in Exercises 2, 3, and 4 and try to ascertain into which of the three families of self-talk your thoughts fell.
2. Over the next two weeks continue to write down vignettes where you behaved assertively, passively, and aggressively, and list the self-talk that accompanied each.
3. For situations where you behaved passively, dispute and debate the self-talk that interfered with your being assertive.
4. For situations where you behaved aggressively, dispute and debate the self-talk that led you to such behavior.
5. Try to be aware of situations where you find yourself tempted to hold back, not saying what is on your mind, relinquishing your stand. Debate and dispute the self-talk that causes obstacles to your being assertive.
6. Push yourself to behave assertively in situations where you usually do not by being clear about your opinion or desires, and ensure that you are simultaneously being considerate of the other person. Note how the other person responds.
7. An important part of assertiveness is recognizing and articulating the difference between facts and opinions. Facts are supported by clear, undeniable evidence and may be confirmed or disproved. Opinions are simply preferences, beliefs, and points of view. For example, the idea that it's warmer in Florida than in Minnesota is a fact. The idea that rock and roll

is superior to classical music or jazz is an opinion. Write down several examples of facts and opinions that you've encountered in recent weeks.

8. If some of the facts were actually opinions masquerading as facts, how did you respond? Was your response effective? If not, how will you respond when the situation arises again? For example, you might choose to say something like "You seem to have strong views on this subject. My own thoughts are . . . " If someone insists that his or her position is based on facts, you have a right to ask for the evidence. Now, think of three new statements you can use when confronted with an antagonistic discussion partner.

9. At the end of the two-week period, write down how many times you behaved assertively, passively, and aggressively. Note whether there is a positive change over this time period. If there is not, repeat these exercises.

PART IV | The Interpersonal Realm

This realm of emotional intelligence concerns what are known as people skills. Those who function well in this area tend to be responsible and dependable.[1] They understand, interact with and relate well to others in a variety of situations. They inspire trust and function well as part of a team.

Chapter 9

Interpersonal Relationships

"Consider the following. We humans are social beings. We come into the world as the result of others' actions. We survive here in dependence on others. Whether we like it or not, there is hardly a moment of our lives when we do not benefit from others' activities. For this reason it is hardly surprising that most of our happiness arises in the context of our relationships with others."

—TENZIN GYATSO, 14TH DALAI LAMA

DEFINITION:

By interpersonal relationships, we mean the ability to establish and maintain mutually satisfying relationships that are characterized by the ability to both "give" and "take" in relationships, and where trust and compassion are openly expressed in words or by behavior. Mutual satisfaction includes meaningful social interchanges that are potentially rewarding and enjoyable and characterized by give and take. Positive interpersonal relationship skill is characterized by sensitivity toward others. This component of emotional intelligence is not only associated with the desire to cultivate friendly relations with others but with the ability to feel at ease and comfortable in such relations, and to possess positive expectations concerning social intercourse.[2]

Roger and Gary met as young men during their first week of dental school, and seemed an odd couple. Roger was the archetypal extrovert. His two passions in life were good food and having fun. As a result, he was out each night until the small hours, and was overweight. He did reasonably well in his studies but, when it came time to graduate, was bouncing around in the bottom half of the class. He didn't care. One year, he'd been elected class president, which pleased him hugely. He was now considerably overweight and quite bald, but he loved people and they loved him in return.

Gary, on the other hand, was slim and fit, an absolute perfectionist, who studied long and hard. This seemed to pay off; his marks were spectacular. In contrast to the gregarious Roger, he confined himself to a small group of like-minded peers. When other students needed help in their courses, he was considered the man most likely to know the answer to a difficult question. He was also considered the man most likely to succeed.

Both men planned to specialize after they graduated—Roger in endodontics, and Gary in periodontics. Roger knew that his lackluster marks boded ill for acceptance into even a garden-variety graduate program, but one of his professors, who believed in his talents, had a word with a friend who happened to teach at Harvard. Roger was accepted into the graduate program at Harvard and proceeded to have even more fun. As for Gary, he applied to several prestigious schools, all of which were eager to have him aboard. He took his pick, which happened to be the University of Washington, and began to apply himself even more diligently than before.

Both men completed their programs, married, and began to raise families. But their approaches to their work were as different as their personalities. Roger delighted in attending all sorts of dental functions and talking to fellow practitioners—just as he enjoyed talking to everyone who crossed his path. He therefore built up an enormously useful network of referral sources. As a result of this, his practice thrived from the very first day he opened his office door. Because his patients thought he was the best dentist they'd ever met, they too were keen to recommend his services. Eventually Roger was elected president of a major dental association, and lived happily ever after.

Not so Gary, who struggled to get his practice off the ground. He didn't believe in marketing himself—indeed, he said the word with a contemptuous sneer. He avoided professional gatherings and did not socialize with other dentists. He knew that his work was of the highest quality, but couldn't bring himself to advertise the fact. He sent lengthy and detailed reports to dentists who referred patients to him which stopped just short of criticizing their work. What he thought of as "small talk" evaded him; he had, in short, no chair-side manner. Nor, unlike Roger, could he initiate and cultivate a relationship.

As far as Roger was concerned, people were great. He was genuinely keen to learn more about them and remembered the minutest details of their lives. His enjoyment and interest were evident and infectious; people felt good around him. These factors marked the difference between his success and Gary's failure to fill his appointment ledger.

Roger's ability to build robust personal relationships with others, intertwined with his capacity to show interest in them and their concerns, was far more important in driving his success than were his technical skills. On the other hand, Gary's aloof and critical style alienated prospective referrers as well as patients, despite his Harvard post-graduate training and his impeccable technical skills.

Key Skills for Better Relationships

In many occupations, good relationships with a wide range of other people are necessary and expected. They come with the territory; they're part of the job description. It's difficult to imagine a salesperson, a politician, a member of the clergy, a social worker, or a teacher with poor interpersonal skills—but our research has shown that these skills are also advantageous in fields that don't immediately spring to mind as "people professions." Such seemingly unlikely groups as computer programmers, engineers, mechanics, accountants, scientists, and plumbers all achieved a higher rate of success if they had high EQs. The reason is simple. If large numbers of people in a given field are all more or less on par in terms of their professional competence, what could enable some of them to move ahead of the pack? Having read this far, you know that the answer is emotional intelligence.

What are the secrets to initiating and maintaining good interpersonal relationships? As with every component of emotional intelligence, there are specific skills involved—and once again, the good news is that they can be learned, as proven by the noted psychologists Drs. Samuel Turner and Deborah Beidel, who've developed a program known as Social Effectiveness Training,[3] designed to assist people who suffer to some degree from social anxiety. By understanding how some of us perform exceptionally well in social situations and by studying others who are experiencing social problems, they've uncovered several key skills that will, with practice, make a difference.

These skills may strike you as quite basic, verging on simplistic. But we've found that even the most mature and otherwise successful individuals are often unaware of these principles. When we sit down with them and work our way through a particular interaction that in some way proved detrimental to them, they're constantly surprised.

Basically, the Turner-Beidel program is divided into three parts. The first involves becoming aware of your social environment; it teaches you when, where, and why to begin and end a variety of interactions. The second part—interpersonal skills enhancement—covers verbal and non-verbal aspects of these interactions: how to be a good listener, how to switch topics, and so on. The third part centers on presentation skills. If you're comfortable talking to a group of people, you have a far better chance of developing useful networks and cultivate long-lasting, meaningful relationships.

Let's look more closely at some of these skills. If you want to initiate conversations with ease, you must pay attention to the social environment. Perhaps you want to introduce yourself to a stranger you happen to see at the bus stop every day, or be ready to respond when you bump into co-workers in a different setting (say, a mall or at a theater). Perhaps the environment is more or less purposeful and structured—a PTA meeting or an aerobics class—or a "forced confinement" situation such as an elevator.

How do you approach people in these diverse settings? First, you want to make sure you have their attention. Are they busy with an activity, or do they acknowledge your presence and smile?

If the latter, the easiest ice-breaker with a stranger is simply to smile back and introduce yourself. You might want to comment on something you have in common (the same bus, the same film you've both seen or are waiting to see).

Selecting a topic for conversation is more important. Three general areas can be regarded as "safe" to discuss: current events, careers, and shared interests. Most of us, if we're inclined to talk at all, have something to say about what's happening in the world or our working lives, or our hobbies.

Keeping the conversational ball rolling is easier if you start with tangibles—a person's car, or his or her choice in office art. With strangers, the idea is to draw them out by asking questions that begin with specifics (how long have they been coming to wherever you happen to be) and move to more open-ended queries (what other places have they been).

Here's a typical situation that you can easily play out in your mind: You're waiting in line at a local store, and you notice that the man in front of you is someone you've seen before. He notices you and smiles—a cue that he's open to passing the time. How will your conversation unfold? Imagine what you'd say about a number of topics, and how you'd shift gears if things started to go a bit flat. See how long you can keep this imaginary dialogue going, and look toward ending it on a graceful note.

While you're doing this, be aware that a conversation flows more freely if you pay attention to the other person, remembering clearly what he or she has said. Sometimes when we meet someone, we're so concerned about our own issues—how we look, what sort of first impression we'll create, whether or not we'll say the right things—that the conversation dwindles into separate monologues, instead of establishing or increasing the bond between the two parties.

But you can practice paying attention to others, just as you can practice all the other components of emotional intelligence. In fact, this skill is closely tied to empathy (see Chapter 10). Think back now to several people you've recently met. What stands out most in your mind? Would you find it useful to keep brief notes about them and others you meet, so that you'll be able to recall important details? You'd be surprised to know how much it means to people in this busy and impersonal world if you remember things about them, demonstrating that you value them and took something away from your previous meetings.

Another important conversational skill is the ability to change topics smoothly and appropriately. Once again, be alert to cues that indicate that it's time to do so. Simple transitional phrases such as "come to think of it" or "that reminds me" may do the job. Be careful, though, to stick with a particular topic as long as it's mutually worthwhile. People who seem to jump around all over the conversational map are sometimes thought of as shallow or superficial.

Give and take is the key to building successful relationships. Individuals who only give are often experienced by others as lacking self-regard and as being too compliant. Such people may have difficulty being assertive, which fuels their "over-giving." Individuals who only take in a relationship are ultimately experienced by others as selfish or bullying. They, too, have difficulties with assertiveness, confusing it with aggression (as explained in detail in Chapter 8). And both individuals—those who give too much and those who take too much—are generally unsuccessful in building solid relationships.

People who are proficient at building strong interpersonal relationships intuitively know that such relationships are founded on mutuality: reciprocity of "give and take." Relationships that flounder can usually be traced to a lack of reciprocity: either one of the two individuals weakens the relationship because he or she is always taking and never giving, or is always giving and seems unable to receive.

In the former situation, a person will undermine the relationship because he or she is experienced as exploitive, parasitic, opportunistic, and being only a "user." In the latter case, one of the potential partners—always giving and unable to receive—weakens the relationship because he or she, through that behavior, is experienced as being too needy, not believing him- or herself worthy of friendship and thus having to "buy" it. That person's behavior can also cause others to feel guilty, obligated, or dismissed—feelings that work against forming strong relationships.

Successful workers at all levels of an organization—from front-liners to CEOs—intuitively know that relationships are built on reciprocity of give and take. They know one other crucial factor in building firm and resilient relationships: they listen more than they speak, and they listen deeply and intently to the person speaking to them. Of these workers, others say, "He really took me seriously... I felt as if I were the only person in the whole room in whom he was truly interested... for those five minutes I felt valued, appreciated, taken seriously, and the center of his attention."

Why such responses? Because authentic, active, deep listening forges strong relationships. When listened to in this manner, the speaker feels valued, attended to, and interesting. Too often we think that developing a relationship means that we have to talk a lot, impress others with our achievements, let the world know of our past accomplishments and future dreams. Not so. That behavior risks us being experienced as braggarts, interested only in ourselves. As one CEO jokingly told me, "God gave us two ears and one mouth as a message to listen at least twice as much as we talk!"

Making and Keeping Friends

Good, supportive friends are among life's greatest rewards. They're the people we turn to in times of happiness and distress, or simply to talk to about life's daily grind. The give-and-take of these vital relationships pays off in small, almost imperceptible ways in the short term, but pays big dividends over time.

Where can you meet new friends? How can you establish new and interesting relationships? Well, there's no shortage of places to meet people—churches or synagogues (which obviously suggest a shared spiritual bond) or adult education classes (that just as obviously attract people with similar interests) are great places to start. Fitness is good for both body and soul, and health clubs and sports events attract a wide cross-section of men and women of every age. You might enjoy looking into one of many community and school organizations, or working with a political party. Of course, kids are second only to pets as an ice-breaker. Are yours into baseball or hockey, dance or drama? Many a friendship has been struck while cheering on a child.

But knowing where to meet people is only a first step. Next, you have to initiate contact by recognizing the cues that suggest another person is interested in pursuing matters. Conversation leads to invitation, starting with smaller, noncommittal activities (coffee before lunch, lunch before dinner). Present the invitation in a way that will allow you to gauge the other person's interest, perhaps by suggesting that you might do something "sometime." A positive response means go ahead; a neutral one means try again some other day.

Once you've established a relationship with someone, the next phase involves continued contact in person, by phone, or by e-mail. This is important so that both parties know the other hasn't lost interest; by staying in touch, you give the new friendship time to develop and grow.

Exercises

There are very few, if any, successful hermits. Part of success is the ability to cultivate and develop meaningful relationships with others. Close interpersonal relationships add to the richness of life and provide valuable support in times of need. For example, social support has been found to be a significant variable in helping people cope with serious illnesses.

Self-Assessment

1. Generally speaking, do you prefer being with people or alone? In which situations do you like being alone? In which situations do you prefer to be with other people?

2. What do people generally like about you?
3. What do they dislike?
4. Which of these activities makes you feel uncomfortable: meeting someone new, going to a party, speaking up in a group situation, asking a stranger a question, having a serious conversation with someone, getting to know someone better, teaching someone close to you to do something new, being intimate with someone?
5. Which of the above—or some other selection of your own—makes you the most uncomfortable? Why do you think this is so?
6. Briefly describe the last time you felt uncomfortable in one of the above situations. What were your feelings? Were you aware of the feelings of the other person or people involved? What thoughts went through your mind? How could you have better dealt with this situation?

Self-Assignments

1. Think of five situations when you might need to introduce yourself to someone new (e.g., a new employee at work, someone who just moved into the neighborhood) and, in each case, write down five different forms your introduction could take (e.g., "Hello. My name is John Smith. I don't think we've met before," or "Welcome to the neighborhood. I'm Jane Doe.").
2. Over the course of the next week, introduce yourself to a stranger and start a conversation. Use open-ended questions, along with the skills you'll learn from the chapter on empathy (Chapter 10). Describe the interaction in your notebook. Include the person's name, the topics you discussed, the person's reaction, and how you felt about the interaction.
3. Suppose you've met someone you'd like to know better. Based on your first impressions, write down questions you could use to initiate a conversation, sustain it, switch topics, or seek a graceful exit while looking forward to your next meeting.
4. Taking an interest in others means asking them personal questions. Many people shy away from this, because they think it may be seen as intrusive, but wrongly so—people love to talk about themselves. Most of the time, people will appreciate that you are taking an active interest in who they are and what they are saying. Listen deeply and ask questions that facilitate their telling you even more.

The questions you ask will depend on the nature of your relationship with the other person. In your notebook, write down some of the questions you might ask to get to know your co-workers, a partner or spouse, or a friend better.

5. Invite someone you know to an activity (out to coffee, a movie, etc.). In your notebook, describe how the person reacted to your invitation, what activity you agreed upon, and whether the interaction was a success.

6. Keep a list of the people you contact each week—acquaintances, friends, and relatives. Are you satisfied with the nature of these contacts? How about the frequency? Are there people you would like to be closer to? Are there relationships you are dissatisfied with? What can you do to change the nature of these unsatisfying relationships?

Chapter 10

Empathy

"Seeing with the eyes of another, listening with the ears of another, and feeling with the heart of another."

—ALFRED ADLER

DEFINITION:

Empathy is the ability to be aware of, understand, and appreciate the feelings and thoughts of others. Empathy is "tuning in" (being sensitive) to what, how, and why people feel and think the way they do. Being empathic means being able to "emotionally read" other people. Empathetic people care about others and show interest in and concern for them.[1] It is the ability to non-judgmentally put into words your understanding of the other person's perspective on the world, even if you do not agree with it, or even if you find that perspective ridiculous. Being empathic shifts an adversarial relationship to a collaborative relationship. Empathy has nothing to do with being "nice" to others. Empathy is simply a skill that allows you to see and experience the world from another person's perspective. Putting that understanding into words solidifies your relationship with that other person, and shifts it from an adversarial into a collaborative relationship.

It was the morning of their big sales presentation and Edmond had been unable to put together the numbers Roxanne, the lead presenter, needed for her PowerPoint show because his daughter was ill the night before. He spent hours in the emergency ward waiting for her to be seen. Roxanne was fuming when Edmond indicated he had not yet finished his part. The first words out of her mouth were, "I hate it when you don't pull your weight. If I had known I couldn't depend on you I would have worked with Joanne. Now I'll have to spend the rest of the morning finishing your work. I already had other things I was planning to do for this presentation. Did you even think about how this would impact on me?"

Edmond could have simply replied, "My daughter was sick, I was at the hospital—I couldn't help it."

What Edmond did say was, "I'm sorry I don't have the numbers. It must seem to you that I'm not taking this seriously, and you must be frustrated that I haven't kept my commitment to you."

Roxanne replied, "That's right, that's just how I feel. So what happened? Why don't you have the numbers worked out?"

Edmond's empathic comment—putting into words Roxanne's feelings of annoyance and frustration—helped to calm her down and shifted the adversarial tone of their relationship to a much more collaborative one. With this new collaborative tone, Roxanne was now willing to hear his reason for not doing his work, without perceiving it as an excuse. When she heard that his daughter was ill, her anger dissipated entirely: "That's too bad. Sorry I got so angry. You know how I hate to be behind on projects."

What Empathy Is Not

At its core, empathy is the ability to see the world from another person's perspective, the capacity to tune in to what someone else might be thinking and feeling about a situation—regardless of how that view might differ from your own perception. It is an extremely powerful interpersonal tool. When you make an empathic statement, even in the midst of an otherwise tense or antagonistic encounter, you shift the balance. A contentious and uneasy interchange becomes a more collaborative alliance.

When a relationship is an effective collaboration, you maximize your ability to get what you want or need from the other party. After all, no one is going to give you what you desire if they feel misunderstood or attacked.

In that case, you'd be viewed with mistrust or anger. By contrast, every time others feel as if you're in tune with them, they feel validated. The emotional bond between you strengthens, and the other person is more apt to work with, not against you.

But, for such a powerful tool, empathy is underutilized. There are three main misconceptions about empathy that prohibit many people from turning it to their advantage.

First, they sometimes confuse empathy with being "nice"—with making generally polite and pleasant statements. This is not what empathy means. For example, in the airport scenario described in Chapter 2, John told Sally the ticket agent that it must be hard for her to deal with stupid and abusive patrons. He was very accurately putting into words his perceptions of her thoughts and feelings, but he wasn't being particularly nice. The ticket agent didn't know—and didn't need to know—whether John was nice to everyone he met. He may well have been, and chances are he was, but it wasn't important to their interchange. As a result of his empathic comments, Sally felt a sense of connection with him, and became actively interested in doing her best to get him on board a flight.

Second, many people confuse empathy with sympathy, but the two are actually quite different. Basically, sympathy puts the speaker first, by putting into words our reactions to and feelings about another person's situation. In the airport scenario, John eventually expressed sympathy by saying that he felt sorry about what Sally had to put up with. But to have begun their conversation with that remark would have been a mistake on his part. Instead, he wisely considered her thoughts and feelings paramount. Empathic statements usually begin with the word "you"—as in, "you must be feeling or thinking [a certain way]." Sympathetic statements begin with "I" or "my," and reflect the speaker's perspective. For example, you might attempt to comfort someone who's suffered a loss by saying, "I was sad to hear" about it, or, "My condolences to you and your family." These are welcome sentiments, and wholly appropriate to certain situations. But they're not empathic, and don't have the power to change relationships.

Third, some people believe that, by making an empathic statement, they'll seem to be agreeing with or approving of the other person's position, when in fact they might be opposed to it. Not so. Empathy is simply an acknowledgment that the other party holds that viewpoint. By expressing empathy, you admit its existence without passing judgment on its validity.

Unfortunately, empathy often falls by the wayside because when we need it most, we're least open to using it—that is, when we're under stress, misunderstood, irritated, or defensive. At times like these, our comments automatically reflect our perspective. We're quick to argue our position, defend our behavior, and attack the other person's stance. They, in turn, tend to react in exactly the same way. The result is a lockstep escalation of emotional push and counter-push, which of course ends up being counter-productive for all concerned.

Put Emotions on Hold

If you are prone to short temper—as all of us are, at one time or another—why not learn to take your emotional temperature before it climbs into the red? That reading can serve as a kind of radar or early warning system that guides you through your interactions with others by offering signals that allow you to better navigate your environment.

Let's imagine, for example, that your child comes home from a baseball game. He and his team just lost. He speaks to you in a rude and disrespectful tone. Your first inclination is to respond in kind, snapping back at him. After all (at least in the glow of false nostalgia), you never treated your parents that way. Or you might say the wrong thing—in this case, "So, you lost another game." This ups the ante and he will explode in earnest.

Saying something like "You sound upset. Are you?" is an empathic comment on what you think might be his inner experience—one of being upset. Empathic comments such as this allow the recipient to feel understood, and in feeling understood, they strengthen the sense of being on the same side.

Another result of an empathic comment is that it allows the recipient a chance to talk more about what is truly bothering him or her. In this example, the youngster replies, "Of course I'm upset! We just lost the semi-finals." Which leads to an empathic response such as: "That's just terrible. You guys worked so hard. This must be so disappointing and angering."

Instead of being reactive, slow down. Stop and think for a second. Your child's purpose in behaving this way isn't to get you upset. The wise approach on your part is to switch on the radar. Your anger serves as a red light. Something is bothering him, and it's important for you to hold back until you realize what's going on. You detect that he's not upset at you, but at himself and his team for losing. He's not angry at you, but at the other team for winning, and at himself and his team for not playing well.

Now is the time for you to be understanding, to defuse the confrontation rather than give into your own anger and allow it to escalate.

There's a twin challenge here: to use self-awareness to gauge our mounting irritation, contain our impulses, and act sensibly in the face of provocation; and to call upon our empathic side in order to grasp the other person's position.

This is what John the airport traveler from Chapter 2 succeeded in doing, whereas Sam, his hostile fellow passenger, failed. Sam spoke exclusively from his own selfish point of view, railing on about his importance, his inconvenience, his promised retaliation. John put his reactions on hold and put into words how he believed the ticket agent must have felt. She in turn felt relieved, validated, and understood, with the result that John succeeded in his aims.

Ask Excavating Questions

Of course, empathy (or any other component of emotional intelligence) isn't a magic wand. An encounter may not immediately take a turn for the better if one party expresses empathy. In fact, the other person's anger may momentarily increase. Knowing that someone sees her point of view, she may feel more comfortable about freely venting displeasure or hurt feelings. As well, a long-standing relationship between two people may serve to muddy or complicate what kind of statements can productively be offered in an empathic way. If there's an atmosphere of distrust or a hierarchical power imbalance, especially in the workplace, it can be even harder to call upon your empathic abilities.

It's tempting to believe that if we know a person reasonably well and can recall his thoughts and feelings as expressed in previous and vaguely similar encounters, we can make a fairly accurate guess as to what his feelings are likely to be in the present tense. But it's a mistake to assume too much about anyone—whether a stranger or a friend. That's why what we call excavating questions are an important prelude to expressions of empathy.

Excavating questions help you dig for the truth of the matter. They uncover another person's innermost emotions by requiring that person to provide more information about him- or herself—information that will enable you to formulate a response. These questions can't be answered with a simple yes or no. They're personal and open-ended, though very often outwardly nonspecific and general: how did you feel (or what did you think) about this or that; what did you wish might happen?

To express empathy, you need to elicit and pay close attention to two types of information: the words another person uses to describe thoughts and feelings, and those used to describe desires and expectations.

Consider this exchange between Greg, a 16-year-old with a problem on his mind, and his father, Howard.

> Greg: I can't believe it's Monday, and the exam's tomorrow. I figured I could get in three hours of studying a night, but no way. I wish I was ready for it.
>
> Howard: Well, if you'd organized your time and watched less TV, you wouldn't be in this mess.
>
> Greg: Yeah, that's right. Climb all over me the day before the exam. That's just what I want to hear. And how do you know how much TV I watch? You're not around here often enough to know.

How do you think Greg felt in this instance—understood and soothed? What about the relationship between him and his father—is it one of alliance or contention? Clearly, Howard spoke from his own perspective in an entirely critical way, spurring Greg's angry and petulant response.

Now let's alter the dialogue slightly, and see where it leads.

> Greg: Here it is, Monday, and I'm not ready for the exam tomorrow. I tried to get in three hours of study a night, but there was no way.
>
> Howard: Don't worry about it. It won't do any good. It's too late now; there's nothing you can do.

In this case, do you think Greg felt reassured or coldly dismissed? Does he think his father knows or cares about what he's going through? Do you predict a bright future for their relationship? Now let's shift the dialogue again. This time, after Greg confesses his unease, Howard connects with his son's feelings and emotions, and calls upon his empathic skills.

> Howard: Gee, that's too bad. Sounds like you're pretty worried about it. Do you think you'll be able to pass?
>
> Greg: I don't know. I'll take a shot, but it doesn't look too good. Guess I should have used my time better.

| Howard: | Is there anything I can do—anything you want to bounce off me between now and tomorrow? |
| Greg: | Well, now that you mention it... |

This time, Howard showed concern and a degree of empathic understanding of his son's situation ("Sounds like you're pretty worried about it"). That's exactly how Greg felt. Feeling that his father grasped and acknowledged his perspective, Greg was more open and willing to listen. Howard followed up by waiting for his son's response, and then suggested—but didn't impose—a possible solution. Even if the last-minute cramming session doesn't work, the relationship is in far better shape.

Focus on the Other's Subjective Perspective

What makes some people naturally empathic, and others less so? One factor, as noted, is the ability to ask questions that take the interchange away from superficial concerns to focus on understanding more about the other's perspective, especially if it is different from your own view. As Stephen Covey writes in his book, *The 7 Habits of Highly Effective People*,[2] "Empathic listening is so powerful because it gives you accurate data to work with. Instead of projecting your own autobiography and assuming thoughts, feelings, motives, and interpretation, you are dealing with the reality inside the other person's head and heart."

This can be particularly difficult in a complex and long-standing relationship, as shown in the following conversation between another father and son—Earl and Wayne.

Wayne:	I didn't make the varsity hockey team.
Earl:	Gosh, that's too bad.
Wayne:	[after a moment's sullen silence] You don't know what that's like.
Earl:	It must feel awful. I know you had your heart set on it.
Wayne:	What do you know? You told me you were the only kid in town who couldn't even skate.
Earl:	Okay—but I've had lots of letdowns.

Wayne: I'm not talking letdowns—I'm talking hockey.

Earl: Yes, I know, but . . .

Wayne: No, you don't. You don't know and you don't understand.

How is Earl doing here? At first glance, he's trying to do all the right stuff. He talks about how disappointed Wayne must be, which seems to him an empathic comment. In fact, it is, but it doesn't go far enough. Wayne's response shows that his father isn't homing in on what he's thinking and feeling.

Then Earl compounds his error by talking about himself and other unspecified disappointments in his life, which in Wayne's mind pale beside hockey. By doing so, he moves further away from seeing matters from his son's perspective.

Let's continue the dialogue and aim for a more satisfying conclusion. Now, Earl tries to stifle his defensiveness and experience the moment from Wayne's standpoint. He gets part of the way there, and gets at least an inkling of what it might be like for an athletic kid who lives and breathes hockey to even think about discussing his woes with a father who wouldn't know the difference between the third period and the sixth inning.

Earl: I guess it's hard talking to me about this. You figure I don't know anything about it, and it means so much to you.

Wayne: Yeah, well . . .

Earl: Maybe it doesn't get any easier when all the other guys have fathers who do know about it and take them to the games.

Wayne: Well, you show up and you cheer, but we're not really together, are we? And we don't talk about it. And I don't think you understand how important it is.

At about this point, Earl might begin, again, to get a bit defensive. He knows perfectly well that Wayne is out playing hockey five times a week; he'd have to be an idiot to miss that. He also knows that he's paying the bills for the practice time and the equipment. These are objective truths, but they're not the point of the conversation. On this score, Earl would, so far, get low marks for empathy, because empathy has relatively little to do with objective truth. Rather, it hinges on grasping the other's subjective truth—in this case, Earl's ability to tap into what Wayne feels about his failure to make the team, and about his father's failure to grasp the significance of that event. The point isn't what Earl sees from his adult, bill-paying perspective. The point is how a 17-year-old experiences his father and whether or not his father knows how vital hockey is to him. This is what Earl must focus on, so he changes tack.

> Earl: Okay, let's talk about this. Maybe I don't know how important hockey is for you. What would the other guys' fathers be doing or saying right now, to let their kids know they care about what's happening?

> Wayne: Well, just talking like this helps. You're taking it seriously, right? So that's a help.

> Earl: I guess it's not much, but I can promise you I'll still be at your games. And maybe you and I could go and watch the Leafs play sometime. We've never done that, but I'd like it. How does that sound?

> Wayne: Sure. That would be okay.

Perhaps you're wondering what might have happened if Earl had made this offer earlier in the conversation, when Wayne was really upset. Most likely it wouldn't have worked; Wayne would have smelled an attempt to placate him and buy him off. Instead, he had to feel understood, to know that his father could at least partially see the world from his perspective. That's why Earl's empathic comments were vital. He had to solidify a ruptured bond before Wayne would value any sort of peace offering.

Exercises

The power of empathy is that if you can grasp what another person is thinking and feeling—even if it differs wildly from your own perspective—and put your comprehension into words, the other person feels understood.[3] This offsets any degree of tension that exists between the two of you and forges a strong bond of collaboration that helps you get what you want: to solve problems and create successful interpersonal relationships.

Self-Assessment

Do you take the time to listen to what others are telling you? Do you accurately understand what they're saying before you respond to them? Remember, at this stage, it's important to be a sort of neutral recording device. This is not the time to superimpose your own version of what they're telling you or jump in with statements of your own feelings, thoughts, and opinions.

Below are three comments made by three different speakers. For each one, from the group of responses, decide which possible responses are empathic and which are not. Before looking at our answers, jot down the reasoning behind your decisions.

1. Sheena, a 26-year-old single woman, is describing what went on between her and her two sisters the day before: "It was so-o-o nice of them. Yesterday was my birthday and my sisters surprised me by taking me out to lunch at this terrific restaurant. I couldn't believe it! They gave me all these little presents!"

    To these comments you reply:
    a) "It sounds like you should have really thanked them and let them know how much you appreciated what they did."
    b) "It sounds like you had a terrific time."
    c) "It sounds like they wanted to give you a day to remember."
    d) "You were really surprised by their thoughtfulness!"

    Answers b), c) and d) are empathic. Why? Because, from her words, Sheena sounds surprised by her sisters' thoughtfulness, it certainly sounds like she enjoyed herself, and there is a suggestion that she viewed her sisters as wanting to give her a day to remember.

    Answer a), on the other hand, reveals more of a "reality oriented" perspective, and additionally there is nothing in Sheena's tone or words that implies that she felt she should have thanked them.

2. Still unable to master the computer program, Dillon turns to you for the third time that day seeking help and direction. He states, "I *still* can't figure out how to master this damn program. And you do it so flawlessly!"

    You reply:
    a) "Are you this slow on the uptake with everything?"
    b) "You'll catch on. I had the same trouble initially, too."

c) "These programs can feel really frustrating and make you think you'll never catch on. But it does get easier."

d) "Learning these programs can make you want to just put your fist through the screen. But it does get better."

e) "I know how it feels not catching on right away. I was really aggravated at the beginning, too."

Answers c) and d) are empathic. They capture the sense of frustration that Dillon is experiencing.

Answer a) is a judgmental comment that speaks to how you feel about Dillon turning to you yet again, and does not capture Dillon's feelings, thoughts, or behavior. Answer b) is not empathic either; it is more a sympathetic, reassuring comment. It may be helpful but it is not empathic. Answer e)—though heading in the right direction, in that it is reassuring—is from the speaker's perspective, not from Dillon's perspective. It, too, speaks more to sympathy than empathy.

3. Your spouse gets home at 5:30 p.m., turns to you and sighs, "I didn't get the promotion; Ralph got it. I just got a speeding ticket on the way home, and I've got a four-alarm headache."

You respond:

a) "Didn't get the promotion! We've been banking on it. We've been counting on the increased income. What went wrong?"

b) "Don't worry; you're smart. I've got confidence in you. Another opportunity will show up."

c) "You should have seen this coming. Ralph is a hotshot, he's everybody's friend, and he does have more experience."

d) "Oh, what a day you've had. You must wonder if it can get any worse."

e) "Geez...you must feel like nothing's going your way."

f) "Boy, you must feel like crap. Come here and I'll give you a back rub."

g) "Oh, dear, it sounds awful, but others have it worse. Remember Philly? He lost his job last month, and his wife walked out four days later."

Answer d) is an empathic statement. You are putting into words what your spouse's statements and behavior tell you about his or her internal experience. Answers e) and f) are also empathic. Once again, you are capturing what is probably your spouse's internal experience and perspective: nothing is going right. Additionally, you offer some nurture with your supportive offer to give a back rub.

With answer g), although you start off in the direction of empathy with your words "Oh, dear, it sounds awful," you quickly veer away from that empathic stance by pointing out that others have it worse. That may be reality. It may be true, but it is not an empathic statement. It is not going to allow your spouse to feel understood and supported. Rather, he or she is probably going to respond by feeling that his or her experience and trouble are being minimized by you.

Answer a) is not empathic. It is a comment made from your perspective. Answer b) is a reassuring comment; it may make your spouse feel better, but it is not an empathic comment. Answer c) is a comment, again, from your perspective. It is not empathic. Worse still, it would probably feel like a criticism (Ralph does have more experience) and a put down (Ralph is a hotshot).

To continue this scenario, let us assume that your response was g), where you point out that it could have been worse. Your spouse responds to this comment by saying "I tell you how terrible all of this is for me, and all you do is tell me how much worse it could have been!"

Given what you have learned in these examples, what do you think your response should be?

a) "I'm sorry. You're absolutely right. Here you are telling me what a disastrous day you've had and all I give you is stupid comparisons and meaningless platitudes."

b) "Well, I'm just trying to cheer you up!"

c) "Here we go—I'm wrong again! It seems I can't do anything right in your eyes."

The empathic statement is a), because with this statement you put into words what he or she is thinking.

Self-Assignments

1. Ask someone you know well how he feels about a given topic—something as simple as a recent film, or an event in which both of you participated. Then let the conversation roll for five minutes. At that point, describe to the person your version of what he thinks and feels. You may be surprised—to put it mildly—to find a difference of opinion.

2. In general, stop and listen more to others. If someone's feelings and opinions are of value to you, check to see how accurately you've understood her.

3. Keep a journal recording your correct (hits) and incorrect (misses) impressions of other people's feelings and thoughts. For each miss, record why you think you were off the mark.

4. Before meeting with someone important to you, prepare by thinking about your expectations of the person. Prepare, as well, for these expectations to be wrong. What would you like to accomplish as a result of the meeting? In which areas would you like to know more about this person?

5. During the encounter, focus on the other person. Make eye contact and pay close attention to facial expressions and body language. Check your interpretations of what's happening by means of questions like "Are you saying that . . . ?"

6. After your meeting, review the results. What did you learn about the person? How did she feel about things that are important to you? What things were important to her? How can what you learned be useful in your future relationship? What did you do that let the other person know how you feel about her?

Chapter 11

Social Responsibility

"If a free society cannot help the many who are poor, it cannot save the few who are rich."

—JOHN F. KENNEDY, 1961

DEFINITION:
Social responsibility comprises the desire and ability to willingly contribute to society, your social group, and generally to the welfare of others. This component of emotional intelligence involves acting in a responsible manner, even though you might not benefit personally, doing things for and with others, accepting others, acting in accordance with your conscience, and upholding social rules.[1]

Socially responsible people have social consciousness and a basic concern for others, which is manifested by being able to take on community-oriented responsibilities. They possess interpersonal sensitivity and are able to accept others and use their talents for the good of the collective, not just the self. People who are deficient in this ability may entertain antisocial attitudes, act abusively toward others, and take advantage of others.[2] It's doing something for the team, the division, the organization, or for society at large that does not benefit you directly.

Following one of our presentations on emotional intelligence at an event sponsored by a major social service agency, we were approached by a local rabbi. His reaction was unusual; we'd never come across it before. He began by talking about EQ's intrinsic morality. We asked him to explain what he meant. "Cognitive intelligence is amoral," he said. "Anyone can have a high IQ—it's a matter of luck. Murderers, criminals, and Nazis could have all had high IQs. But by their deeds, they could not have had high EQs. Thus, EQ involves morality. I like that."

We do, too. By definition, EQ includes social responsibility—a concern for the welfare of others, the ability to integrate yourself into the community at large, and a desire to further the betterment of your time and place. At a time when much of the so-called personal growth movement that started so promisingly can appear almost Machiavellian in nature, designed primarily to achieve a particular, often self-absorbed and inward-looking end, it's refreshing to note that emotional intelligence refers to—indeed, demands—a well-rounded and outward-looking approach to life.

The Queen of Hearts

Diana, Princess of Wales, continues to fascinate the world even after her death. What was it about her that spurred such a global outpouring of grief? Why did people feel a personal loss at her passing, and feel so drawn to her while she lived? What did she do to transcend the bounds of mere celebrity?

The Diana phenomenon cannot be explained by her royal status. Barring the late Queen Mother, whom everyone liked, and perhaps Diana's son Prince William, few people really care deeply about the rest of the House of Windsor. Diana's beauty certainly played a part. Had she been plain—a latter-day Eleanor Roosevelt—we might not have followed her doings quite so ardently. But many other equally beautiful women and handsome men fail to elicit the same reaction.

Nor did Diana's riches account for her popularity. Other fabulously wealthy people go almost unnoticed about their business. Nor was Diana's appeal based wholly on social responsibility, as some have claimed. Yes, she engaged in tireless volunteer work—but so did Mother Teresa, who died at about the same time. The world mourned her passing as well, if not quite so intensely. And Mother Teresa, in fact, gave more of herself to her chosen causes than any other public figure of our time, devoting her entire life to the world's most downtrodden.

What was unique about Diana? We believe it was the powerful combination of social responsibility and empathy. She embraced causes that were dear to her heart, going far beyond what was expected of her or what her advisors considered prudent. It was apparent in the way she talked to people and in the way she promoted her chosen causes that she genuinely cared about those on whose behalf she worked. Such commitment is rare, particularly in the rich and famous. Diana could have made obligatory appearances, lending her name to various charities. Good would have come of this; the media would have paid attention. But she went beyond that, and her deeds and appearances were characterized by emotion and authenticity of expression.

This sort of thing cannot be faked for long. Diana was no stranger to galas, but when she attended she made sure the spotlight shone on those in need. People whom she touched directly responded to her, even loved her. Those who witnessed her touch others loved her for doing so. She could empathize with the elderly, with children, with the sick, and those in the terminal stages of AIDS. She had no fear of approaching them or comforting those who'd lost limbs to land mines. She would look into their eyes, listen to them, and speak to their concerns. She also showed her own vulnerability, something everyone could relate to. Despite her exalted position, she suffered through an unhappy marriage, anorexia nervosa, and the suffocating attentions of the British press. That emotional sincerity, coupled with her social conscience, made her, as she wished, the Queen of Hearts.

Of course, Diana was not alone in her espousal of good works. Renowned film stars such as Elizabeth Taylor, Jane Fonda, and Barbra Streisand are dedicated to using their privileged positions to give something back. So are the many businesspeople who establish foundations, endow scholarships, and so forth. More good works are done behind the scenes than we know about, but more are needed.

We ourselves know something about the sometimes surreal world of professional sports. We've worked with hockey players—some of them barely in their 20s—who earn from $400,000 to $10 million for a season's work. What a boon it would be if all professional athletes associated themselves with charitable causes—a children's hospital, research into a fatal or wasting disease. There's no shortage of worthy causes that go begging for funds: programs that benefit the aged and disabled, newly arrived refugees, or single-parent families. By pledging a percentage of their vast salaries as well as making personal appearances, athletes would earn our respect. By giving back to society in a way that ordinary people cannot, they'd serve as role models and set an example we could all be proud of.

Corporate Social Responsibility

Until quite recently, social responsibility had no place in the boardrooms of the nation. Today, however, we see pulp and paper conglomerates pledging to preserve our forests. Oil companies tout the necessity of pristine oceans and reducing dependency on fossil fuels; brewers urge moderation and exhort us to intervene if our friends intend to drink and drive.

Social responsibility has always made good sense, but only recently has it begun to make good business sense as well—witness the courses in corporate ethics now prevalent at every major business school. Our research identifies a watershed event in this evolution: the creation, in Britain, of a chain of cosmetic stores called The Body Shop. Its founding president, the late Anita Roddick, launched her products by advertising the fact that none was laboratory-tested on animals, and announced that her business was dedicated to the pursuit of social and environmental change. At the time, most people didn't know that animal testing went on. But the campaign proved a success—and since then, many firms across different industries have followed suit.

Did Ms. Roddick believe passionately in animal rights or did she simply intuit and decide to capitalize on what advertisers call a unique selling proposition? In a sense, it doesn't matter. The Body Shop did well, and a more humane approach was forced on its competitors across the board.

Examples of this new mindset abound. For example, a woman named Christine Magee owns and operates a chain of bedding shops called Sleep Country Canada. It's always been her practice to donate customers' old but salvageable mattresses to suitable charities; the firm picks these up and delivers them at no cost.

Of course, we aren't suggesting that corporate social responsibility is a quality unique to businesswomen. A number of years ago one of us (Steven) spoke at a human resources conference in Cape Cod. There was a presentation scheduled at an earlier time slot on staff retention. The speaker, a CEO named Jeffrey Swartz, was to talk about his experience at Timberland, the boot, shoe, and outdoor clothing manufacturer. His presentation was something of a metamorphosis where he related his ascension to CEO of the family business. Starting out as a "spoiled rich kid," he was transformed through an experience of donating shoes to homeless people in Boston. As a result he refocused the company's mission, with social responsibility as one of the pinnacles.

His company was singled out in *Business Ethics* magazine's top 100 American corporate citizens list where it stated:

> One of the most impressive advances on the list was made by Timberland, which jumped from No. 74 last year to No. 6 this year. Timberland has one of the strongest employee volunteer programs in the country, with its decade-old "Path of Service" program giving employees 40 hours of paid time to contribute to the community during working hours. Now the Stratham, N.H., footwear and apparel company, with $1.6 billion in sales, is placing greater emphasis on environmental programs. In early 2006 Timberland announced a new shoebox "nutritional label," detailing where the product was made, how it was produced, and its impact on the environment and communities. "We thought about how closely consumers read nutritional labels on food products and thought, why doesn't this happen in our space?" recalls Dave Aznavorian, a senior global brand manager at Timberland.[3]

You may have wondered, what does that have to do with staff retention? Well the moral of Swartz's story was that after turning Timberland into a caring, socially responsible company, the firm's staff retention went up significantly. People now think of themselves as being part of an organization that makes the world a better place, as opposed to just working at a shoe manufacturing company.

The worldwide administration of the EQ-i and EQ-i 2.0 reveals that women score higher than men in social responsibility. However, women point out, correctly, that the glass ceiling still exists, that they may have come a long way, but there's still a long way to go. While women make up only 2 percent of bosses of America's largest corporations, there are (at the time of this writing) 15 female CEOs of Fortune 500 companies. These include CEOs Carol Bartz (Yahoo!), Angela Braly (WellPoint), Ursula Burns (Xerox), Lynn Eisenhans (Sunoco), Christina Gold (Western Union), Ellen Kullman (DuPont), Irene Rosenfeld (Kraft Foods), and Indra Nooyi (PepsiCo), among others.

Young girls are entering science classes in greater numbers, cheered by the knowledge that DuPont—tagline: "The miracles of science"—a leader in the field of science-based solutions in agriculture, nutrition, electronics, communications, safety, transportation, and apparel technology, has a female

CEO also. And so does Xerox, which currently bills itself "Ready for Real Business." These women earned their positions in direct competition with the best and brightest men—but we believe that they were aided in their success equation by their empathy and social-responsibility skills.

Helping Others Helps Yourself

Those skills are part of a balanced package that's being increasingly recognized as desirable in today's business climate and in everyday life. The best news about social responsibility is that—because it's directed outward—it's perhaps the easiest component of emotional intelligence to change. As it changes, other skills tend to slipstream along behind it and fall into place.

Here's a typical example. A friend whom we'll call Alex experienced a bout of apathy, low energy, and general depression during his first year away from home at university. We suggested that he become a Big Brother to a fatherless boy who was giving his mom a hard time. Not only did the child's behavior improve beyond everyone's hopes, but the weekly outings helped remedy Alex's fit of the blues. His self-regard improved, he was better able to set priorities, and he entered with renewed enthusiasm into campus life.

Being socially responsible has a demonstrable upside: it tends to pay off big and sometimes unexpectedly for modest effort. By helping others you often gain more meaning in your own life. By focusing on the more serious problems and dilemmas of others, you gain new perspective on your own. This alone can be therapeutic.

And it can pay off in more tangible ways as well. Confirmation of this comes from an unexpected source: two professors based at the universities of Oxford and Vienna who set out to discover why people cooperate with each other, and developed a mathematical model that pinpointed the benefits.[4] If we subscribe to survival of the fittest, there doesn't seem to be a scientific rationale for getting along with our fellow humans. We're probably programmed to put up with our relatives (this is known as kin-selection or the selfish gene), and if two people believe that they'll meet again, they'll be apt to make a stab at behaving half-decently. The challenge, though, was to figure out what drives the good Samaritan—someone who helps another person with no expectation of being helped in return at some future date. The explanation seems to be that word of your good deed will spread. Others will hear about it, view you as a kindly and altruistic individual, and be far more likely to do you a good turn when the time comes.

If so, think of social responsibility as a series of pebbles thrown into the water. The ripples will spread in unexpected ways. Let's look for a moment at Sam and Janet, who both started working as account executives at the same wholesaling company. Both were conscientious workers, but Sam tended to live and die by his job, staying late and putting in too much extra time for his own good. Janet, by contrast, felt it important to involve herself in all sorts of community activities, acting as a Big Sister and serving on the board of directors of a mental health treatment center for pre-school children.

In time, Sam began to feel he was getting stale at work—treading water by exerting himself more and more, but getting no further ahead. He felt, rightly, that he'd dedicated himself to the company, but began to suspect that his salary didn't reflect this contribution—in other words, that he'd never "get back" in some form what he'd put in.

Meanwhile, Janet's activities were doing her a world of good. First and foremost, she felt that she was contributing to the betterment of society. She donated money to worthwhile causes, but her personal involvement set her apart and gave her a real sense of fulfillment. Her outlook changed when it came to the inevitable aggravations at work and home—things that Bob, for example, took hard. A minor setback in one of his projects was immediately magnified into a full-blown disaster. Janet saw things in a different way. She knew what real disaster looked like, having witnessed it first-hand in the lives of those she helped.

As well, word of Janet's activities got around. As a board member at the treatment center, she made many contacts that proved enormously helpful at work and in her personal life. Soon she was bringing new clients to her firm. Another board member, who owned a public relations firm, helped her convince her superior to devise a more aggressive marketing campaign that included public relations, which eventually resulted in tens of thousands of dollars in new business. Janet also met a wide range of other professional men and women—people who may, at some point, prove of the utmost benefit to her if she decides to change fields or seek new opportunities.

In addition to volunteer or philanthropic activities, social responsibility in the workplace also encompasses your ability as a manager to contribute to your team or your department by following the direction that the team or department wants to take, even if the direction is not your number one choice. The direction suggested to you may be your second or perhaps even third choice (but certainly not your last). It should be a choice that you are comfortable and can live with, even though it is not your first. If the team or department's decision fulfills the objective decision-making criteria, social responsibility is the capacity to put your preferences aside, and follow what the team or department supports. A corollary of this is that excellent leaders can compromise and put their preferred decision aside when the team or department's decision is appropriate. Doing so solidifies team spirit, is evidence of your grounded flexibility, and demonstrates that good leaders are also good followers.

Seinfeld and the Good Samaritan

Is the New Testament story of the good Samaritan a bygone biblical homily? Not at all. Just as individuals clearly derive important benefits when they exercise social responsibility, so society itself has moved toward viewing helping others as a necessary component of community life—not a luxury, an indulgence, or an extra.

The final episode of the *Seinfeld* television show had an interesting plot-line (for a self-confessed show about nothing). In this program, Jerry and his friends fail to help a person whom they see being held up by a gunman, and are promptly charged under a fictitious good Samaritan law. While on trial, the self-absorbed quartet are forced to watch a parade of the moral misdemeanors they'd committed throughout the previous seasons.

But a very real law of this type was passed in Israel in 1998. It's based on the commandment cited in Leviticus 19:16—in essence, that a person is legally obligated to help another whose life is in danger, or who faces great risk to safety or health, as long as that help can be reasonably safely given. That is, you aren't compelled to rush into a burning building in order to save the occupants, but you must summon the fire department. Our ancient and collective understanding demonstrates that these actions on behalf of the common good are the glue that binds our society together. A high level of social responsibility means a better, more fully functioning emotional intelligence.

Exercises

Being successful is not a solo activity. Real success comes from being a valued, contributing member of a social group. Caring about and sharing with others, no matter how rich or poor you are, gives real meaning to your life and your success.

Self-Assessment

1. What community organizations are you involved in?
2. What active roles do you play?
3. What political party do you support?
4. What role do you play in it?
5. Do you participate in charitable activities? If so, list them and describe your role.
6. Do you feel that you donate enough money to charitable causes?
7. Do you feel that you contribute enough time to these same causes?
8. How can you involve your friends, family, and co-workers in an effort to be more involved in charitable events?
9. What have you done recently to help people who could use a hand?
10. What have you done recently to help strangers in need?
11. Give three examples of situations in which you were sensitive to the needs of friends, acquaintances, or co-workers. In each case, what did you do?
12. Reflect upon three situations when you did not go along with your team's (or department's) decision, and three examples of when you did go along with your team's (or department's) decision, even though it was not your number one choice. Detail why in particular circumstances where you did, and in particular circumstances where you did not. Did the reasons have to do with evidence-based criteria, your flexibility, your rigidity, your caving in to group pressure, your feelings that you always have to be right, your support of the team's (or department's) decision-making process, or your ability to live with the team's (or department's) decision?

Self-Assignments

1. In your notebook, write down five things you could do that would be appreciated by people in need.
2. Now think of one thing you could do this week that would help others.
3. Write down the three most worthy causes, charities, or non-profit organizations you can think of. Next to each, record the single most important thing, other than donating money, that you could do for them. Then select one action and follow through on it.

PART V | The Decision-Making Realm

This realm of emotional intelligence concerns your ability to use your emotions in the best way that helps you solve problems and make optimal choices.[1] Success in this area means that you can grasp problems and devise effective solutions, deal realistically with situations, and manage impulses that may disrupt effective decision making.

Reality Testing

Chapter 12

"All theory is gray, but the golden tree of actual life springs ever green."

—JOHANN WOLFGANG VON GOETHE, 1808

"There are some people who live in a dream world, and there are some who face reality; and then there are those who turn one into the other."

—DOUGLAS H. EVERETT

DEFINITION:
Reality testing is the ability to assess the correspondence between what's experienced and what objectively exists. Reality testing involves "tuning in" to the immediate situation. The best simple-sentence definition of reality testing is that it is the capacity to see things objectively, the way they are, rather than the way we wish or fear them to be. Testing this degree of correspondence involves a search for objective evidence to confirm, justify, and support feelings, perceptions, and thoughts. The emphasis is on pragmatism, objectivity, the adequacy of your perception, and authentication of your ideas and thoughts. An important aspect of this component involves the ability to concentrate and focus when trying to assess and cope with situations that arise.[2]

Reality testing is associated with maintaining a focus on the outside world, particularly when facing unpleasant situations, rather than burying one's head in the sand. It is the ability to tune in to the immediate situation with lucidity and clarity in perception and thought processes. In simple terms, reality testing is the ability to accurately size up the immediate situation rather than turn a blind eye to, or rationalize away, very real problems. It is also the capacity to curtail a tendency to "catastrophize" real problems. That is, it is the ability not to make "mountains out of molehills," but rather when a problem exists, to face it without always believing it is overwhelming and insurmountable.[3]

As they passed in the hallway, Dinah smiled at Roxanne, the new vice-president. Roxanne did not smile back. "Oh, my God," thought Dinah, "she doesn't like me. That's all I need. I must have done something to offend her. What am I going to do? I hate it when people don't like me."

Dinah's reality testing was compromised by unsubstantiated fears. She was unable to accurately and objectively judge her interaction with Roxanne; instead, she catastrophically interpreted it as confirmation of her worst fear: she was a person whom others didn't like. Had she been more objective and analytical, and less haunted by a basic sense of insecurity, she might have recognized that Roxanne was not slighting her but, rather, was preoccupied with her own concerns.

Be Objective

A police officer's job is not an easy one, for any number of reasons. One of the major challenges is dealing with, say, three witnesses to a car crash, who, commonly, produce three radically different versions of the event, leaving the cops to sort out what actually happened.

This same phenomenon unfolds daily in every human interchange. An old saying captures it well: there are three sides to everything—yours, mine, and the truth. When we experience an event, how close do we come to perceiving matters as they really unfolded, rather than coloring them by our fears, wishes, prejudices, and a host of defensive or offensive emotions? Discerning the difference between the way things are and the way we fear they are or hope they might be is the essence of reality testing.

How do we go about this necessary task? It involves a search for objective evidence that will confirm, justify, and support our thoughts and perceptions. As well, reality testing is the capacity to "read" situations accurately, to size up what's going on. At its most sophisticated, it allows us to tap into a group's emotional currents and power relationships, the shifting political alliances and allegiances that swirl beneath the surface. Reality testing lets us tune in to a situation while keeping it in a broader and correct perspective, without excessive fantasizing or daydreaming. It enables us to concentrate and focus on ways of coping with what we discover and to keep our emotions in check, uncolored by illusion.

People with a strong capacity for reality testing see the world around them in an objective, clear-eyed manner. They are quick to recognize where problems exist, and can perceive opportunities when they come into sight. Those who have weaker reality-testing skills either keep their heads in the sand to avoid facing problems or can see (and magnify) only risks and, as a result, are unable to take advantage of opportunities.

Don't Fear the Worst . . .

Let's see how reality testing plays out in one or two scenarios. First, we'll eavesdrop on Bob and Neil as they take a coffee break at Acme Industries. Bob is on the boil about the new CEO: "This guy isn't one of us; he doesn't understand what goes on here. They parachuted him in from Philadelphia. I don't know what to make of him, but I do know he's moving too fast. He's been here two months and he's turning the place upside down. All these changes are getting to me. I've dusted off my résumé and I'm starting to look around, but I'm not happy about it. I like this job, and Lord knows I need it. I've got a monster mortgage and I don't know who else is going to pay the freight. How about you?"

Neil, having taken all this in, replies, "I don't know much about the CEO either, but I've got friends in Philadelphia, and they say he seemed pretty fair. I'm not all that concerned. Why should I be? My division makes money and morale is good, so why should he tear it apart? I don't think there's been a problem with my performance evaluations, so why should he kick me out the door? Anything can happen; maybe he wants to bring in his own people. But I've been here a while, and they'd have to give me a package. That would give me time to look around. I was at Frontier for 10 years, so I know there's a life after Acme. I haven't got my head in the sand, but I think there's a future here for me. I'm not going to screw it up by spending all my time worrying. I can handle change as well as the next guy. It doesn't threaten me; it's more of an opportunity. Actually, I feel pretty good and pretty settled these days."

How would you rate Neil's capacity for reality testing? His views are well thought out, well argued, and based on a pragmatic assessment that seems to be supported by the evidence—neither his division nor his job is in peril. He's willing to work with the new administration, and intends to remain a valuable employee, but is confident that he'd be able to prosper elsewhere if necessary. He's unfazed by the prospect of change, and will probably continue to function as effectively as before.

Bob, on the other hand, has given way to fearful fantasies, has begun to catastrophize for no valid reason, and will only end up increasing his level of stress, which will interfere with his ability to do his job effectively—and may even result in his getting fired.

. . . But Take off Those Rose-Colored Glasses

In Bob's case, his baseless dread interfered with his ability to lucidly assess his situation. But other people who are deficient in reality testing rush to the opposite pole, adopting a naive, starry-eyed attitude, in spite of mounting evidence that all may not be rosy.

Nowhere is this reaction more prevalent than in the field of romance. Love is blind, and many a relationship (especially when it begins) finds both individuals painting their partners in idealized terms—as in this monologue delivered by Anna on the subject of her new boyfriend: "I know you think I'm nuts, but I really love him. He's changed, he really has. I have faith in him, and I know that my love has made a difference. Okay, he used to run with a bad crowd, but what do you expect when he got shuffled off into all those foster homes, and there was that thing with the drugs. But he was just holding on to a package; he didn't know what was in it. And he's older now. And I know all about the other women—real weirdos, like the one that got pregnant, but that was a long time ago, and . . . " But why continue? Anna's reality-testing skills obviously need work; she has her head in the sand and is denying very real evidence that her new boyfriend is trouble.

Whether you're forging a relationship (or trying to turn a difficult one around), assessing the magnitude of a problem, or evaluating the benefits of an emerging opportunity, seeing the situation as it truly exists is crucial to success—but if you misread the information you're receiving from your environment, you're at a disadvantage from the word go.

Exercises

A clear, unblinkered "reading" of your environment leads to success because it brings with it the capacities for identifying and addressing problems and recognizing and building on opportunities. Finely honed reality testing also allows you to read a group's emotional climate and the power relationships at work. It is a complement to self-awareness, which gives you the capacity to take your "internal temperature." Reality testing allows you to measure "external temperature."

Self-Assessment

1. Although the two vignettes in this chapter—one concerning Bob, the other concerning Anna—represent extremes in reality testing, which of these two vignettes more closely resembles your style? Do you often have unfounded fears about a given situation? Or are you more likely to sugarcoat reality?

2. Rate yourself on the following questions by answering Rarely, Sometimes, Usually, or Frequently.

    a) By and large, does feedback from others consistently tell you that your reading of various situations is objective? Realistic? Sound? Seasonable? In perspective? Lucid? On target?

    b) Do others indicate that you tend to overlook difficulties? Minimize problems? Make mountains out of molehills? Sweat the small stuff? Catastrophize?

    c) Are you often told that you are whistling in the dark? Dreaming in Technicolor?

    For Question a), give yourself a score on each response of −2 for Rarely, −1 for Sometimes, +1 for Usually, and +2 for Frequently. For Questions b) and c), score each response +2 for Rarely, +1 for Sometimes, −1 for Usually, and −2 for Frequently. Total your score. A positive score suggests that your reality testing is headed in the right direction, while a negative score suggests that your judgment may be clouded by fears or wishful thinking.

3. In your notebook, write down as many instances as you can think of that demanded that you evaluate an important situation in which you

had a stake (a decision at work, one concerning your children or your significant other, one concerning a group of people whom you didn't know well). In retrospect, do you think your reading of the situation was clear and grounded in fact? Or was it either too negative or overly optimistic? Bear in mind that we aren't talking about whether the outcome was in your favor—only whether your thinking and perceptions were focused and dead-on.

4. What, if any, feedback did other people who were knowledgeable about these situations give you concerning your style and how you weighed the evidence?

5. In your notebook, describe an episode during which, in retrospect or in the light of feedback from other sources, you believe that your capacity to size up the situation was radically off-base. Now write down whether you were off-base in a fearful or a hopeful manner.

6. Judging from the information gleaned in the questions above, is your reality testing usually on target? Too negative? Too positive?

Self-Assignments

Remind yourself how to set up the ABCDE chart by looking back at Chapter 2.

Strengthening your reality testing depends on two capacities: the ability to identify irrational self-talk that clouds your logical judgment, and the ability to dispute and debate this self-talk as it arises.

1. Looking at the episode you identified in Self-Assessment Question 5, what irrational self-talk was going through your mind? Write it down, and note how you can dispute and debate this clouded thinking.

2. Over the next week, when you're called upon to size up a situation at work (either a problem or an opportunity), note whether your thinking style leads you toward fearful catastrophizing or a head-in-the-sand reaction. Then dispute and debate the self-talk that's leading you to either extreme. By doing this, you'll develop a more pragmatic, show-me-the-evidence view. But be aware of one last caveat: some people fall short when it comes to reality testing because they lack independence. Although they start off with a clear-headed reading of what's going on, they lack the self-confidence that comes with independence, and as a

result have to turn to others to assess the situation for them. If the others are lacking in reality testing, the individual may be swayed by their erroneous views.

3. When you arrive home from work, write down in your notebook the work situation, your initial thoughts, some of the disputing, debating, and discarding that went on, and what your ultimate read of the situation was.

4. Repeat the same exercise, this time focusing on an issue that arises between you and a significant other—be it a spouse, a parent, a child, or a close friend.

Chapter 13

Problem Solving

"A problem is a chance for you to do your best."

—DUKE ELLINGTON

DEFINITION:
Problem solving is the ability to find solutions to problems in situations where emotions are involved, and to understand how emotions impact decision making. Problem solving is associated with being conscientious, disciplined, methodical, and systematic in persevering and approaching problems. This skill is also linked to a desire to do one's best and to confront problems, rather than avoid them.[1]

Susan, a young lawyer, had trouble working her way through the reams of documents that were provided to her for each new case she was assigned. She could eventually pull everything together and see the big picture if she stuck with it, but more often she felt like giving up after two or three attempts trying to organize and assess it all. Her quiet and somewhat less self-assured colleague Liz, on the other hand, was more persistent. As she reviewed her case documents, she would determine the issue and formulate one strategy, then try another if the facts and documentation failed to support it, then another, and so on. She chose not to give up, seeing her work as a challenge. If she hit the wall and grew frustrated, she'd look to her next option—calling on someone for help. Liz had a list of colleagues, including senior partners, she could count on to point her in the right direction by discussing the case, which would assist in cutting through the clutter and help her determine the key issues in ways that made it easier for her to proceed.

In another five years, chances are Liz will have proved to be more successful in her firm, thanks to her approach to problem solving. Notice that one of her skills, common to most people with high EQs, is her ability to keep herself motivated, even when obstacles get in the way. Using emotion to motivate yourself regardless of the nature of the challenge is characteristic of people with well-developed emotional skills.

Susan's tendency to give up is connected to her propensity for responding to difficult situations by quickly feeling lethargic and unmotivated. She then begins to engage in negative self-talk: "Oh, this is all too much! Just look at me, what a dummy I am. I've made two attempts, and I still cannot get it right! I just always screw up!"

If Susan were to use the ABCDEs (in Chapter 2) to "dispute and debate" her self-talk, she would be on the road to becoming less down on herself, less lethargic, and could be far more motivated to successfully return to the task at hand.

Another important emotional skill is knowing when to call on the advice and expertise of others. The key is not to throw up your hands and ask that person to do it for you immediately, which would render you dependent (and likely fired), but to seek aid from diverse sources who'll assist you in reaching your own conclusion.

Six Steps for Solving Problems

Never has it been more important to focus on problem solving. In workplaces everywhere, supervisors are asking their employees to come to them, not with difficulties as they may arise, but with solutions in hand, ready to be implemented. A competitive economy demands that we be problem solvers, not problem reporters or collectors. This demand, if we can meet it, renders us more independent.

Among the pioneers of social problem solving as an intervention are psychologists Thomas D'Zurilla and Arthur Nezu. They have published dozens of research studies demonstrating that training people in better problem solving can greatly influence their ability to deal with problems in every area of their lives: work and career, finances and personal property, health and behavior, relationship and family.[2]

They have defined problems as being a single time-limited event, such as being late for a flight, or an acute illness; a series of similar or related events, such as dealing with a bullying boss, or a daughter who continually violates curfews; or more long-term issues, such as coping with chronic pain, loneliness, or boredom. Note that most problems fall into the "interpersonal" category, while others tend to be more of a "technical" nature. Even with technical problems, however, there is usually an interpersonal component.

Consider for a moment Ed, whose new work role has to do with high-level computer communications, a technical skill which he has yet to master. As a result of not being competent in this part of his work, he is slow and makes many errors, and his co-workers who depend on him for generating and receiving messages become at first increasingly frustrated, and then irritated with him.

As their impatience mounts, they begin pressuring him to keep up and deliver the goods. Under such pressure, his anxiety increases and interferes with whatever skill set he has—making his output even worse. Here, what begins as a "technical" problem soon also becomes an "interpersonal" difficulty.

Next time you encounter a problem, view it as a challenge to be overcome, an opportunity to be seized. Each time you have the chance to beat a problem into submission, grab it and go. You'll become better with practice, by bearing these steps in mind:

State the case. Examine the problem, describing it as accurately and realistically as possible. Try looking at it from other people's points of view, to make sure that your perspective isn't unduly narrow. Part of being objective involves being aware of the impact of your emotions. Our emotions often color our view of problems we encounter. That doesn't mean you should become unemotional; rather, beware of your emotions and the biases they bring to the table.

Generate alternatives. Think of as many solutions and approaches as you can. This is a brainstorming session, and some of your ideas won't hold water. Don't worry. At this stage, don't evaluate your ideas—just let them come. Again, think of ways that other people might tackle the same dilemma.

Evaluate each alternative. When you've got all your options firmly in mind or—better still—down on paper, look at each one and consider the probable outcome. Prioritize them, from best to least favorable. Also, do a "gut check." Pay attention to how the potential solution feels to you. Sometimes we reject options because they just don't feel right. You don't need to explain why, that alone can be important information. Pay attention to the reverse as well. Some solutions just feel better for us. If it feels right, then you may be moving in a good direction.

Choose the best option. Now is the time to take the plunge, recognizing the risk involved. No one can predict the success or failure of a given course of action with 100 percent certitude. Gain confidence from the knowledge that you assumed the risk and took action based on sound information gathering and an analytical process.

Implement your solution. Press on without getting bogged down in what-ifs and maybe-we-should-haves. Perhaps you'll have to make adjustments along the way, but resist the temptation to go back to square one. Give your chosen strategy a chance to work. Remember, settling on it as opposed to your other choices was the hard part. So reward yourself—pat yourself on the back for moving beyond the quagmire of indecision.

Assess the outcome. Evaluate whether your solution has solved the problem. If it has, great. If not, begin this process again. When the problem seems to be of a technical nature, do not overlook any interpersonal difficulties that may have emerged as a result of that technical issue.

Now, let's see how these techniques play out when applied. Linda, a very personable and congenial young woman, came close to finishing her nursing certification, but decided instead to join the army and train as a medic. Although aware of her lack of formal education, she had a wide variety of interests and a keen, inquiring mind. In fact, she ran into trouble in the army, because she kept challenging the drab and lock-step routine. "Why do we have to clean our bed rolls three times a day?" she'd ask. "Wouldn't it be better to clean them once, and then wrap them up in plastic? Then we could get on to other stuff." Her superiors viewed these very sensible suggestions as borderline insubordination, with the result that Linda eventually switched to the navy, which she found far less regimented and much more to her liking.

In time, Linda married Jack, who served in the marines. She liked to say that he was more broad-minded than the run-of-the-mill leatherneck, which was quite true. In fact, he appreciated her novel solutions to everyday woes and recognized her superior negotiating skills. Jack was more than happy to let her lead the way, while he upgraded his own skills by moving from radar systems into other forms of computerization.

When she resigned from the navy to start a family, Linda became concerned about their suddenly decreased income. She said nothing directly to Jack, who liked and was very adept at his military duties. Still, she began to subtly prod him into thinking about the possibility of civilian employment. The couple lived in California's Silicon Valley, and she knew that Jack would have little difficulty in making the transition.

After the birth of their second child, Linda began working part-time with the Red Cross, organizing blood donor clinics at various corporate headquarters. Pretty soon, she had a plan in mind. Everywhere she went, she chatted with a wide range of employees and, if possible, senior executives, asking them every question she could think of about their firms. After a clinic was wrapped up, she'd stay a while in the staff cafeteria, where people were pleased to talk to so interested a visitor. In time, she'd personally investigated and individually rated dozens of computer firms. She also got a "gut feeling" from each organization as to how the culture felt to her.

Thus, Linda had identified the problem—finding a great place for Jack to work as a civilian. She studied the problem during her own employment—finding out about the different companies in the vicinity. She brainstormed by coming up with numerous questions to ask at each workplace, and carefully recorded her findings for later reference. The next steps would involve proposing solutions, selecting one for implementation, and monitoring the outcome.

One day, Jack—unaware of all these activities—took Linda out for dinner and announced that he'd come to the conclusion that it would be wise for him to investigate a change of career. Without missing a beat, Linda brought out her notebook, which the two of them continued to examine and discuss for several nights. Fortunately, she had the interpersonal finesse to pull this off without bruising her husband's ego. On the contrary, he was delighted and flattered that she'd saved him so much research, legwork, and doubt. In no time, they'd narrowed his choices down to three companies that Linda felt strongly would suit his personality and abilities. Jack applied to all three, and eventually got the job of his—and Linda's—dreams.

Externalize, Visualize, and Simplify

Taking a slightly different approach, let's look at externalization, visualization, and simplification, the three rules of problem solving formulated by Marvin Levine, author of *Effective Problem Solving*.[3]

Externalization involves displaying the information you're working with. Write things down, or draw a graph to define more complex relationships. That way, you'll have all the elements in front of you.

Visualization might include imagining yourself going through the various steps involved in dealing with a problem before you carry them out, or picturing the outcome of a possible solution. A variation on this technique has proved very successful in helping professional and Olympic-caliber athletes. We have them rehearse in their minds the most challenging and typically encountered aspects of their sport, and conjure up a clear mental image of themselves performing at peak, eluding opposition players, and scoring goals, runs, or touchdowns. They can do this anywhere, anytime—on the team bus en route to an arena or as they go to sleep the evening before a game. By preparing to meet obstacles as they arise, you'll be much better prepared for the real thing when it comes along.

Finally, simplification involves breaking the problem down to its simplest common denominators. If you focus on the most relevant information, keeping things as specific and concrete as possible, even the most seemingly convoluted difficulty becomes easier to get a grip on.

How does this work in practice? Let's consider Darlene, a 32-year-old woman who wanted a challenging and enjoyable job. The classified ads of her local newspaper were of little help, so she went through the externalization/visualization/simplification process. First, starting to externalize, she wrote down in as much detail as possible the sort of work she'd prefer. Then she came at the problem from different angles, thinking about the jobs she'd had in the past, and what she'd liked or disliked about them. This exercise helped her identify what had given her the most satisfaction in the working world, and in life.

Next, continuing with her externalization, she began to think about all her current and previous co-workers, as well as her friends and acquaintances. Some were obviously happier with their jobs than others, and she tried to analyze why this was so. Then she thought about what others had (or might have) said about her in her previous positions. Were her memories and perceptions in tune with their probable readings? Did she strike them as happy and fulfilled?

Then Darlene tried to visualize herself in all sorts of different jobs that in some way caught her interest. She ran through the entire gamut: jobs that involved a high degree of interaction with others, solitary jobs, jobs that involved technical skills that she had or could perhaps acquire, jobs that required artistic flair, jobs that took place indoors and out, and even jobs that she could perform at home. As she visualized, she paid attention to her gut feelings—the internalized emotions she associated with each option, as well as the self-talk connected with these emotions that might also be interfering with her performance.

She learned from this visualization that she was primarily interested in and emotionally tuned in to creative work, rather than something highly technical. She liked working with others and didn't want to be tied to a desk or a cubicle. And an unsuspected theme emerged: she was happiest and most at peace with herself when she was cooking.

Was cooking a job? Of course it was, and it could be analyzed too.

Darlene started this exercise with externalization: making a list of every position associated with the food and restaurant industry, describing them in detail. She thought about her résumé and visualized how she'd present herself in an interview, and about past experiences that were at all relevant to each job category. Having noted the pros and cons of each, she selected a few that seemed likely to appeal: an apprenticeship as sous-chef at a restaurant, a staff position with the test kitchen of a food manufacturer, and a similar post with a catering company. She did as much research as possible, visiting the library and reading all sorts of trade magazines, calling anyone she knew who had contacts in the three fields, and paying personal visits to prospective employers. In time, her knowledge and enthusiasm paid off: she was hired by a local restaurant and soon became indispensable to its operation.

Our advice, then, is to take heart from Darlene's experiences. Problems are normal events, part of everyday living. Everyone goes through them, so don't take them too personally or imagine that they're aimed at you alone. Successful problem solvers see them as challenges to be overcome or learning experiences that will lead to strength and growth. By starting with a positive approach and putting your emphasis on their solution, the rest of the steps involved will be that much simpler, easier, and more effective.

Exercises

Problem solving, as we've seen, is associated with being conscientious, disciplined, rational, methodical, systematic, and persevering. The key is a desire to do your best in the face of doubt or adversity—to confront problems rather than avoid them.

But people who successfully solve their problems have two other capacities. First is intuition—commonly known as hunches and impressions. The trick is not to follow intuition blindly or give it too much credit, but to explore it in a logical and realistic way. In fact, intuition can be an early warning signal, identifying problems that haven't fully emerged but are beginning to edge onto the scene. If you can pick up on these almost subliminal signals—and then examine them pragmatically and methodically rather than dismissing or overlooking them—you'll have a head start when the problem lands with both feet.

Successful problem solving is also bolstered by innovation—the capacity to come up with fresh new ways of viewing the issue at hand and brainstorming alternative solutions. Like intuition, though, innovation must be tempered by a clear-headed calculation of the risks involved in these unusual approaches.

In sum, the most adept problem solvers have a vital edge because they can identify obstacles that might prevent them from attaining their goals in a family, social, or workplace setting, and they overcome them by a blend of intuitive and logical means. Those who don't have this capacity often fail to see the obstacle until they run into it—or, if they recognize it, they become flustered or demoralized. They cannot correctly spot the problem until it bowls them over, and they wind up stymied in their desire to achieve what they want.

Self-Assessment

1. In your notebook, write down a problem you've experienced in the past week.
2. Describe it, as either a technical problem (meeting a budget deadline, figuring out which of two insurance policies to buy) or an interpersonal difficulty (something that affected a relationship at home, at work, or in a social situation).
3. Describe how you attempted to solve the problem.

4. Was the outcome positive or negative?

5. In your notebook, write down the steps of problem solving described earlier: sensing the problem exists and feeling confident and motivated to deal with it effectively; defining and formulating it clearly by gathering relevant information; generating multiple solutions through brainstorming and innovative thinking; and weighing the pros and cons of each, choosing the best, and moving to its implementation and outcome-assessment. Next, write down whether you worked your way through each step and, if so, what it was you did.

6. Was there a price you paid for skipping a step? Or was the outcome still positive? Remember that if you brought intuition and innovation to bear on the problem's solution, it might seem that you missed a step when you were actually using these capacities.

7. In what ways did you try to look at the problem from a fresh perspective?

8. In addition to following a logical, sequential method of generating possible solutions, did you brainstorm others as they came to mind, whether or not they seemed appropriate or workable?

9. Did you pay attention to hunches, instincts, curiosities, or a "sixth sense" as early indicators of the problem or its solution?

10. If so, how did you firm up these hunches by subjecting them to realistic evaluation?

11. Even if your problem seemed to be confined to the workplace, was it (as is very often the case) compounded or worsened by personal issues?

12. If so, how did you address these issues? Was the outcome positive or negative?

13. If negative, write down how you might have successfully addressed these issues, using your capacities for empathy, assertiveness, independence, and interpersonal relationship building.

Self-Assignments

1. Over the next two weeks, be attuned to problems as they arise, and use information gained from your self-assessment to better solve problems—recalling that problems are usually a blend of the technical and the interpersonal.

2. Each evening use the above self-assessment questions to grade how you approached the problem and refine your approach so that over time you become more adroit at problem solving.

Chapter 14

Impulse Control

"I can resist everything except temptation."

—OSCAR WILDE, *LADY WINDERMERE'S FAN*

DEFINITION:

Impulse control is the ability to resist or delay an impulse, drive, or temptation to act. Impulse control entails avoiding rash behaviors and decision making, being composed, and able to put the brakes on angry, aggressive, hostile, and irresponsible behavior. Problems in impulse control are manifested by low frustration tolerance, impulsiveness, anger-control problems, abusiveness, loss of self-control, and explosive and unpredictable behavior.[1] Impulsive people are often described as tempestuous, hot-headed, and "leap-before-they-look" people.

Following a presentation on emotional intelligence to a group of business executives, several members of the audience approached us to continue the discussion. One man, accompanied by a slightly younger woman, waited impatiently for his chance to speak. When his turn came, he began by admitting that he agreed with much of what we'd said, but took great issue with one point. According to him, we were miles off base when it came to impulse control.

He himself was very impulsive, he said, and always had been. If he hadn't been, he believed, he'd never have gotten anywhere in life. He alluded to the millions of dollars he'd made and mentioned other equally successful entrepreneurs. Controlling their impulses would have dragged them down and held them back. Snap decisions were his life's blood; he was renowned for them and he wouldn't apologize to anyone. He trusted his own intuitions, his own judgment. Nor was he afraid of acting as quickly as he made up his mind; he didn't let anyone stand in his way. If he and the people whom he mentioned had attempted to deny their impulses, it would have gone against their natural grain, and they'd have wound up as failures.

This was interesting logic, and it seemed to impress the members of the audience who overheard his comments. But it called for some follow-up on our part. We asked if he'd ever lost out on a business deal because of his impulsiveness. Of course, he replied, that's the way the world works. You win some, you lose some.

Well, then, we wondered—was he married?

"Three times."

"Any kids?"

"Yes, four."

"Do you get to see them often?"

"Sure, every couple of months or so. What does that have to do with anything? Anyway, about impulsiveness . . . I just thought I'd let you know." With that, he turned and joined the departing crowd.

When he left, his companion remained behind for a minute or so. She identified herself as his second-in-command at head office.

"You're right, you know," she said. "I have to work with him. He arrives in the morning and starts to snap at everyone in sight. It puts them off; they're demoralized before they even start their day. He wants them up to speed—his speed. He flies strictly by the seat of his pants, and nobody else gets a chance to wear them. A lot of the time, he's right—but when he's wrong, he's wildly wrong. I've seen it happen time and time again. I can handle him, but then I have to turn around and make sure he hasn't bludgeoned the rest of the staff into submission, or left them in the dark about what he's up to. His personal life is another story, but there you are."

All pretty much as we'd suspected—and as you guessed when you saw his replies to our questions. Fortunately for him and his company, the impetuous businessman was smart or lucky enough to have hired the ideal second-in-command, whose career appeared to consist largely of compensating for his weaknesses. Her patience, calmness, thoughtfulness, and superior interpersonal skills held the office together, while he went on his pyrotechnic way. That's a good fit, while it lasts—although how long she'll be able to carry such a heavy burden is debatable. But just imagine how much more he might achieve in both his working and personal relationships if he were able to operate less impulsively.

Look Before You Leap

Note that the businessman in the true story above credits impulsiveness for his success, but muddies the waters by talking about trusting and acting upon his true instincts. No one suggests that effective impulse control involves stifling or disregarding valuable gut feelings. Instead, it's the capacity to look before you leap—to manage a wide range of volatile emotional states and urges wisely and coolly.

We know that people have trouble with impulse control when others describe them as rash, hot-headed, impatient, or (at best) mercurial. They have a low tolerance for frustration; they're fine one minute and difficult the next. They tend to make poor decisions under pressure and spend money unwisely. Their love life is hyperactive, but relationships go nowhere because they can't sustain a relationship. They don't act in their own best interests; they get carried away by the moment. The "instinct" referred to by the businessman is in truth usually a series of knee-jerk responses to events.

Individuals with effective impulse control, by contrast, have the capacity to think first rather than responding reflexively. It allows them mental space for weighing alternatives and assessing options so that their actions and expressions are reasoned and well considered. This leads to wise decision-making and responsible behavior. Plans made after a period of reflection always have a much greater chance of success. Who, after all, is going to be more apt to achieve their aims—people who don't pause to consider the facts and respond immediately to any idea or thought that pops into their heads, or those who calmly plan their words and deeds, remaining unperturbed even under trying circumstances? Who is going to be more adept at turning around relationships that have gone sour, dealing with unsettled clients, and listening thoughtfully and respectfully to an upset significant other? It's no contest, is it? People who exercise healthy impulse control—while still retaining flexibility and spontaneity, so that they don't come across as stilted or stick-in-the-mud—will remain cool under pressure and will come out ahead of the game every time.

Each time we hear of an outburst of road rage, we know that we're dealing with serious impulse control impairment. (Of course, the use of alcohol and other drugs plays havoc with our ability to keep ourselves in check.) Spousal abuse and date rape are among its other more tragic manifestations. The majority of lapses occur in less dramatic ways—but they occur daily, in most people's lives.

In any discussion of impulse control, it's tempting to focus on the failure to deal with anger and aggression. No doubt these feelings and behaviors are among the most likely to get us into big trouble—but we don't think you'll have all that much difficulty thinking of occasions when someone you know has overstepped the bounds of fair business competition and resorted to bulldozing and intimidation; come on too strong in a sexual encounter; given in to a desire to purchase something for no good reason (and perhaps with insufficient funds in the bank); or simply taken an undue risk based on insufficient knowledge and consideration of the outcome. Whenever we leap before we look, we may be acting impulsively.

How can we guard against doing so? By reviewing our ABCs—our Activating events, Beliefs, and Consequences. All of us are prone to behave impulsively when our thoughts and feelings are heating up. We feel we've been unfairly criticized, so we lash out. We see an opportunity that's too good to ignore (and probably too good to be true, but we don't take the time to recognize that fact), so we try to grab it at any cost. We want instant retaliation or instant gratification, as the case may be. What are we really doing? We're not only leaping before we look, we're leaping directly from A to C. Feelings are translated into action with the speed of light. There's no opportunity to bring logical evaluation to bear, to ponder the Bs, let alone the Ds and Es described in Chapter 2. As a result, we respond reflexively, crudely, and inappropriately, alienating the people we want to win over and, in so doing, undercutting our chances of success in attaining our goals.

The Impulse Gate

You'll remember our airport scenario from Chapter 2, during which Sam flew off the handle and, as a result, remained on the ground, whereas John, his far more savvy fellow traveler, was able to get to his destination with the help of the long-suffering airline agent. Sam—and anyone else who has severe problems with impulse control—also has a defective emotional safety valve called an impulse gate. Here's how it works, in the context of the ABC technique.

We'll remember that the Consequences (C) of an Activating event (A) and our intervening Beliefs (B) involve both feelings and behaviors. That is, our emotions give rise to a course of action. Here's where the impulse gate comes into play. Imagine a little gate that swings open and closed between feelings and behaviors. If it's working properly, feelings get stacked up on one side for a while. The impulse gate puts them on hold. We're aware of them, but we don't do much about them right away. Frustration, hostility, destructiveness, and a host of other potentially wounding emotions are left to cool their heels. They've got nowhere to go; they can't get through the gate and be acted upon.

If the impulse gate is faulty—if it's stuck wide open and doesn't swing to and fro—what happens? All those feelings come rushing through like shoppers at a door-crasher sale and turn into instant action. There's no time to evaluate the probable outcome, to rate the chances that the action will succeed, or to weigh the price we'll pay for its implementation. We may think or feel we've achieved a short-term gain (the release of tension that immediate action brings), but we've dealt ourselves in for long-term pain (by failing to reckon the costs and benefits attached).

Can we work on the defective impulse gate, oil its hinges, and make sure it's swinging properly? Yes, we can—by taking care to work our way through the ABC procedure whenever possible. To jump from A to C is always a mistake. It effectively takes us out of the equation, because we don't explore and test the validity of our beliefs. We can't, therefore, influence the consequences by gaining perspective and talking ourselves out of automatic responses.

And this can be done one emotion at a time. Early in this book, we pointed out that EQ, unlike IQ, can be worked on and changed because emotions aren't fixed. They come and go; we can subject them to logical processes and turn them to our advantage. They only seem powerful and permanent because we don't know how they operate.

Well, here's an example of the way a fairly intense emotion can vanish in an instant. You're in a crowded elevator; people are crammed in like sardines. Someone behind you brushes against you—not once, but twice. It's sort of a probing, poking motion, and damned annoying. What kind of idiot would shuffle around under these circumstances? Justifiable irritation swells into righteous anger, and you prepare to confront the perpetrator—until you glance over your shoulder, only to find a blind person with a cane. What emotions sweep over you now, other than embarrassment and shame? If you'd taken the trouble to turn around and see what was happening, or counted to 10, you wouldn't feel like a fool. How appropriate was your initial response, and where did your anger go? It wasn't analyzed away; you didn't let it out through catharsis. So, too, can other emotions disappear or change into their more suitable counterparts, either because of changing circumstances or by a conscious effort on your part to deal with them more appropriately.

The Marshmallow Test

All of us, as reasoning and reasonably self-aware adults, have the ability to practice impulse control—even though, for some of us, it's a bit late in the script. Remember that the human infant has no impulse control at all. Babies are remarkable though fairly straightforward pieces of work. When their bladders are full, they urinate; when frustrated, they scream. Then they start to observe and listen to their earliest emotional coaches—a fancy term for parents.

Sometimes the lesson takes hold, but sometimes it doesn't. A precedent is set early on. One of the more enduring illustrations of this fact was a study conducted in the 1960s by the psychologist Walter Mischel at Stanford University—the so-called marshmallow test.[2]

Mischel's experiment involved a number of four-year-old children. Each child was seated in a room that contained a chair, a table, and a single marshmallow. The person who was conducting the test informed the child that he or she had to run an errand, then made an offer the kid might (or might not) refuse. If the child wanted to eat the marshmallow immediately, that would be okay. But if the child waited until the adult returned, the reward would be a second marshmallow.

The kids made their choices, and Mischel noted the results, which were interesting in themselves. Two-thirds of the children managed to hang tough and earn the second marshmallow. The rest did not. But that wasn't the end of the experiment. Because they were mostly the children of Stanford professors, graduate students, and employees, Mischel was able to locate them 12 and 14 years later, when they were about to graduate from high school. At this point, he gained access to their academic records, and asked their parents to evaluate how successful they had been in and out of school. What do you think he found?

The kids who had gobbled up a single marshmallow were having one or two problems. As a group, they were less adept at making social contacts, more prone to be stubborn and indecisive. They yielded readily to frustration as well as temptation. Those who had put their gratification on hold—and by doing so, doubled their pleasure with a second marshmallow—were more successful: they showed more social skills, exhibited superior coping mechanisms and, in general, were ahead of the game. This was reflected in their grades. They were, simply put, better students, and had scored remarkably better on their SAT tests.[3] It sounds incredible—but the ability, at age four, to wait for a second marshmallow was twice as accurate a predictor of a kid's future SAT score than his or her IQ.

A more recent study drives this point home on a much larger scale. We are now learning the seriousness of the effects of poor impulse control over decision making throughout the lifespan. A study carried out in New Zealand followed 1,000 children from age three until they were age 32. They were tested on a number of dimensions of self-control from the beginning (age three)—using observations, self-reports, parent and teacher reports, etc.—and throughout their childhood and adolescence and into adulthood.

The bottom line of the study's findings was that children with lower self-control were three times more likely to develop multiple health problems, struggle financially, or be convicted of a crime. In one example of this, 13 percent of children with high self-control were convicted of a crime by age 32 as compared to more than 40 percent of children with low self-control. Also, multiple health problems showed up in 27 percent of low self-control children as opposed to 11 percent of high self-control kids. In the study, only self-control was looked at, factoring out intelligence, social class, and mistakes made as teenagers.

The study identified several gateways, or what it called "snares," encountered by low self-control children in their teenage years that increased the probability of the outcome findings. For example, poor self-control children were more likely to start smoking at age 15, drop out of school, or become teen parents.

Terrie Moffitt, a Duke University psychologist and one of the lead investigators of the study, nicely summed up the role of self-control: "Self-control is a vital skill for scanning the horizon to be prepared for what might happen to you, for envisaging your own future possibilities, for planning ahead to get where you want to go, for controlling your temper when life frustrates you...We all use it every day, but some of us use it more skillfully than others." The authors go on to recommend that we implement interventions which could help children and adolescents improve their self-control and prevent many problems later on in life.[4]

Exercises

People with effective impulse control look before they leap, consider before they act, and are able to resist and delay the urge to react in a knee-jerk fashion. Those with difficulty controlling or delaying impulses are burdened by low frustration tolerance and vulnerability to stress, and behave in compulsive, arbitrary, and thoughtless ways. They tend to have difficulty controlling their anger, and so are hot-headed, tempestuous, given to abusive outbursts, rage reactions, or explosive and unpredictable behavior.

Now think of an individual with good impulse control and one with poor impulse control using the descriptions just listed. As mentioned previously, individuals who respond immediately to any idea, thought, or impulse that enters their heads; who do not take the time to consider the facts or information; and who respond to frustration with tempestuous outbursts are not going to experience success in life. Individuals who consider aspects before reacting; plan instead of lunging forward; weigh pros and cons; and remain relatively unperturbed and calm even under trying circumstances will be successful. They'll be better at turning around relationships that have gone sour, dealing with demanding and unsettled clients, and listening thoughtfully to significant others who are upset.

Impulse control should not be confused with inflexibility. People with healthy impulse control can still be flexible and spontaneous. If someone with what seems like highly effective impulse control comes across in a stilted, inflexible manner, this is more a reflection of a deficiency in the component of flexibility.

Self-Assessment

1. Do the following statements apply to you? (Respond in your notebook with the answers Never, Rarely, Seldom, Frequently, or Always.)
   - I tend to leap before I look.
   - I become impatient easily.

- Others seem too slow in making up their minds.
- I often regret not giving more thought to decisions.
- I often make impulse purchases.
- Others tell me that I tend to be hot-headed.
- If other drivers cut me off, I pursue and make obscene gestures at them.

If you've answered either Frequently or Always for most of these statements, chances are you have a degree of difficulty with your impulse control.

2. Answer the following statements Yes or No.
   - During the past three years, I have struck someone in anger.
   - During the past three years, I have thrown objects out of a sense of frustration.
   - During the past three years, I have made a rash decision that I have regretted.

   If you answered Yes to any of the statements, you have difficulty with impulse control.

3. In your notebook, describe a situation that has occurred during the past few weeks in which you wish you'd paused and thought through your response before taking action. It needn't involve behaving in an angry, tempestuous manner; it might simply have to do with making a rash or unwise decision.

4. Write down how you would handle the following situations in terms of your thoughts, your probable actions, and any alternative courses of action you might pursue.
   - While waiting in line at a movie theater, the person in front of you sees several of his friends and invites them to cut in.
   - While you are watching a TV show you enjoy, your child comes in, decides it's boring, and switches the channel to watch music videos.
   - A relative or close friend reveals that she's always thought you were lazy.
   - A member of your team at work fails to do his part in a major project that's due for presentation to an important client the next day.

   Did your responses show you to be generally assertive, empathic, or impulsive? Did your self-talk play a role in causing you to behave in passive or aggressive ways, in un-empathic ways, or in overly impulsive ways? If so, how might you change your self-talk in each situation so as to behave more appropriately?

5. Often the self-talk that's associated with impulsive outbursts stems from interpreting the behavior of others as abusive, insulting, or overly personal. Just as often, the self-talk that accompanies rash decision making is related to very strong wants or needs, or an excessive desire to impress some other person. Does this hold true for your self-talk in these sorts of situations?

Self-Assignments

Remind yourself how to set up the ABCDE chart by looking back at Chapter 2.

1. Over the next week, pay close attention to anger or frustration as it begins to build, monitoring and understanding your feelings and self-talk. Debate and dispute it at the time, if you can. In any case, later in the day, summarize these incidents in your notebook, and see whether your efforts allowed you to get a better handle on your emotions.

2. Often, if your anger escalates too quickly, you may lose the capacity to deal with self-talk in the midst of a stressful incident. That's when you have to lower the temperature of your emotional state. As an extreme measure, you can simply walk away, excusing yourself and stating as calmly as possible to the other person involved that you'll return. Failing this, the stress control exercises described in Chapter 16—belly breathing, acupressure, or purposeful distraction—may give you sufficient time to put a cap on impulsive behavior.

PART VI | The Stress-Management Realm

This realm of emotional intelligence concerns your ability to be flexible, tolerate stress and be optimistic[1]. Success in this area means that you are able to remain calm and focused, change direction or beliefs when presented with new evidence, demonstrate resilience, maintain a positive attitude, and constructively withstand adverse events and conflicting emotions without caving in. In the workplace, these skills are vital if you customarily face tight deadlines or must juggle many demands on your time. At home, they enable you to simultaneously maintain a busy household and be mindful of your physical health.

Chapter 15

Flexibility

"It is not the strongest of the species that survive, nor the most intelligent, but the one most responsive to change."

—CHARLES DARWIN

DEFINITION:
Flexibility is the ability to adjust your emotions, thoughts, and behavior to changing situations and conditions. This component of emotional intelligence applies to your overall ability to adapt to unfamiliar, unpredictable, and dynamic circumstances. Flexible people are agile, synergistic and capable of reacting to change, without rigidity. These people are able to change their minds when evidence suggests that they are mistaken. They are generally open to and tolerant of different ideas, orientations, ways, and practices. Their capacity to shift thoughts and behaviors is not arbitrary or whimsical, but rather in concert with the shifting feedback they are getting from their environment. Individuals who lack this capacity tend to be rigid and obstinate. They adapt poorly to new situations and have little capacity to take advantage of new opportunities.[1]

Back in the early 1980s, Mary was happily employed at a large mental health center. Her close companion and trusted tool was an IBM Selectric typewriter—the one with the revolving ball—that weighed in at half a ton and never broke down no matter how you abused it. She was accustomed to her machine, and felt that it enabled her to get the job done—which, for its time and place, it did.

Eventually, though, the organization decreed that electric typewriters were passé, and stocked up on the latest leap forward in office technology: a dedicated word processor. Mary's boss was thrilled. Mary was not. Only after weeks of pleading and cajoling did she wave farewell to the trusted Selectric and plug in the new device.

Soon, to her surprise, Mary became familiar with the word processor. She admitted that she had tried to cling to the past and that the word processor really did make her work easier. She typed away for a year or so—until personal computers came down the pipeline. The office bought one for each employee, loaded with a program called MultiMate. Once again, Mary's boss was pleased as punch. Once again, Mary was dismayed—but once again, she took the requisite lessons and mastered new skills. But when WordPerfect came on the market, and the boss announced that everyone would be switching over the following Tuesday. Mary took the weekend to think about it and, on Monday, handed in her resignation.

Both she and the facility that had employed her for so many years lost something valuable in this unhappy scenario. Mary had bent as far as she was able, and then could adapt no further. (Oddly, it's possible that she'd have been able to learn WordPerfect and its many successors in another environment. That is, if she started anew with another workplace, she'd have a fresh outlook and be more open to the possibility of change.)

Good Leaders Don't Go Down with the Ship Anymore

If we look back at business leaders of the past, we'll see that *consistency* was a signature characteristic. When yesterday's CEO made a decision, that decision was defended by everyone in the organization—from top to bottom—even when contradicted by the data.

Taken to the extreme, leaders were expected to go down with the ship. The ability to "stick with it" and "ride the tide" was important for leaders who were ego-driven. That is, they feared *looking* bad as much as they feared doing bad. Changing your mind (or altering course) was perceived as an unbearable weakness. It was the kiss of death upon which the leader would lose respect and no longer be able to face his workers.

Who epitomizes this type of leadership? An example can be found by looking at one of the icons of corporate leadership during the first half of the last century—Henry Ford. Being steadfast and staying the course were significant characteristics in Ford's early success. However, there came a time when flexibility, willingness to change, and listening to others would be even more important.

Take, for example, the following quote from Lee Iacocca's seminal article on Henry Ford in *Time* magazine: "The problem was that for too long they [Ford] worked on only one model. *Although people told him to diversify, Henry Ford had developed tunnel vision. He basically started saying 'to hell with the customer,' who can have any color as long as it's black* [italics added]. He didn't bring out a new design until the Model A in '27, and by then GM was gaining."[2]

Getting stuck at that time gave Ford's biggest competitor, General Motors, the break it needed to take significant market share. It was Ford's son who stepped in and finally insisted on bringing out new models (such as the Model A) needed for the continued survival of the company.

The other key aspect of this leadership style is that these leaders were driven by the past. They looked at the past to guide their future. What seemed to work before should continue to work again. This of course supports the need to be consistent—but at the cost of being unable to take advantage of new technologies, the changing economy, and the shifts in what the customer desires.

Today's Leaders

On the other hand, let's look at how one of the 20th century's icons of corporate success—Bill Gates—faced a changing business landscape. Gates has always projected enthusiasm about new technologies and their potential to improve our lives. But some people have forgotten that, when it came to the early days of the Internet, Gates was decidedly pessimistic and slow off the mark.

One of us (Steven) remembers attending a presentation given by Gates in Toronto sometime during the early 1990s (along with about 2,000 others).

At the time Gates talked about how Microsoft had spent several million dollars looking at the potential of the Internet. He concluded that the best commercial use would be for video-on-demand (which people could already get via cable and satellite transmission), and that the bandwidths required would be insufficient until the year 2010. As a result, Microsoft chose to take a pass on the Internet.

The following quote is taken from a speech Bill Gates gave around that time: "Bandwidth is a big issue. Unfortunately, it's not like microprocessors where every year you're going to see exponential improvements... *But to make this happen will take something like 20 years* [italics added]. And the main reason is that to get these high-speed connections to be pervasive, particularly getting them into homes around the world, will take a long time."[3]

Then something happened that changed everything. Silicon Valley veteran Jim Clark got together with a fresh University of Illinois computer science graduate named Marc Andreessen. In Clark's kitchen they created a small company with a plan to simplify and speed up access to the little-known World Wide Web. They called their enterprise Netscape. As soon as their little company went public, it changed the landscape of initial public offerings—it also changed the world as we knew it. With one blow, Microsoft was lagging behind when it came to a new, cutting-edge technology.

And Microsoft, in the public's mind, meant Bill Gates, who in numerous forums had staked out a position that now looked untenable. He was captain of Microsoft, and old-style captains of industry have traditionally gone down with their sinking vessels. At best, they'd find ways to shore up and continue to defend their positions—because the worst thing a leader could do would be to publicly change his or her tune. Being inconsistent was worse than being wrong; it would be considered as weakness and waffling under pressure.

But what did Gates do? After all, he was already one of the richest human beings on the planet. Would he stick with his decision to pass on the Internet? Or would he risk publicly changing his mind? Would he base his decision on what others would think of him? Was he concerned about his ego? Come on, do you really think Bill Gates would make that kind of decision based on what people would think of him?

Gates turned a multi-billion-dollar organization around, and went flat out after the Internet. Microsoft Explorer was developed and eventually became the world's most widely used Web browser. As documented in *Time* magazine: "The World Wide Web emerged in 1994, making browsers necessary, and Netscape was founded that same year. Sun Microsystems developed

Java, the Internet programming language. Gates hung back. It wasn't until 1996 that Microsoft finally, according to Gates himself, 'embraced the Internet wholeheartedly.'"[4]

Why did he behave that way? Because Gates, like many of today's successful leaders, was and remains more concerned with success than with what people might think of him. He is driven by the future and its opportunities, not by the past or his ego. Learning from the past is valuable, but preserving it can waste energy. Worrying about looking good, being consistent, or keeping the status quo were yesterday's virtues, but today's kiss of death. Successful leaders put their egos behind their missions, move forward with the times, and aren't afraid to alter their positions as necessary.

As, in the future, will successful employees in every field. Today's teenager can expect to change careers—not just jobs, but careers—six times before he or she retires. Many of tomorrow's employment opportunities don't as yet exist. Our children will do things we simply can't imagine, changing and upgrading their skills on a constant basis.

Flexibility Can Be Learned

Flexibility involves being able to train yourself to reinterpret unexpected situations that may at first inspire gloom or alarm. These range from the merely annoying (the babysitter suddenly develops a pressing engagement elsewhere) to the major and life-altering. Consider the situation where a couple decides to have a child based on the fact that the husband runs his business from home. Then, in the seventh month of his wife's pregnancy, the father-to-be receives a lucrative job offer that involves extended absences. In this case, flexibility can make all the difference between an irreparable strain on the marriage and a new beginning for the family.

Inflexibility, after all, represents an extreme form of the homing instinct—we become over-attached to familiar ways of thinking and behaving. This can be changed, although not without disruption and a period of adjustment. Consider something as simple as sleeping without a pillow, or with a differently shaped orthopedic pillow. At first, it will feel odd, which you'll interpret as discomfort. For several nights, you may not be able to relax. Then it will start to feel normal, and your sore neck and shoulders will improve. Remember also that the ABCDE technique described in Chapter 2 can help you unlearn long-standing though counterproductive behavior patterns.

By the way, as any parent knows, kids are often the most set in their ways, yearning for McDonald's to the exclusion of all else, turning up their noses at anything resembling a vegetable, and refusing to go near any other restaurant. One way around this is to appoint the finicky eater a food critic, and turn home menus and restaurant outings into opportunities to explore and severely rate other foods. Chances are, McDonald's will still come out on top, but the exercise opens up new vistas and, with luck, enables you to shoehorn in a couple of vegetables along the way. And, in the process, you'll be developing your child's flexibility.

Be Open to Change

In sum, the flexibility component of emotional intelligence concerns our overall ability to adapt to unfamiliar, unpredictable, and fluid circumstances. Flexible people react to change without rigidity, are able to change their minds when the evidence suggests that they're mistaken, are open to and tolerant of different ideas, orientations and ways of doing things, and can smoothly handle multiple demands and shifting priorities.

Remember, though, that flexibility doesn't equal impulsiveness. Impulsive people typically react in an arbitrary manner, without sufficient thought, rather than in response to new and valid information. By contrast, people who lack the capacity to be flexible are resistant to new ideas and incapable of adapting. They cling to old behaviors in novel situations, even though their actions are clearly insufficient and ineffective.

Note also, that flexibility is not the same as being unassertive. Unassertive people cannot "stand their ground"; they cannot defend their position, nor take an unpopular stance. They simply cave in under pressure. Flexible people, although at first glance they may be confused with those wrongly called "unassertive," are not. They don't change their mind, their direction, or their stance because they cave in. They change their position because they are able to adapt to, and take advantage of, new information to which they had not previously been party to.

Remember also that flexibility is tied to reality testing. If you can't read your environment accurately, you'll be hampered in picking up new signals that ought to lead you to appropriate responses. A football quarterback, for example, had better be highly flexible. He may have a particular plan in mind when the ball is snapped, but he must depart from it if he sees that the action is unfolding in a different way. Were he to stick to the agreed-upon play at any cost, regardless of what was happening on the field, he'd be doomed to failure.

Exercises

Flexible people have the capacity to smoothly handle multiple demands, shifting priorities, and rapid change. Particularly in today's business environment, this capacity is important for success because it allows you to take advantage of new information as it arises, adapt to change as it occurs, and respond to shifts in priorities.

People who lack the capacity to be flexible continue to practice old behaviors in new settings where they may prove ineffective and inefficient. They are resistant to new ideas and, being unable to adjust to changes, are unprepared when new and different ways are required. As a result, opportunities for success slip through their fingers.

Self-Assessment

1. In your notebook, write down a number of set routines that play out regularly throughout your day.
2. Do you ever vary these routines? If so, how often? Do you do this in response to new information? If so, why?
3. List three things you'd like to alter in these routines.
4. How do you think your spouse, friends, co-workers, or supervisors would like to see you change? Has anyone suggested that you make this sort of change?
5. When the time seems right, ask any of the people listed in the previous question where they think you fall on the rigid–flexible continuum.
6. If you were to change just one thing about yourself, what would it be?
7. Centering on that single change, how would you go about it? Who could help you put it into place? What would that other person do?
8. How do you think this change would impact on your life?
9. Answer the following questions with Always, Usually, Sometimes, Infrequently, Rarely, or Never:
   a) When you eat out, do you order the same things?
   b) Do you find yourself doing (or not doing) innocuous things because they might bring you luck?

c) Do you tend to get upset over little things such as not being able to go to a movie you would like to see?

d) Do others tend to call you a back-seat driver?

e) Are you the kind of person who likes everything in its place and a place for everything, either at work or at home?

f) Do you avoid trying new things?

Score yourself as follows: −4 for Always, −2 for Usually, 0 for Sometimes, 2 for Infrequently, 4 for Rarely, and 6 for Never.

If your score is in the negative, you might wish to examine whether you are sufficiently flexible; if your score is positive, you can probably consider yourself flexible enough.

Self-Assignments

Remind yourself how to set up the ABCDE chart by looking back at Chapter 2.

Flexibility is built on twin foundations: a strong sense of reality testing and an ability to manage stressful situations, as discussed in the following chapter. At this point, it makes sense to revisit your reality testing—because if you can't assess what's going on in your environment, you'll have difficulty adapting your responses to new information. For example, economic changes that affect your workplace can't be ignored or misinterpreted. If you're blind to them, you won't be able to develop new plans that will allow you to seek a more stable occupation.

Another key to flexibility is self-awareness, which allows you to tap into unrealistic fears (typically, concerns about losing control or being pushed around) and damaging self-talk. If you can identify and deal with these impediments, your innate flexibility will grow.

1. At the end of each day, jot down in your notebook a situation which, in retrospect, you view as a failure to be sufficiently flexible—for example, if you refused to change a position or didn't move quickly enough. Using the ABCDE chart, record your self-sabotaging self-talk. After several days, you may see a pattern emerging. Perhaps most of your fears center on losing face, losing control, being criticized, or simply making mistakes. If so, concentrate on this category by using the chart to dispute and debate the self-talk. This way, you'll be prepared to monitor other

situations as they arise, and be able to judge whether your efforts have led to a shift in behavior. If they haven't, spend a bit of time revisiting silent self-talk that might have escaped your notice. Again, dispute and debate.

2. Over the next days and weeks, when you find yourself behaving in a less than flexible manner, make an effort to find new ways of dealing with these situations. Perhaps you'll be successful right off the bat—or you may find that new, previously buried self-talk bubbles to the surface and tries to block your path. If so, write it down in your notebook, and proceed to a fresh round of disputing and debating.

   Chances are you'll have to do so, because improving your flexibility requires practice and patience—especially if you like to get things right the first time, and respond to any lack of initial success by becoming even more rigid and self-critical. Press on; your efforts will be rewarded in the end.

3. Be aware that what may at first seem to be flexibility might in fact represent a lack of assertiveness. Similarly, what may seem at first glance a very assertive stance might in fact be a sign of inflexibility. Remember that assertiveness means standing up for your rights, expressing and defending your thoughts, feelings, and behavior. But if you continue to defend a position despite receiving rational and valid information that negates your stance, you are really being inflexible, not assertive. And if you are too frequently bending to the wishes of others, you're not being flexible, you're being unassertive. In your notebook, use the ABCDE chart to assess whether your self-talk and behavior in certain situations speaks to flexibility or unassertiveness; to assertiveness or inflexibility.

4. Any time you see yourself being inflexible, push yourself to be more open to new ideas and new ways of doing things. Later that day, write down what transpired and how successful you were.

Chapter 16

Stress Tolerance

"It is not stress that kills us. It is effective adaptation to stress that allows us to live."

—GEORGE VAILLANT

DEFINITION:
Stress tolerance is the ability to withstand adverse events and stressful situations without developing physical or emotional symptoms, by actively and positively coping with stress. This ability is based on (1) a capacity to choose courses of action for dealing with stress (being resourceful and effective, being able to come up with suitable methods, knowing what to do and how to do it); (2) an optimistic disposition toward new experiences and change in general, and toward your own ability to successfully overcome the specific problem at hand; and (3) a feeling that you can control or influence the stressful situation by staying calm and maintaining control.[1]

Stress tolerance includes having a repertoire of suitable responses to stressful situations. It is associated with the capacity to be relaxed and composed and to calmly face difficulties without getting carried away by strong emotions.

People who have good stress tolerance tend to face crises and problems rather than surrendering to feelings of helplessness and hopelessness. Excessive anxiety, which often results when this component is not functioning adequately, has an ill effect on general performance because it contributes to poor concentration, difficulty in making decisions, and somatic problems such as sleep disturbance.[2]

Kevin, today's designated car-pool driver, is at the end of his rope.

"I don't know how much more of this I can stand," he tells his buddy Lawrence. "I've got two major projects to wrap up by the end of the month. My partner's sick, so all his files have landed in my lap. Sandy just flew to Detroit to be with her mother—another bout of who knows what. That leaves me with the kids. To top it all off, we just found out that Tanya has a learning disorder. Nothing serious, but she's going to need a tutor, and you know how much that costs."

Lawrence shakes his head in sympathy. "You've got a lot on your plate," he says. "I don't know how you manage to hold up."

"I've got a secret," says Kevin. "I'm not holding up. My neck is killing me. I wake up at two in the morning with work on my mind and can't get back to sleep. Half the time I can't catch my breath. And yes—I went to see the doctor. He says I'm still alive—no heart problems and my lungs are okay. But he did say I'm really stressed out, and he's right."

Kevin was certainly wise to check with his doctor—unlike many men who grin and bear it until they're dead and buried. The symptoms of stress can indeed mimic signs of heart, lung, or thyroid disease. And his doctor's diagnosis was correct: stress overload is one of the most common maladies of our time. The way we feel has been proven to have an enormous impact on our bodily functions—our heartbeat, breathing rate, and blood pressure. Over the long term, a person's emotional equilibrium has a circular effect on stress tolerance. The more centered you are, the better you'll be able to absorb life's blows, and the healthier—both physically and mentally—you'll feel. The inability to manage stress can often result in anxiety, depression, poor concentration, flawed decision making, and sleep disturbances, along with a range of even more debilitating physical symptoms such as breathing difficulties, chest pains, diarrhea, shortness of breath, heart palpitations, and nausea. We think we know what stress means and how it affects our lives. But even if our understanding is correct, we have difficulty doing something concrete about it amid our increasingly hectic schedules.

The Evolution of Stress

Our understanding of stress has changed dramatically over the past three decades. In fact, the term did not originate in psychology or physiology, but came from physics. It referred directly to a mechanical force acting on a body. The reaction to that stress was called strain.

The notion of stress was first applied to animals and humans in the 1930s, when evolutionary scientists demonstrated how, in the past, threatening situations caused states of physical arousal. Outside events or perceived danger primed the body for a "fight or flight" response. If early humans (or lions and tigers and bears) elected to fight, they'd better have had what it took to ward off an intruder. The alternative (for them or smaller creatures) was to make a run for it.

These automatic physiological responses were crucial for our primitive ancestors, and we are their inheritors. But such deep-seated biological impulses can be a mixed blessing for us today. When both our minds and bodies instinctively react to a considerable and immediate barrage of stress, the result can be devastating. Of course, our responses are somewhat more varied than fight or flight. In the 1960s, Dr. Hans Selye identified what he termed the General Adaptation Syndrome—our innate methods for coping with stressful events. Basically, he believed that we go through three stages: alarm, resistance, and exhaustion. All this is more or less automatic, hard-wired into our genes. But, Selye believed, conscious interventions to better process these three stages can modify their impact. These interventions underpin effective stress tolerance techniques, some of which are outlined in the exercises later in this chapter.

The Indicators of Stress

As with many other components of emotional intelligence, the first step in confronting stress is to engage your self-awareness and look for physical and mental sensations. Which ones apply to you? You might feel wound up, wired, or overwhelmed; experience tension in the neck, back, and shoulders; or suffer from headaches, dizziness, or shortness of breath. Sleep patterns may be disrupted, and you might experience loss of appetite, heartburn, or a variety of aches and pains.

Under stress, our mood turns sour, and we have to fight off depression and anxiety. Thoughts run along the lines of "This is too much to bear"; "I just can't face it anymore"; "How do I get out of this?"; "I wish my problems would all just disappear"; "Can't somebody do something to help me?"

As for behaviors, stress is usually apparent to both the person who's suffering from it and to an astute or even casual observer. When you're under pressure, perhaps you can't sit still. You pace to and fro and wring your hands or run your fingers through your hair. The opposite end of that spectrum is the tendency to sit gazing into space, flopping like the proverbial potato in front of the TV for hours on end or retiring early to bed, where you stare at the ceiling.

If you take a minute to run through these admittedly glum responses, and write down any others that you might have experienced—physical sensations, emotional state, habitual thoughts, and observable actions—you'll have a clear picture of your personal stressed-out profile.

Keep Your Perspective

Effective stress tolerance serves as a preventative measure, helping to protect us from high blood pressure, heart disease, and ulcers. It involves a repertoire of suitable responses to trying situations. It's the capacity to be calm and composed, to face difficulties without getting carried away or hijacked by strong emotions. It allows you to tackle and take control of problems one by one, rather than surrendering to panic. As we've seen, the alternatives are less than attractive.

James O. Jackson, a senior writer and editor at *Time* magazine, is one of those rare professionals with an admirable threshold for stress. The nature of his business finds him facing a barrage of last-minute assignments, yet he's able to concentrate, assimilate vast amounts of information in mere hours, and produce beautifully written prose. All the while, he somehow manages to keep his sense of humor, has time for the problems of others, and meets erratic behavior and unreasonable expectations on the part of his frazzled colleagues with unflappable equanimity.

How does he do it? In his words, "it helps to have been raised in New Mexico, where the only stress is imported by visiting Texans, New Yorkers, and Californians." The key, he says, is to remain inside your "envelope of competence." That is, be assured of what you can do, do the best you can, and don't let anyone or anything nudge you into unnecessary frenzy. Most important, according to Jackson, is a sense of perspective: "What will it all mean in 100 years or 100 days or 100 hours? Today's magazine is tomorrow's birdcage liner." And, with typical self-deprecating wit, he points out the value of laziness, because "lazy people find quick, easy ways to get the job done." This from a man who has run field bureaus in Bonn and Moscow, was the first American journalist to interview Mikhail Gorbachev, wrote a spy thriller in his spare time, and enjoys gardening at his Massachusetts summer house.

Jackson's formula centers on three key elements: the capability to plan a course of positive action to limit and contain stress; the ability to maintain an optimistic attitude in the face of sudden change and negative experiences; and the capacity to feel that you have control, or at least influence, over stress-inducing events.

Don't Be Your Own Worst Enemy

Stressed-out feelings are very often stoked by the ABCDEs described in Chapter 2, and by self-sabotaging self-talk. It is very easy to catastrophize the situation, along the lines of "I'm going to have a nervous breakdown. It's absolutely impossible for me to do this." Off-kilter beliefs such as these are guaranteed to keep the vicious cycle of stress running at full throttle. It's difficult—if not impossible—to address the true external cause of your stressful feelings without first getting them under control.

Let's go back to Kevin, the stressed-out car-pooler, and take a look at his ABCDEs. His activating events are clear: he's juggling two projects; his co-worker is sick, with the result that he has to juggle even more; his wife has gone out of town to deal with a family crisis; and his daughter has been diagnosed with a learning disability. He then describes the consequences: he's tense, anxious, and overwhelmed. He doesn't know which way to turn; he can't sleep and fears for his health.

At least Kevin has wisely visited his doctor, who advised him to be wary of stress. A good start—but now he must look at the beliefs that conspire to make him feel overwhelmed. If he succumbs to stress, he'll be in trouble. He'll try but fail to postpone dealing with his woes. He'll shuffle them aside and attempt to get some rest, but rest will evade him. So—under the terms of our optimistic scenario—let's say that he examines what's going on. He's harried, but still coping. His wife hasn't left him, and his daughter's problem has been identified in time. By debating and defusing these admittedly serious problems, he may well find a way to deal with them.

The first step in combating feelings of being overwhelmed and powerless, which are associated with being stressed out, is to regain control. Simply writing down all the many situations with which you are dealing moves you from a passive position to an active stance. Psychologically, this shifts the emphasis from your being a helpless victim of circumstances to an active agent in mastering these circumstances.

Next, combine related pressures into a single category. With Kevin, he began by writing down the amount of work he had, the absence of resources, the rushed deadlines—all of these he listed under "work-related stressors." Next, he wrote down the other simultaneous pressures to which he was exposed: wife gone, no one to talk to about these difficulties, having to cook for himself, make the beds, and walk the dog. All of these went under the category of "spouse away."

Again, the process of writing these down made the stressors more concrete, and in doing so, more manageable—far more than the amorphous feeling he previously had—than being bombarded by ill-defined issues.

The third step is to take a "bite-size" chunk. For example, one problem only, and address it. In reflecting on this, Kevin realized that most of the work problems were the result of insufficient resources. He could handle this by speaking to his boss about whether the workload he is suffering under may be shared with other co-workers, or whether the deadlines might be shifted. Again, the idea that there are other alternatives—whether they work out or not—psychologically gives Kevin a sense of control over what previously felt like an uncontrolled downpour of demands on him.

Kevin might also try to prioritize what "bite-size" tasks he was going to address first by doing so along the lines of what seems to be the most important, what seems to have the shortest timeline, or what would be the easiest to successfully manage.

While doing this mental planning, Kevin might also pay attention to activities that could diminish his sense of physical and emotional exhaustion. Becoming involved in a physical activity like running, squash, and/or working out will, through the release of endorphins, have a "de-stressing" effect on Kevin's physical and psychological symptoms of being stressed out. Listening to soft classical music also has a tranquilizing effect on one's mood, thoughts, and behavior.

Resolving to phone his wife each night to demonstrate that he's taking her mother's ailments seriously helps him both connect with his wife and strengthen their relationship. Then he ponders the need for cash to pay for his daughter's tutoring. That's manageable. He hasn't touched his line of credit for a while, and his finances are in good shape. He can afford to get a part-time nanny until his wife returns, so he can begin the search for a suitable tutor. Going through this exercise, his panic subsides, he perceives a number of sensible courses of action, his mood brightens, and his stress—while still present—begins to feel more controllable. His next medical checkup will, with luck, yield far more hopeful results.

Can you strengthen your resilience to stress and actively increase what might be called your hardiness? Indeed you can. Stress tolerance can be learned (as we'll demonstrate later on in this chapter). Once learned, it offers relief and improved health in both the short and longer term. That, in turn, allows us to become more flexible and adaptive when further, more severe hardships come our way.

The attempt to understand the relationship between negative events and our ability to cope with them has a long history. As early as 1915, Freud was postulating what he termed a "defense mechanism," a largely unconscious process involving deep-seated internal repression and rationalization.[3] But Freud's theories were updated in the late-1970s by researchers who believed that, on the contrary, stressful situations usually unleash conscious strategies or styles that people under stress have developed over time to suit themselves.[4]

This is good news for those who wish to handle stress better. If Freud had been correct, unconscious processes would have had to be probed and uncovered by means of extensive therapy—an arduous prospect. But if stress can be eased (or worsened)—sometimes instantaneously—by the people involved, depending on what they tell themselves and how they behave, then the condition is much more open to improvement on an individual basis.

The exercises that follow will help you learn to better cope with stress.

Exercises

If we develop stress responses to demanding and challenging situations, we always run the risk that the emotional experiences of anxiety, panic, or hopelessness will erode our ability to reality test, problem solve, and behave with confidence and certainty. Our physical symptoms of chronic tension, shortness of breath, etc., will deplete our sense of vitality and make it difficult for us to concentrate and focus. All of these debilities will make it less likely that we can be successful.

In short, if we "cave in" to minimal environmental demands, we will not have the presence, the hardiness, or the resilience to behave independently and assertively, and all of this will undercut our attempts to be success-ful. Individuals who do not have good stress tolerance tend to "fall apart" or become "overwhelmed" in two ways: some feel highly anxious and agitated, flustered and worried, helpless and hopeless, demoralized and apathetic; oth-ers may not experience uncomfortable emotional states, but may develop physical symptoms of insomnia, rapid heartbeat, breathing difficulties, nau-sea, diarrhea, unrelenting headaches, or rashes.

Individuals who have developed the ability to tolerate stress do not develop these symptoms, but rather stay calm and focused under pressure. They do not visit their difficulties on others. They have the capacity to relax and wind down emotionally. Those who tolerate stress well are also described as hardy and resilient. They can present themselves with confi-dence, think clearly, and assess their environments realistically.

Stress tolerance is linked with success because it brings with it the capac-ity to focus and weather storms without allowing unpleasant feelings or disturbing bodily symptoms to interfere with moving forward and reaching a goal. Without the capacity for stress tolerance, reality testing, problem solv-ing, flexibility, and impulse control are all eroded. And as these abilities are undermined, individuals become less and less able to function successfully.

Self-Assessment

Remind yourself how to set up the ABCDE chart by looking back at Chapter 2.

1. Think of a demanding, unpleasant, or unexpected situation that has arisen recently at work. It might be a deadline that looms when you're already snowed under, a lost promotion, or the prospect of losing your job itself.
2. In your notebook, write down the unpleasant feelings you experienced, any unexplained physical sensations that accompanied the incident, and the ways in which your work suffered because of your difficulty in managing the stress.
3. Now think of a similar situation that has arisen in your personal life, such as encountering problems with your significant other, parents, or

children. Again, record your feelings, your physical reactions, and the negative impact of the stress on your relationships with these people.

4. Think back to several recent stressful incidents, and make a note of the event that sparked the stress. Do these events form a pattern, revealing your areas of vulnerability to stress; that is, are the majority work- or family-related? Which, if any, produced a feeling of helplessness and inability to effect change?

5. Once again, for each of these incidents, make a note of your feelings and bodily sensations. Does a pattern emerge here as well? Some of us tend to be either "feelings" or "body" responders to stress; while others get hit both ways at once. If you are this type, how does your stress first manifest itself?

6. Pay specific attention to the thoughts you are experiencing while "stressed out." They may be thoughts such as: "I'll never get out of this. I feel completely overwhelmed, and I'm going to fail at everything. Why am I such a loser?" Apply the "D"(from the ABCDE method) and "debate and dispute" their validity. Also ask yourself: "Where's the evidence?" that you will never get out of this, and you will cave in completely.

    Similarly, pay attention to words like "always" and replace them with "sometimes," so that phrases such as "I always screw up," become "I sometimes screw up." This shifts "hot" emotions to more "cool" emotions, and diminishes the sense of stress and strain.

    Take another polarizing word such as "never"—as in "I never do the right thing"—and change it to the word "sometimes." I.e., "Sometimes I don't do the right thing."

    The same thing is true with other polarizing words such as "should." Rather than using "should," use the word "prefer" instead. For example, the phrase: "I should be able to get this done in 10 minutes," becomes: "I'd prefer to get this done in 10 minutes, but it's no catastrophe if I don't."

    This is also true with the word "must"; substitute the word "prefer" instead. A phrase such as: "I must catch this subway," thus becomes the less frenzied: "I really would prefer to catch this subway." Making these word substitutions diminishes your psychological "fever," and takes the edge off the experience of stress.

7. How do you deal with stress at present? List even those methods that aren't effective and that you'd like to change.

8. Which of the following tactics are you most apt to resort to:
   - taking a deep breath
   - going for a walk
   - counting slowly to 10
   - ignoring the problem and hoping it will go away
   - passing the buck to someone else
   - looking for alternative strategies
   - making lists
   - letting emotions surface
   - exercising
   - using alcohol, tobacco, or other drugs
   - meditating, practicing yoga, or listening to soothing tapes
   - taking a tranquilizer or other medication?
9. How would you prefer to deal with stress as it affects you and as you understand it? What, in your case, do you think is the ideal solution?

Self-Assignments

A number of physical exercises can help shift our unsettled emotional states to calmer, more relaxed feelings—as well as to actually alter to some degree the body's physiological responses. For maximum effect, they should become part of your daily routine. Don't wait until a crisis emerges and then plunge into them, looking for a quick fix (although two of them can also be resorted to when emotions are running hot).

These exercises take only five or 10 minutes each—a small price to pay, considering the time you might spend on coffee breaks or watching TV.

Because it releases endorphins, exercise has a potent effect on reducing the signs and symptoms of stress. Also, it cheers you up; you feel (correctly) that you're actively doing something constructive, instead of passively experiencing various sensations. This in itself imparts a sense of control over your body—and, by extension, the situation that keyed the stress in the first place.

1. *Diaphragmatic or "belly" breathing* sounds peculiar at first, and somewhat unnatural. Usually we fill our lungs with air by lifting the ribcage when we inhale and letting it fall again as we exhale. But this normal state of affairs can actually magnify our hot emotional states. Belly breathing involves holding the ribcage fixed and activating the diaphragm, located lower down in the stomach. Here's how you do it:

- Find a quiet carpeted area, free from distraction. Loosen your shirt or blouse and take off your shoes. Lie down on your back and close your eyes, then place one hand on your chest and the other on your belly. Breathe normally, and observe what happens—then concentrate on changing that instinctive pattern.

- Keeping your chest and ribcage as immobile as possible, breathe through your nose and allow your belly to expand and power the inhalation. Then exhale slowly through your partially opened mouth. With practice, you'll be able to let your expanding belly do the inhaling for you, and allow your contracting belly to direct the breath out. Repeat this cycle for five minutes, by which time you'll feel refreshed, relaxed, and alert.

During moments of stress, you can still resort to belly breathing while sitting, standing, or even walking. If you can't close your eyes, focus on a nearby object and repeat the breathing cycle as many times as you wish.

2. *Acupressure* works on the same principle as acupuncture and shiatsu massage. A simple exercise will show its advantages. Using the thumb and forefinger, squeeze the fleshy area between the thumb and forefinger of the other hand. The sensation should be slightly uncomfortable, but not painful. Maintain pressure for about five seconds, repeat on the opposite hand, and then repeat the entire cycle two more times. Your sense of tension should recede.

3. *Progressive relaxation* was introduced by the psychologist Edmund Jacobson[5] and further refined by Robert Benson at Harvard and the renowned psychiatrist Joseph Wolpe.[6] If practiced daily, it's been proven effective in reducing high blood pressure, irritable bowel syndrome, and general anxiety levels. But it's less effective during sudden or acute anxiety attacks, which are best remedied by means of belly breathing and acupressure.

   - Again, this involves a quiet, carpeted area. Remove your shoes, loosen your clothing, lie down on your back, and close your eyes. Clench both fists tight for 10 seconds and focus on the degree of tension in your hands. Then ease your grip, and you'll notice a sensation of heaviness and warmth. Do not repeat this. Instead, go on to flex your biceps and forearms for the same length of time.

   - Proceed to wrinkle your facial muscles, then work your way through your shoulders, chest, stomach, lower back, buttocks, thighs, calves, and feet. Throughout, tell yourself that you are indeed becoming more and more relaxed. When finished, lie still for a while before you slowly get up. At first, you may feel a trifle light-headed. This is perfectly normal, but take care to move carefully for the next few minutes. One caveat: do not attempt these exercises if you suffer from any muscle ailments. You can probably modify them to suit your condition, but you must check with a health-care professional first.

4. *Purposeful distraction* serves to combat stress, and you can pursue it in several ways. First, try writing down a list of things that you can do when in the grip of stress. The very act of putting them on paper offers a sense that you've planned ahead, which also boosts a feeling of control. Next, you can distract yourself when worrisome thoughts appear by replacing them with pleasant and peaceful mental images such as a seashore, a forest, or shifting clouds. Or, having learned which activities exacerbate your sense of stress, you can discontinue them. For example, if you're stuck in a traffic jam and find yourself looking at the car clock every 30 seconds, distract yourself by switching the dashboard display to a temperature reading. Instead of listening to the local rock and talk station (which will tell you only what you already know—you're stuck in traffic), tune in to classical music or jazz.

5. Another effective way to relieve stress is to give yourself a "worry break" by consciously setting your woes aside and promising that you'll revisit them at a specific time later in the day. List your worries on a sheet of paper, seal the paper in an envelope, and mark a specific time on it, such as 7:15 p.m. Now that your concerns have been sealed away, promise yourself that you will not think about them until the time you have designated. At that time, open the envelope and revisit your concerns for three minutes. Then put your list back in the envelope, write a new time on it, and repeat the process.

6. Practice your "Ds," asking yourself "Where's the evidence?" and "debating and disputing" your self-sabotaging catastrophizations. Additionally, search out "hot" words like "never," "always," and the miserable-making "musts" and "shoulds," replacing them with "prefer." Doing this transforms sentences like: "I should be able to finish this," or "I must get this done," to "I prefer to finish this," or "I prefer to get this done."

Chapter 17

Optimism

"The optimist proclaims that we live in the best of all possible worlds, and the pessimist fears this is true."

—JAMES BRANCH CABELL, 1926

DEFINITION:
Optimism is the ability to look at the brighter side of life and to maintain a positive attitude even in the face of adversity. Optimism is an indicator of one's positive attitude and outlook on life. It involves remaining hopeful and resilient, despite occasional setbacks. Optimism is the opposite of pessimism, which is a common symptom of depression.[1]

Reuben Rodriguez is a vice-president of human resources at Grupo IMSA (now known as Ternium Mexico S.A. de C.V.), a manufacturer that, with over US$5 billion in sales and 14,000 employees, is among the largest 25 firms in Mexico. About 15 years ago, in his position as an export sales manager, Reuben was having trouble closing a deal with a major client who looked as if he might be ready to take his business elsewhere. Reuben was perplexed and upset; he grew more worried by the day. He couldn't focus on his work, and his personal life began to suffer. Defeatist thoughts threatened to overwhelm him for the first time in his career. Then a seemingly trifling incident drove home to him the positive power of optimism and the negative effects of dwelling on the downside.

One Saturday morning, in the midst of Reuben's most stressful period, a traveling vendor came to his door with an order of fresh strawberries for Reuben's wife. The vendor was accompanied by another shabbily dressed man, carrying a tray of fruit candies whose virtues he kept pitching whenever the conversation lagged. Reuben fended him off at first but, when the man persisted, Reuben lost his temper. "Don't you understand?" he shouted. "Can't you hear? I don't want any candies. Go away and stop bothering me. Learn to get the message—no means no!" With that, Reuben took possession of the strawberries and slammed the door behind him.

But he'd slammed it so hard it popped open, and he had to go back and close it again. This time, he overheard the two men as they walked away. The strawberry vendor was trying to cheer his friend, but the candy vendor didn't need cheering. "No problem," he said. "This guy is going to be my customer next week. Just wait and see. He's in a bad mood today, but sooner or later he'll buy."

Reuben stood on the doorstep, as a mental light bulb came on. There he was, the highly trained professional with a college education, receiving a lesson in salesmanship 101 from an unexpected source. The peddler had showed persistence, optimism, and generosity of spirit. On a day when everything went wrong, he saw future opportunity. In fact, the opportunity materialized at once. Reuben called the man back, bought some candies, and tipped him lavishly. "You have no idea how helpful you've been," he said.

So the vendor made his sale—but did Reuben? In fact, he didn't, but he accepted this setback and went on to achieve greater success. He'd learned a lesson that stayed with him—one that he applies to this day while training his employees. Optimism has nothing to do with how rich or poor you may be. It's an inner resource—the ability to believe that times may be rough but, with renewed effort, they'll improve, and that failure and success are, to a great degree, states of mind.

Turn the Three Ps Around

Like assertiveness, optimism is very often misunderstood. It's not a tendency to believe that things are going to turn out for the best no matter what. That inclination reflects a weakness in our reality testing. It is also abdicating our part in the equation—risky behavior that can blind us to the real challenges that must be faced and overcome. Nor is it the capacity to indulge in a perpetual pep talk—to keep repeating positive things about yourself. This too can lead you up a blind alley. Rather, it's the ability to stop thinking or saying destructive things about yourself and the world around you, especially when you're suffering personal setbacks. True optimism is a comprehensive and hopeful but realistic approach to daily living.

The psychologist Martin Seligman has discovered three major attitudes that distinguish optimists from pessimists.[2] First, they view downturns in their lives as temporary blips on the radar. The bad times won't last forever; the situation will turn around. They don't feel doomed to walking through an unfolding disaster movie of sadness, disappointment, and underachievement. Basically, they see troubles and difficulties as delayed success, rather than outright and conclusive defeat. Second, they tend to view the misfortune as situational and specific, not as yet another manifestation of a long-standing and inescapable doom. That way, even a really bad experience can be examined and dealt with individually—it's not the last straw. Third, optimists don't immediately shoulder all the blame. If their examination turns up external causes, they take these into consideration.

This is in contrast to the three Ps of pessimism: Permanence, Pervasiveness, and Personalizing. Pessimists will tend to experience each and every setback as just the latest in a long line of past and (quite probably) future failures that they're fated to suffer. Any lapse will be seen as yet another example of how they screw up everything all the time. Why do bad things keep happening? Because pessimists decide that their own incompetence or ineffectiveness is to blame.

The optimist turns those three Ps around—not by some so-called power of positive thinking, but by disputing inappropriate self-blame and feelings of helplessness. Consider Rob, who lost a good job opportunity after getting caught in a traffic jam that made him late for a crucial interview. If he were a die-hard pessimist, his responses might be: It figures. Nothing ever goes right for me (Permanence). No wonder this happened; things always go wrong (Pervasiveness). I'm an idiot for starting so late and taking that route (Personalization).

In contrast, if Rob took an optimistic view, he might respond like this: Geez, what a downer. But I've got another interview next week. (The outcome, while undeniably unpleasant, isn't the end of the world.) Bad luck—but I've missed appointments before, and I'm not on the breadline yet.

(The present situation is unique, not a reflection of how things "always" turn to ashes, and needn't be repeated.) It wouldn't have made any difference which route I took; the whole city's gridlocked. (An external force played its part.)

Note that it would have been a mistake for Rob to try to blame all his woes on heavy traffic. That would have been looking for excuses, an abdication of all responsibility for how things turn out. The traffic was a factor, to be sure, but he could have gotten up at the crack of dawn and played it extra-safe. Perhaps he will the next time around. Pinning all the blame on external factors is just as bad as pinning it all on ourselves. The healthy approach lies somewhere in between the two extremes.

Flexible Optimism versus Blind Optimism

Another danger is the tendency to put on rose-colored glasses. If our attitude is too positive, it may lead us into uncritical assessments of a given situation. That's why optimism is tied to reality testing—our ability to read our surroundings accurately. Seligman uses the term "flexible optimism" for this grounded-in-the-real-world hopefulness, and distinguishes it from "blind optimism"—an essentially pie-in-the-sky and un-self-critical approach. Blind optimists are the Pollyannas among us. They're in denial—for them, no problems exist, and success can be obtained against impossible odds and in the face of logic. They also overlook or skate around the cost of failure.

As an extreme example, if you spend large sums of money buying lottery tickets, you marginally increase your chances of winning, but the odds remain stacked against you and the price of losing increases, because you've devoted even more of your income to a fool's errand. Sometimes a child can see what the blind optimist cannot—it's time to back down and take another approach. Generally, these are times when the potential cost of a particular decision is enormously high, even if the risk involved may appear to be somewhat low.

Given these distinctions, how can we increase our sense of realistic or flexible optimism? Adversity and disappointment strike us all, but our responses vary. An optimistic approach is vital for enhancing resilience—the capacity to bounce back from frustration or failure. Why do optimists experience life's inevitable downturns so differently from the way pessimists do? Both, over the long haul, probably encounter the same number of defeats (although pessimists, because they expect the worst, are perhaps looking for trouble, and find it more often). One answer is that the difference lies in what optimists say to and about themselves following an adverse event—the self-talk identified in our ABCDE model in Chapter 2.

As noted earlier, everyone responds to various events with specific thoughts, which drive feelings and behaviors. Pessimists tend to follow a particular cycle. Their thoughts are angry or hopeless—they want something, can't get it, and are convinced that they never will. Not surprisingly, the resulting feelings and behaviors are sadness, guilt, helplessness, passivity, inaction, or (worse) destructive action. The optimist guards against these feelings and behaviors by breaking the cycle of destructive signals that get passed down the line when misfortune strikes and replacing them with more appropriate ones. Think of this as recording over an existing tape. The result now becomes enthusiasm about new alternatives, confidence that renewed or alternative efforts will succeed, creative planning, goal-oriented activity, and healthy living.

Give Yourself a Break

Remember that it's always advisable to look for plausible alternatives. Pessimists head straight for the worst-case scenario and, as explained earlier, take it personally. For example, consider the luckless handyman who tries but fails to fix a leaky faucet. What does he do next? He loses his temper, wrecks what few tools he has in his possession, and decides to shoulder the blame by means of poor-me self-talk. He's all thumbs, there's something the matter with him, he'll never learn, and so forth. To appreciate how counterproductive these thoughts are, imagine someone else saying these things to him. They'd be considered offensive and inaccurate, and the handyman would leap to his own defense.

Well—in his defense—maybe the lighting is poor, the tools aren't right, the washer is the wrong size. Maybe, given everything else he's done that day, it's a mistake to get bogged down in fiddly stuff. Maybe it's just time to stop. So he should focus on what's temporary and changeable (washer size, lighting, and time of day); specific rather than all-encompassing (this is a hard job and there've been other jobs that didn't defeat him); and above all non-personal (all of the above, which means it isn't entirely his fault).

Alternatively, he could just call the plumber, or a friend who is handier than he is. This is called the "so what" technique, and isn't to be scorned or sneezed at. You got the worst mark in class? You got turned down for a promotion or by someone you had asked out on a date? Well, so what? Just let it go. Recognize your legitimate feelings of disappointment, but don't let them debilitate you. Use the setback to spur yourself on. Take another class—perhaps one more suited to your skills and interests, and you'll score higher. Another firm, or another department, may recognize your talents; another application will yield the result you seek. As for your love life, even a host of rejections doesn't mean that there's no one who's right for you. Romance is a mysterious endeavor at the best of times; you never know when Mr. or Ms. Right will come around the corner, and you'll be better prepared if your head isn't buried in a pessimistic sand pile.

Even if some of the negative thoughts that crowd your mind have some degree of validity at the moment, you can move on, taking steps that will enable you to handle similar situations better in the future. Don't repeat your mistakes. It's surprising how many people—especially those with pessimistic tendencies—continue to bang their heads against the wall, perhaps as a way of punishing themselves for not being able to attain success in one particular task. This leads nowhere. We aren't counseling you to give up in the face of adversity. We are saying: Take a "time out," step back, look at yourself objectively, and don't force yourself to do something over and over if you know that it's not one of your strengths. That realistic self-examination is a strength in itself, and will lead to brighter days.

Exercises

In his book *Learned Optimism*,[3] the psychologist Martin Seligman details a number of scientific research studies that show that optimistic people live longer, have fewer illnesses and lower blood pressure. They tend to be more successful in all their activities. Is this surprising? Not really. Realistic optimism is the ability to look at the brighter side of life and maintain a positive attitude in the face of adversity. It is a positive approach to daily living. Optimistic people recognize when they are in difficult situations, but have a positive regard to how things will turn out—based on acknowledgment and recognition of their own skills, the capacity to actively address problems, and the ability to recall other situations where they have successfully overcome obstacles. In this way, realistic optimists differ greatly from those individuals who maintain a positive outlook despite objective evidence that they are confronted with very difficult and real problems. These people are not realistically optimistic; they have significant difficulties with their reality testing. They keep themselves blinded to the very real problems they face by maintaining a "head-in-the-sand" attitude.

Optimistic people are resilient and hardy; they face adverse situations with a realistic "can do" attitude. Rather than feeling hopeless, giving up, or turning away from difficult situations, they persevere: they are tenacious; they keep trying. They are also flexible—they try different approaches. These qualities fuel their success.

Self-Assessment

1. Copy the following questions into your notebook and answer them with Never, Seldom, Occasionally, Frequently, or Always.
   a) People say that I complain a lot.
   b) Those close to me say I have a positive attitude.
   c) I believe I have a positive attitude.
   d) I wake up on a typical weekday and look forward to what's about to unfold.
   e) I wake up on a typical weekend morning and look forward to the day.
   f) I have a positive view of the future when it comes to my
      • work
      • career
      • family
      • social life

   g) When something unwanted occurs, I don't let myself get down.
   h) When something unwanted occurs, I tend to reframe it in my mind so that I see it as a challenge to be met.

   Give yourself a score for each response of −4 for Never, −2 for Seldom, 0 for Occasionally, +2 for Frequently, and +4 for Always. Add up your score. If it is negative, you tend toward pessimism. If it is positive, you are likely optimistic in your perspective.
2. Write down what you think you could do to make your future brighter in work, career, family, and social life, in both the short and longer term. What would be a good first step in each area toward achieving your goals?

3. How important is it for you to make these changes?
4. Practicality aside, if you could have three wishes, what would they be?
5. Returning to the practical, if you came home after a bad day at work, what activity would make you feel better?
6. Think of someone you consider an optimistic person, and think about what you could learn from his or her example.

Self-Assignments

Remind yourself how to set up the ABCDE chart by looking back at Chapter 2.

1. Over the next few days, jot down in your notebook any setbacks or disappointments that come your way, along with examples of your self-talk, the thoughts that flow from it, and the feelings and behaviors that follow. These events needn't be earth-shaking. They might range from losing your keys to losing a promotion, from discovering that your child has been pilfering the milk money to being rebuffed by a co-worker.

2. Reading through your responses, you may discover that any pessimistic attitudes are connected to self-blame or accusatory thoughts, dejected and demoralized feelings, or floundering or grinding-to-a-halt behavior. How can you get this process back on track? By means of the ABCDE technique. Negative self-talk can be disputed and replaced by positive messages that get you somewhere. This time around, though, it may be helpful to resort to a couple of props. Try wearing a rubber band on your wrist and carrying a pair of dice in your pocket. This sounds (and may feel) a trifle silly, but it works. When you begin to indulge in negative thoughts, snap the band as hard as you can. The momentary discomfort will break up that self-defeating internal monologue. Now that you've got your attention, shift it elsewhere by running your thumb along a die's surfaces, counting the indentations from one to six. Concentrate on this, and it will keep your mind from returning to a doom-laden rut.

3. Another trick that stops negative thoughts in their tracks is to put them on hold—writing them down as they occur, and making a firm appointment to deal with them at a certain time, say, at eight o'clock that evening. The act of recording them deflates some of their urgency, and reserving a time to come back to them robs them of even more punch.

4. In either case—or if you want to confront these thoughts as they arise—you can swing into the debating and defusing mode. Put yourself on the opposing team and search for evidence that will contradict encroaching pessimism. Do you always fail? Of course not—and you can honestly say so. Congratulations. You just won a battle against negative thinking, but not the war.

5. Over the next few days, note how you respond to new opportunities, outcomes that you'd previously wished for, or disappointments that—despite your best efforts—have come home to roost. Do you fear that the opportunity will disappear or turn out badly, that the positive event will somehow end in ruin, or that the setback is yet another example of the way things always turn out to your disadvantage? If so, your fears would suggest that you have a pessimistic view.

6. Write down typical scenarios during which your pessimism seems to emerge. Then look for and record the self-talk that exacerbates these events, and debate and dispute this negative commentary.

7. Over the next week or so, if a similar situation rears its head, debate and dispute your self-talk as it arises. Try to reframe the situation so you can view it as an opportunity, a challenge, or a test of your ability to affect the outcome in an optimistic and positive way.

PART VII | General Well-Being

This area of emotional intelligence concerns your ability to enjoy yourself and others, and your overall feelings of contentment or dissatisfaction.[1]

Chapter 18

Happiness

"Happiness is no laughing matter."

—RICHARD WHATELY, 1854

DEFINITION:

Happiness is the ability to feel satisfied with your life, to enjoy yourself and others, and to have fun. Happiness combines self-satisfaction, general contentment, and the ability to enjoy life. Happy people often feel good and at ease in both work and leisure; they are able to "let their hair down" and enjoy the opportunities for having fun. Happiness is associated with a general feeling of cheerfulness and enthusiasm. It is a by-product and/or barometric indicator of your overall degree of emotional intelligence and emotional functioning. A person who demonstrates a low degree of this component may possess symptoms of depression, such as a tendency to worry, uncertainty about the future, social withdrawal, lack of drive, depressive thoughts, feelings of guilt, dissatisfaction with life, and, in extreme cases, suicidal thoughts and behaviors.[2]

Anne wakes thinking, "Another day of work, work, work. Oh well, gotta get up." Driving to work, she thinks, "The sun's too bright. I should have brought my sunglasses. Oh well, I'll be in the office soon." At work, she does her job, talks with her colleagues, but keeps her eye on the clock, waiting for quitting time. When invited to join a number of her co-workers for dinner, she thanks them and takes a rain check, stating that there is a TV movie she has her heart set on watching.

Adam, on the other hand, wakes, peers out his apartment window at the blue sky and sunshine and thinks, "Looks great out; a wonderful sunny day."

Driving out of the underground parking, he heads down the street, gazes up toward the tops of the trees that line the street and muses, "Look at the way those branches create an archway; that greenery, it's like driving through a beautiful forested tunnel." At work, he spends some time joking with his colleagues and, although he is looking forward to a sports program on television later that evening, when invited to join co-workers for dinner, replies, "I was going to watch the sports special tonight, but this sounds even better!"

Unlike Anne, Adam felt pleasure at the beginning of a new day, was turned on by seemingly small things like a blue sky and boughs touching, and had a jocular ease with colleagues at work and a sense of spontaneity that allowed him to change his plans and actively and joyously participate with his co-workers at dinner. He had a sense of vitality about, and pleasure in, life.

Happy people have a sense of cheerfulness and enthusiasm about them, a strong capacity to enjoy life, have fun, and be spontaneous. They take pleasure in the small things in life.

Individuals whose capacity for happiness is diminished rarely feel delight, tend to be inhibited in their style, and seldom show spontaneity. At the far end of this spectrum, people who lack happiness may possess symptoms typical of clinical depression: a pervasive feeling of sadness and glumness, a pessimistic outlook, significant guilt over what seem to be minor transgressions, suicidal thoughts, and bodily symptoms of sleep disturbance, weight loss, and lack of sexual interest.

The capacity for happiness is not an isolated ability. It influences and is influenced by other abilities such as reality testing, self-regard, and self-actualization. If, for example, your capacity for reality testing is compromised and you tend to evaluate the environment around you through dark-colored glasses, chances are your capacity to feel happy will be impaired.

On the other hand, a strong sense of self-regard and self-actualization will positively influence your capacity for happiness.

Broadly speaking, there are two reasons why some of us wind up feeling unhappy. First, we hope that we will obtain something we desire, or expect that something good will happen to us. When these hopes or expectations do not materialize, we feel disappointed. We may then start to believe that it is our destiny to be forever unsuccessful. Second, we expect or fear that something bad will befall us. When these fears are realized, we sink into resignation and helplessness.

But, once again, there's good news. If we can modify our wants and expectations, we'll affect both the sense of resignation and the resultant sadness. Through reality testing, we may be able to shift our goals so that they're more appropriate and attainable. Of course, if they're already appropriate and we still can't attain them, we'll be forced to either give them up (which is bound to make us feel sad in the short term) or come at them from another direction by using problem-solving skills. This is a valuable technique, because to abandon hope of achieving what you want may well reflect a pessimistic attitude or faulty problem solving, and not the unavoidable response to a momentary setback.

Nature or Nurture?

The pursuit of happiness ranks right up there with the search for love and the quest for eternal truths as one of the most riveting preoccupations of humankind. Since most North Americans have both time and money on their hands, achieving happiness is a growth industry. Each publishing season, a new batch of book titles speaks to our individual and collective yearning to feel content. Meanwhile, academics and scientists are doing their part, writing and publishing more than 1,000 scholarly articles annually that dissect our quality of life and our chances at self-fulfillment.

This is nothing new. Many ancient philosophers believed in the search for happiness, known as hedonism. In their view, this was a noble goal, the highest and best use of our time on earth. Today, the word has fallen into disrepute, and we think of hedonism as a primarily selfish activity—a short-term scramble for more or less instant gratification. Happiness, by contrast, is thought to be more desirable, more all-encompassing, and a far more worthy aim.

But how to attain it? In 1996, a remarkable possibility was raised by two researchers at the University of Minnesota.[3] They released the results of a study of 2,310 pairs of identical and fraternal twins, which found little variation between the self-reported satisfaction levels of those twins who were raised together and those who were raised apart. Happiness, the scientists surmised, must be partly genetic—somewhere between 44 to 52 percent inherited. The medical and psychological communities took a skeptical view of the so-called happiness gene, and things quieted down for a while. The consensus was and remains that, while we may be born with some kind of predisposition toward being happy, whether or not we actually achieve the state itself depends largely on external factors and our reactions to them.

Wealth Does Not (Necessarily) Equal Happiness

Happiness seems to have relatively little to do with material well-being. The Hungarian-born American researcher Dr. Mihaly Csikszentmihalyi, who has spent much of his career putting happiness under the microscope, has several insights to offer.[4] According to his findings, people worldwide tend to describe themselves as more happy than unhappy. We'd expect, for example, that anyone who's fortunate enough to live in a country that's economically prosperous and politically stable would be ahead of the game, and this is true to some degree—Swiss and Norwegians consider themselves happier than Greeks and Portuguese. But there are exceptions: the Irish claim to be happier than the Japanese. In the United States, studies have consistently found that about one-third of people surveyed say they're "very happy," while only one in 10 describes him- or herself as "not too happy." The majority choose the description "fairly happy"—that is, slightly above what they'd imagine to be the average.

Since the 1960s, an international group of social scientists has been collecting data in 50 countries for a project called the World Values Surveys.[5] It found that happiness levels increase in direct relation to economic development until a country achieves prosperity roughly equivalent to that of Ireland prior to its current financial crisis. Past that point, there seems to be hardly any direct link between prosperity and happiness. The Values Surveys also found that a sudden financial gain—as, for example, a lottery win—can boost happiness for a few months, but that over a 10-year span, it has no impact on happiness.

When University of Illinois psychologist Ed Diener and his colleague David Myers at Michigan's Hope College reviewed a host of other studies for a *Psychological Science* article titled "Who Is Happy?,"[6] they found little difference based on sex, race, and age, and only a small relation between riches and life satisfaction. In the United States, billionaires are only slightly happier than people with average incomes. Personal incomes may have more than doubled between 1960 and the late 1990s in constant dollars, but the proportion of people who described themselves as happy has remained stable at 30 percent. That is, once you're above the poverty line, more money contributes less and less to the happiness mix. More important, according to their research, were traits such as self-esteem, sense of personal control, optimism, and extraversion.

Happiness Comes from the Inside Out

How can we actually increase our happiness level? As we've seen throughout this book, what we do concretely affects how we feel. If we're strong and active we're more likely to be happy. If we can achieve a reasonable quality of life, even in relatively modest circumstances, we'll be happy. If we develop goals that give our lives meaning, and keep mentally and physically alert, we'll be happy. It's important to have dreams and take risks in life, no matter how humble the dreams and modest the risks.

Friends, family, and loved ones certainly enter the picture. Although we can be happy in private moments of reflection and during solitary activities, most of us feel better when we're with others. Individuals with a large social network—those with strong interpersonal skills—tend to be happier than those with few personal contacts. A state of withdrawal does not lead to happiness, which may partially explain why extroverts are happier than introverts. That having been said, achieving happiness really does hinge on yourself alone. Stephen Covey, author and organizational consultant named as one of *Time Magazine's* most influential Americans, is convinced that long-term happiness comes from the inside out—by means of controlling our own lives and putting our short-term desires to higher purposes and principles. In his words, private victories (making and keeping promises to ourselves) precede public victories (making and keeping promises to others). Covey writes, "In all my experience, I've never seen lasting solutions to problems, lasting happiness and success, come from the outside in." He goes on to explore the folly of trying to change the world—let alone your marital partner or your children—without first recognizing and changing the role you yourself play, which is plainly the first step toward real fulfillment.[7]

Happiness Is Attainable Goals

Another factor in the happiness mix is a person's ratio of expectations to accomplishments. Setting goals is fine, but if you set your sights unrealistically high, you may fall short and fall into unhappiness. Even those who accomplish the most may not necessarily enjoy their achievements, simply because they are unable to satisfy themselves. For example, Asian students who arrive at North American schools very often achieve excellent grades, but are less content than classmates who are doing less well. Why? Because the demands they place on themselves are even higher than their formidable accomplishments. Again, one's perception and the ability to set a realistic frame of reference are key to achieving happiness.

Although this was his first year at a new school, Trevor wanted to become president of the student council because he thought it would give him a higher profile, offer him an opportunity to meet new kids, and help him to be seen as a figure of importance. In discussing this with his dad, his father pointed out, "I think it's a great idea that you want to contribute. However, you've only been at this school for a couple of weeks. Most of the other kids have been there for a couple of years. I think chances are good that you may not be successful. Not because you're not a good candidate or haven't got what it takes, but because people just haven't had the opportunity to get to know how good you are. Maybe it would be better if you did something else, where you could still contribute but where your success doesn't depend upon being elected by kids who don't know you. Then, when they get to know you, you'll have a better chance next year."

Trevor listened to his dad, and thought the advice was good. He modified his goal: instead of running for school council, he volunteered for the school newspaper, which would put him into contact with lots of kids, allow him to lobby for school issues, and display his name on the byline once every other week. He felt good about his decision, and ultimately was happy with the experience he had on the newspaper.

Think what would have happened if he had run for president of the school council, given his newness. Chances are he would have been defeated and would have felt quite sad as a result. However, by reexamining and readjusting his goal, he was able to focus on one that was attainable, and from which he experienced a fair amount of enjoyment.

Clearly, happiness is tied to reality testing. Happy people are able to take pleasure in what they have done and can do, rather than being driven to think that they should or must do more. They don't dismiss or denigrate their achievements. If they become unhappy for whatever reason, their self-awareness enables them to note their change in mood, to understand what caused it, and to set about solving the problem in an upbeat way. They're resilient because they have a track record—a trajectory of success that motivates them, providing a source of energy and enthusiasm. This not only propels them along a positive course, it draws others to them. If you're satisfied with your life and not particularly envious of anyone else's, it's much easier to build strong and lasting relationships.

The Wonders of Flow

Again, the idea of wholehearted participation and dedication seems to be integral to happiness. Dr. Csikszentmihalyi noted that many people, while engaging in certain activities, become so focused and absorbed that they reach a heightened state of consciousness, an almost euphoric state of mind. This can happen while they are writing or painting, playing sports or going for a walk on a beautiful day. It occurs unexpectedly, sometimes during something as prosaic as cooking or gardening or cleaning the house. The key element is total involvement—being really involved in the activity.

Csikszentmihalyi calls this phenomenon "flow."[8] The flow state of mind occurs most often when you engage in tasks that demand intense concentration and commitment, when your skill level is perfectly attuned to the challenge posed by the endeavor. As well, the task must entail a clear-cut goal and offer immediate feedback.

In his studies over the past 30 years, Csikszentmihalyi has found that most of us generally live our lives at two extremes. We're either stressed by work or other obligations, or bored by spending leisure time in passive ways; we jitter in response to a given day's bumps and grinds, or collapse in front of the tube. Somewhere in the middle lies a happier, more satisfying life.

And a longer one. As a final inducement, research has proven what many of us have suspected—happier people live longer, while miserable people die sooner.[9] That in itself may be enough to spur us to take the first steps toward learning new skills, reaching out to others and looking for happiness within ourselves and in what we do.

Exercises

Happy people have an infectious, buoyant mood. They are pleased with, receive joy from, and show enthusiasm at play and work, and their attitude infuses their relationships. Happy people tend to have a trajectory of success in both play and work because they are pleasant to be with and, as a result, easily attract and build relationships with others. Their happiness motivates themselves and others, and provides a source of energy and enthusiasm that is lacking in their counterparts. Additionally, people who are happy show the kind of resilience necessary to overcome minor and, at times, major setbacks. Their sense of satisfaction with their lives offsets feelings of envy and greed that have a sabotaging effect on building relationships and motivation.

People who are chronically sad, on the other hand, have little energy or enthusiasm. They experience difficulty getting the job done at work and in the context of their relationships. Their chronic glumness tends to make others avoid them and leaves them without a social support system to help them attain their vocational or personal goals.

A final and important word about this side of the happy–sad continuum. As noted earlier, some people who seem sad may, in fact, be suffering from a clinical depression. The good news is that, of all medical illnesses, depression is probably the most eminently treatable through appropriate medication and counseling. Recovery rates can run as high as 95 percent—much higher than for diabetes, ulcers, or heart disease. However, because many people associate depression with "weakness," and because for many years it has been stigmatized as a "mental" illness, many avoid treatment that could be so helpful. And depression is no more a sign of "weakness" than are other medical diseases such as diabetes or hyperthyroidism.

The signs of depression are many and varied, but here are some of the warning signals. Over the past few weeks, have you felt:

- continuously down and glum?
- that activities that previously gave you pleasure no longer hold the same joy?
- uncertain or pessimistic about your future?
- that you would be better off if you didn't wake up in the morning?

Physical manifestations are also important. For example, have you found:

- that you have difficulty falling asleep or staying asleep? Or do you find yourself waking up at odd hours and unable to fall back to sleep?
- that your appetite seems to have diminished?
- that you have suddenly lost more than five pounds?
- that your interest in sex has diminished?

If you answered yes to three or more of these questions, it would be wise to consult your physician or a trained counselor.

Self-Assessment

1. To get an idea of where you fall on the happy–sad continuum, answer the following questions in your notebook with Never, Sometimes, Frequently, or Almost Always. To make your answers accurate and meaningful, try to think of situations that illustrate and support your response.
    a) Do you consider yourself a cheerful person?
    b) When you wake in the morning, do you usually look forward to your day?
    c) Do certain activities bring you pleasure?
    d) Do other people seem to find you cheerful?
    e) Do others think you have a sense of humor?
    f) Do you think you have a sense of humor?
    g) Are you able to laugh at yourself?
    h) When someone makes a joke about you can you take it in stride?
    i) How often in the last month have you said to yourself that your life is pretty good?

    Give yourself a score on each response of −4 for Never, −2 for Sometimes, +2 for Frequently, and +4 for Almost Always. Add up your scores. The higher your number, the higher your capacity for happiness. If your score is −12 or lower, you might be depressed; revisit the depression questionnaire on the previous page and speak to your physician.
2. What are some of your favorite activities? (Some may date from your childhood days.) When was the last time you carried them out? How frequently do you carry them out now?

3. How do you generally have fun at work, at home, socially, and recreationally?

4. What are your favorite sports? Do you watch them or participate in them?

5. Of all your acquaintances, who do you have the most fun with? How often do you share a sense of fun?

6. When did you last have a really good laugh? What things do you find amusing?

7. How often do you go to movies, plays, or concerts? Do you enjoy them?

8. Do you enjoy travel? What type of activities do you prefer to do when you travel? Are you interested in sightseeing, sports, or cultural activities?

9. When was your last vacation? Did you take work with you while you were supposed to be enjoying yourself?

10. When was the last time you did something truly spontaneous and unusual? Think back to this activity and remember how it made you feel.

11. Think of a number of flow experiences you may have had lately, either active or more passive.

12. If you rarely or never experience flow, close your eyes and think of something you'd really like to do. Don't worry about whether the activity is realistic—that is, don't write off the possibility of flying on the space shuttle, or running a marathon when all you, in fact, do is walk three times a week. Just let the images come. Put yourself in the center of the action, playing the leading role.

13. Then center on something you do, enjoy to a large degree, and would like to perfect or do more often. For example, if you choose tennis, think about how you might serve the ball. Practice both easy and difficult returns—the more variation the better. As you do this, bring as many senses as you can into play. Be aware of the colors around you on the court, smell the fresh air, feel the warmth of the sun and the heft of the racket in your hand, and listen to the ball as it strikes the ground and your opponent's racket. Later, after you've gone through your own "match of the century," watch some championship matches. Sit back, relax, and involve yourself in the rhythm and ebb and flow of the games.

Self-Assignments

Remind yourself how to set up the ABCDE chart by looking back at Chapter 2.

1. In your notebook, describe in detail the most recent time you felt unhappy.
2. Using your self-awareness, identify the precipitating event involved—that is, what goal you weren't able to attain.
3. Next, recall any debilitating self-talk that might have resulted in your feeling sad, and debate and dispute those messages.
4. Then examine the goal itself. Was it realistic? What would your closest friends say if you asked them? List all the pros and cons associated with the goal to help you decide if it was attainable.
5. If you conclude that it was, use your problem-solving skills to write down a number of different approaches that might enable you to achieve it next time around.
6. If it looks unrealistic, write down a number of similar goals that you might find satisfactory. Choose the one that most resembles your original goal, but seems more likely to be achieved. Then write down ways that you can imagine yourself attaining it.
7. Over the next week, keep a list of other goals you wish to attain in the short to medium term. Examine them in the same way, making sure to keep a second list of easier (and thus more readily achievable) goals that could lead to your main objectives.

PART VIII | Putting It All Together

Chapter 19

The Star Performers

"An ounce of performance is worth pounds of promises."

—MAE WEST

"That some achieve great success, is proof to all that others can achieve it as well."

—ABRAHAM LINCOLN

We hope we've conveyed throughout this book that success in any field rests on a number of emotional intelligence factors. Through-the-roof scores in one or two categories don't necessarily guarantee millionaire status, a meteoric rise on the organizational chart, or the realization of your fondest dreams. Rather, think of success as the result of a mix or recipe of several competencies, some of them unexpected. That's why successful engineers—the most pragmatic bunch you can imagine—are distinguished by high scores in self-regard, optimism, stress tolerance, and self-actualization; why the success of human resources professionals (who might be thought to rise or fall on their capacity for interpersonal relationships), in fact, depends most on self-actualization; why (to cite a recent survey) 68 percent of 150 information technology executives in the nation's 1,000 largest companies stated that they believed "soft skills" were more important now than they were five years ago.[1] Suffice it to say that no component of emotional intelligence exists in isolation. All are intertwined; all are valuable and may be brought to bear to enhance your chances for success.

Throughout the book, we have presented various examples of how emotional intelligence works in real life. In this chapter we want to give you selected examples of how emotional intelligence applies to "star performers"—that is, people who have really excelled in some area. We will briefly describe research studies in which groups of people were tested in order to profile these "stars," as well as some individual case studies. At Multi-Health Systems we have tested the emotional intelligence of more people than anyone else—well over one million people in 66 countries. Our data were the world's first to explore the relationships between emotional intelligence and sex,[2] age,[3] culture,[4] and race.[5] The studies and individuals in this chapter highlight some of the first work directly examining the role of emotional intelligence and star performance. More recently, we have tested tens of thousands of North American children and adolescents using our Youth Version of the Emotional Quotient Inventory (EQ-i YV).[6]

EQ and Top Guns

Perhaps the largest study undertaken looking at the role of emotional intelligence and work performance was with the U.S. Air Force.[7] Back in 1996, the air force identified a problem with its recruiters—the people who choose the young men and women who'll be suited to military life. The trouble was that recruiters were coming and going with depressing regularity; the turnover rate was sky-high—approximately 50 percent. Each person who had been selected was trained and very often relocated to another city, or to a far-flung military base. If that person didn't stay at the job and function as he or she was supposed to, the air force was throwing money away. To be more precise, every "bad hire" was costing the air force about $30,000. Of course, there were also human costs involved—including the strain on the recruiters' families, who were forever pulling up stakes.

Former Lieutenant Colonel Rich Handley, who headed up the recruitment project, called us in and asked us to administer the EQ-i to 1,171 recruiters stationed at bases around the world, to see if we could relate their scores to success on the job. In order to get an accurate measure of that success, we wanted to know, first, how they viewed their own performance, and second, how well they met the quotas that had been assigned for their particular region.

Having administered the EQ-i and other tests so many times, we're well aware that self-rating has its limits. A person may say that he or she is doing great, and that may or may not be the strict truth. On the other hand, when people say they're not doing so well, that usually proves to be the case. Having obtained the EQ-i results, as well as the claimed and actual performance ratings, we plugged all the data into our computers, and found that 45 percent of the recruiters' self-reported success was accounted for by their scores in the 15 components of emotional intelligence—a much higher relationship than has been found in other studies that rely on cognitive intelligence alone.

Then we looked at their actual performance, and found that many of these same components came into play. The five factors that were most likely to translate into success on the job may surprise you. In order, they were assertiveness, empathy, happiness, self-awareness, and problem solving. Those recruiters who scored high in these categories were 2.7 times more likely to succeed, and of the 262 recruiters who scored highest on our inventory, 95 percent met or exceeded their quotas.

Our study also went on to shed new light on several possible factors that the air force thought might have contributed to the turnover problem. A recruiter's base of operations—where he or she was stationed—had no direct relation to success. Nor did gender, ethnicity, education, age, marital status (although marital satisfaction was found to be related to job success), or the number of hours worked. Indeed, those recruiters who admitted to working the fewest hours were the most successful.

All these results made sense to us. First, assertiveness is highly desirable in a sales environment, and a recruiter's task is essentially to sell the military to civilian prospects. The air force was surprised to learn that empathy played a role (it had concentrated on improving the recruiters' interpersonal skills, but not empathy per se), but empathy, as we've seen, is all about the ability to read and respond to the emotions of others. The successful recruiters were able to bring it to bear, adjusting their presentations accordingly and—not incidentally—not wasting time on unsuitable candidates, which is why they could get the job done more quickly. Happiness is straightforward enough, as is self-awareness. Superior problem-solving skills were of real value because the recruiters frequently worked alone, isolated from their supervisors or co-workers.

What happened next? The air force quickly reorganized its recruiter-training program to address the determinants of success identified by the EQ-i. It then ordered a customized computer version of the inventory that's been used ever since as part of the selection process for new personnel. The responses of potential recruiters are compared with a database that contains the results of the initial 1,171 tests, and prospects take part in a structured EQ-i interview we developed to confirm the areas of strength or weakness pinpointed by the self-report instrument.

In fact, our work was cited in a report to a U.S. congressional sub-committee, which compared the recruiter selection processes adopted by various branches of the armed forces,[8] and stated that "only the air force's screening process has measurable criteria to evaluate the interpersonal skills of prospective recruiters."[9] It also stated (somewhat to our chagrin) that "in August 1997 the air force purchased [the computerized EQ-i] for less than the cost of putting one recruiter in the field," and concluded that "air force recruiters are twice as productive as recruiters from the other services."[10]

And what's happened in the meantime? A follow-up study—again, sub-mitted to the congressional subcommittee—found that, after a year of using the EQ-i and the specially developed EQ-i interview to help select new recruiters, the retention rate for this position had increased by 92 percent worldwide, at a cost savings to the air force of an estimated $2.7 million. The U.S. GAO (Government Accountability Office) once again praised the Air Force Screening system.[11] (And yes—we've begun working with the navy and the army on similar projects, tailored to their specific needs.)

One of the hardest sells one of us (Steven) ever had to make took place aboard the USS *George Washington*, one of the most technologically sophis-ticated aircraft carriers in the world. The goal was to convince a group of navy pilots and navigators to take an EQ test. Using your visualization skills, picture in your mind the "ready room," where fighter pilots are briefed. Picture also a senior medical officer, who introduces a lowly psychologist named Steven Stein to a highly skeptical audience of men, some of whom had been through the first Gulf War and couldn't care less about emotional intelligence. Empathy does not appear to be one of their strong points, and the psychologist is forced to draw upon his deepest reserves of optimism.

Fortunately, one of the navigators is vaguely familiar with the notion of emotional intelligence and wants to hear about it. The psychologist begins by accidentally stepping on the fighter crew's emblem painted on the floor (and must pay a $2 fine), but recovers and launches into his presentation—basically, that emotional skills are important, particularly in life-and-death situations.

By the end of the afternoon, against all odds and expectations, the entire crew had completed the EQ-i, and several stayed behind to talk about emo-tional issues related to their job experiences. We were impressed not only with their superb technical skills, but with their wide range of interests and back-grounds. All of them had a college education, but the disciplines varied from history to mathematics to engineering to English literature. In fact, no one was sure how he'd been picked for his elite position, and several remarked that they'd certainly have qualified for civilian jobs that would pay far more than their present earnings. On the other hand, in civilian life, you can't fly an F-14.

Steven thought he knew how the majority of the pilots would score on the EQ-i. To his surprise, he was slightly off base.

First, they were among the highest-scoring groups we'd tested to that point in time. We expected them (along with entrepreneurs, physicians, and members of other "elite" occupations) to do well when it came to self-regard, and so they did. But their answers in this category (and in self-awareness) showed them to be devoid of arrogance, overconfidence, or blind faith in their abilities. In other words, because they knew exactly how good they were, they had absolutely no need to exaggerate.

They also scored well when it came to reality testing (a good thing when they have only a fraction of a second to decide whether or not to fire at what may or may not be an approaching enemy) and to impulse control (again, a vital attribute when pushing the wrong button can spell the difference between life and death for others and for yourself).

They also excelled at stress tolerance, as well they might—but they weren't hesitant to pinpoint the cause of their greatest anxiety. Steven asked them (and don't forget, most had seen live combat in the Gulf) what fright-ened them the most. They said they could handle bombing missions and the sight of an enemy plane or missile with aplomb; their major worry was coming "home"—landing on the pitching deck of the carrier at night.

EQ and the Oval Office

Moving from the theater of war to the political arena, let's see how emotional intelligence affects our elected leaders. President Bill Clinton's indiscretions are receding from memory, but they may yet endure as the hallmark of his term in office, pushing aside his many achievements.

The question repeated over and over at the time was why in heaven's name did Clinton behave that way? Did he harbor a self-destructive streak that pushed him perpetually toward irresponsible acts? We certainly wish that we could administer the EQ-i to him, or to his wife, Hillary, who stood by him to an unusual degree. But in the absence of their EQ results, we can make one or two educated guesses about the president's emotional intelligence levels.

We'd expect that, like the majority of successful politicians, Bill Clinton would score high across the board, particularly on interpersonal skills. He'd also likely do well when it came to stress tolerance, empathy, and social responsibility. His style indicates that he's a strong "people person" who's maneuvered his way through many political and personal minefields. His empathic abilities are clear; whenever he speaks, listeners feel as though he's communicating and connecting directly with them alone.

Clinton's Achilles' heel is equally clear: in his personal life, he's had difficulty exercising impulse control. Finally, this shortcoming led to a national trauma. Whatever his feelings about Monica Lewinsky and numerous other women, it's obvious that he'd have been far wiser to keep his impulses in check, as he himself admitted in numerous apologies to the American people. But still—because of his charisma and interpersonal flair—he survived these incidents. Even after the Starr Report was made public, when Clinton's very public humiliation was being paraded on the newscasts night after night, his approval rating among voters never dropped below 60 percent.

EQ in the Political Realm

Clinton is certainly not the first politician (nor will he be the last) to get into hot water due to faulty impulse control—witness headlines from around the world that describe leaders who engage in dalliances while calling for a return to family values, or are discovered with their hands in the till, having won an election on a house-cleaning platform.

Perhaps out of a sense of self-preservation (not a component of emotional intelligence, but a long-standing prime political imperative), very few elected officials are keen to take the EQ-i—or, if they do, to have the results made known. One who dared is Bill Vander Zalm, a former premier of British Columbia, Canada. Not only did he cheerfully complete the test but he agreed to talk about his scores as part of a Canadian Broadcasting Corporation (CBC) television program about our work, and gave us permission to publish his scores in this book.

Vander Zalm was, and remains, a flamboyant personality. He was forced to resign his premiership in the wake of a conflict-of-interest scandal. When we tested him, he said that he had nothing more to hide and was interested in learning what, if anything, the EQ-i would reveal.

And what exactly was that? Vander Zalm achieved his highest scores in the Intrapersonal (now referred to as Self-Perception and Self-Expression) and Interpersonal realms. The "average" EQ score is 100; Vander Zalm was quite high (or significantly higher) in several categories, scoring 126 in independence (in keeping with his reputation as a leader who stood up, took charge, and led his party to victory), and 123 in both self-regard and happiness. Clearly, his defeat (about which he joked while completing the questionnaire) did not diminish his capacity to enjoy life—he continues to this day to evidence an upbeat demeanor, at least in his public persona.

Vander Zalm's lower scores are equally revealing. For example, he did not (to put it charitably) excel in problem solving—a shortcoming that plagued his government and led to his being labeled a person who shoots from the hip, only to shoot himself in the foot. Another low-scoring category was, as expected, impulse control, in which he managed only 86.

We don't know if Vander Zalm will rival Clinton's legendary resilience, and spring back, phoenix-like, to life. Our advice, if he hopes to re-enter public life or gain elected office again, is to work on his two most deficient areas of emotional intelligence. He'd do well to stop and reflect before he speaks, refrain from answering questions unless he's sure of his ground, and rely on solid advice to sort out reasoned approaches to the tough issues, rather than winging it on his own. If he does, he stands a decent chance of putting the past behind him and re-establishing a positive public image.

"He Shoots, He Scores!"

The Toronto Maple Leafs hockey team, once the pride of the National Hockey League, had racked up several bad years, not only failing to win the Stanley Cup championship, but missing the playoffs altogether. Suddenly, in the 1998–99 season, they were on a comeback, moving from 25th to fifth place in the standings, and ensuring themselves a playoff berth.

But they'd paid a heavy price, and the team had suffered a number of injuries, putting several of their top players on the sick list. This situation became critical by the third game of the second-round playoffs against the notoriously physical Pittsburgh Penguins, and the Leafs, having assessed their bench strength, came up with a bold and unusual plan. They brought in an 84th-round draft pick named Adam Mair, who'd never played an NHL game in his life and had been biding his time with the Leafs' farm club in eastern Canada.

Mair skated onto the ice at the Igloo, Pittsburgh's home arena. No one in the full-house crowd noticed him—otherwise, he'd have been roundly booed, along with the rest of the Toronto players. But the television commentators were struck by his almost unprecedented arrival, spent a moment speculating on his likely fate at the hands of the Penguins, and scheduled a between-periods interview with whatever was left of him when Pittsburgh got through welcoming him to the big time.

Instead, he made himself known at once. Mair scored a goal, becoming only the second player in Maple Leaf history to debut in the playoffs and put a puck in the net. (For trivia fans, the first player to do so hit the ice in 1948.)

We don't wish to appear smug about it, but we weren't in the least surprised by Mair's performance. Why? Because we'd tested his EQ, along with the EQ of 28 other Maple Leaf prospects, at a pre-season training camp. His scores stood out from all the rest, and marked him as the most likely to succeed in whatever he attempted.

His overall score was very high, indicating excellent general adjustment. He was then only 19, but his highest component score was in reality testing, indicating that he had a keen sense of his situation, which would prove helpful in accepting his farm-club status. If you're suddenly selected by a major league team, it's easy to indulge in unrealistic fantasies. Next week, you're bound to be a league-leading goal scorer, adored by all and paid in keeping with your station. The idea that you have a lot to learn gets lost in the shuffle, which impedes your necessary development. But not so with Mair. Instead, he spent his time well, working hard, polishing his skills, and preparing for his chance.

His second-highest score came in problem solving—for any athlete, an important predictor of success. Knowing how to think on your feet in the middle of ever-shifting circumstances, deciding whether to pass the puck or shoot from a less than ideal angle, meanwhile avoiding a swarm of defending players, can spell the difference between victory and defeat. Superior players hone these responses by means of the visualization technique, mentally rehearsing how to overcome obstacles as they arise.

Again, we come back to the importance of emotional intelligence in a particular field. Any hockey player who's taken at all seriously by an NHL scout or coach is on a certain plateau, in possession of a certain level of athletic talents and skills (that are, of course, miles beyond what most of us could ever hope to command). He's got strength and stamina; he's good at the game. But what will enable him to become great?

As we continued to test the Maple Leafs' draft picks over a two-year period, we identified several components that seemed to be directly linked to success in professional sports. Many people would identify stress tolerance, and it's in the running, but by far the most vital factor was optimism. When a team loses by a narrow margin, the player who gets angry, blames others for the loss, or goes into a tailspin from which he takes three more games to recover is not professional material. Instead, his attitude had better be "Well, if we'd only had a few more minutes, we could have made it. And here's what we're going to do next time around." The ability to learn from mistakes and misfortunes differentiates the stars from the rest of the pack.

Another perhaps unexpected factor is happiness. We'd thought, as we set out to test the hockey prospects, that this would surely be the happiest time of their lives. The dream of making it to the NHL was within their grasp; they'd been chosen over hundreds if not thousands of their peers from all over North America, Europe, and the former USSR. But for many of them, happiness remained elusive (as did a berth on the team), whereas those who were genuinely glad to be getting their chance tended to perform at a higher level.

By the way, we also identified one component of emotional intelligence that had a reverse effect on sporting success. This was independence. Players who went their own way tended to underachieve; at this early stage in their careers, they'd have been better advised to learn the team's system, heed the coach, and listen to and follow directions to the letter.

EQ and the Skier

Another athlete we tested is Shirley Diertshi, a (previously) nationally ranked skier from Oregon. She and her three brothers were raised on the slopes, and Shirley achieved great success in both downhill and slalom junior competitions—until one weekend on Mount Hood when she was bowled over by another skier (in fact, by an instructor who'd been doing freestyle flips in mid-air and didn't see her and her companion ahead of him until it was too late). She was sent airborne by the impact and dislocated her hip. Six hours later, having endured excruciating pain while the ski patrol got her down the hill on a sled, she wound up in hospital under general anesthetic. When she awoke, she demanded to get out of bed and back to training for the next weekend's race—a plan the doctor vetoed. In fact, he said, she might very easily have lost her leg, and she faced a long and agonizing rehabilitation.

She remembers that every night she prayed that it would rain, so her brothers couldn't go skiing. To conquer these unworthy thoughts, she contacted her art instructor at the Portland Art Museum, where she was taking courses at the time, and asked for hospital-bed assignments, practicing calligraphy ("every letter in the alphabet at least a million plus times") and developing the ability to focus on something completely different.

Her first day on crutches, she headed for the local Jewish community center and found the therapy pool. Soon she was swimming laps, and was hired as an instructor and lifeguard. Then she got her old job back as a teacher's aide at a public school, walking there and back (a five-mile round trip) on crutches. Later still, when she could walk unaided, she began to run ("little did I know I had aerobic endurance genes"), went back on the slopes, this time as an instructor, and wound up in New Zealand, where friends asked if she'd like to join them in a marathon. Her immediate reply was "Sure, how far is it?" To give her an idea of its rigors, her so-called friends took her 14 miles out of town, dropped her off, and told her to come home under her own steam. A week later, in the actual race, she finished ahead of the expected winner, leading the organizers to suggest that she go back to Boston and try her luck there. The first time she entered that city's well-known marathon she came in 15th. The next, she led all the other American women and set a personal best of two hours, 39 minutes, and 17 seconds.

Her note to us concludes: "I didn't stop running then and I still run now, except now I coach others to reach their potential. My experiences motivated me to pursue further education in an area in which I could contribute to the betterment of other athletes, which is why I chose to attend graduate school to earn a Ph.D. in sports psychology. I had no idea I would travel so far, using the skills I'd developed—commitment, dedication, discipline, and a willingness to work hard and hang in until reaching the finish. I'm currently teaching the psychology of exercise, health, and wellness, and am coaching a cross-country and track team. I still have energy to burn, and I try to aim it in a positive direction, to encourage others to dream and to strive for their desires." As well, Shirley is the consulting psychologist for the U.S. Winter Olympic team.

It will come as absolutely no surprise when you learn that Shirley's EQ-i results evidenced high scores in self-awareness, optimism, self-actualization, stress tolerance, and interpersonal relationships.

EQ in the Financial Sector

Now, let's take a look at some of the other fields in which emotional intelligence plays a role. We've assembled data for so many groups that it's difficult to pick and choose, but we'll settle on a few highlights. Numerous studies have shown that emotional intelligence can be conclusively linked to workplace success. The first one was undertaken, back in 1997, in Manila, Philippines, and was conducted by Joseph Hee-Woo Jae,[12] then a graduate student at the local university. He administered the EQ-i to 100 front-line workers at the Planter's Bank, the country's fifth-largest financial institution. They also took a standardized IQ test, and their supervisors carried out and submitted independent work appraisals. When all the results were tabulated, the IQ test results accounted for less than 1 percent of their work appraisal scores, but their EQ scores could be linked to 27 percent of their success.

Another study that proves the link between emotional intelligence and success on the job stems from our work with the Canadian Imperial Bank of Commerce, one of Canada's largest financial institutions, and concerns the elite Global sales unit, headed at that time by Brian Twohey.[13]

As head of Global Private Banking and Trust for the CIBC, Brian believed that EQ skills were key to his team's performance. Its members are responsible for handling the accounts of wealthy clients whose investments transcend national boundaries. They must therefore be familiar with both Canadian and international tax law and (in short) a maze of rules and regulations. But each member of the unit is in essence a salesperson and has targets to meet. Their sales fall into two categories: those that have already been completed (or booked), and those (known as pipeline sales) that are waiting for certain events to transpire before they can be closed.

Brian was extremely interested when we suggested that his team complete the EQ-i, to see whether its findings might be used as a predictor of sales success. The results show conclusively that they can. Briefly, an individual's test scores accounted for 32 percent of his or her booked sales and 71 percent of pipeline sales.

It's always interesting to compare these results against an employer's or another authority's preconceptions. For example, most people would assume that a successful salesperson would excel at interpersonal relationships. Indeed, the Global sales force's performance hinged on both interpersonal relationships and self-actualization. Team members who really enjoyed their work, set personal goals, and put in the extra effort to excel were the ones who came out ahead. The third most important skill (one shared by sales professionals in many other fields) was empathy—the ability to put yourself in someone else's shoes. Following close behind were flexibility, stress tolerance, and reality testing. Putting these factors together in a formula, rather like the one we created for the U.S. Air Force, we came up with a powerful tool for Brian to use both in his selection of new personnel and in his attempts to improve the already superior skills of his current staff.

Another well-documented example of the way emotional skills can be improved in a work environment comes from Kate Cannon, formerly at American Express Financial Services.[14] Kate designed a very effective program to achieve this aim, and used the EQ-i to evaluate its effectiveness by comparing the test results obtained from 52 sales consultants with their subsequent performance. Not only did the salespeople's performance improve at work, many of them also reported greater success in dealing with situations that arose in their personal lives. In Kate's group, the EQ factors that showed the most change—especially for those who initially scored rather low—was in the areas of assertiveness, empathy, reality testing, self-actualization, and self-regard, as well as optimism.

All of which makes sense. When you're trying to sell something to or (in the case of the collection agents we'll describe below) get something from someone, assertiveness comes in handy. Combined with empathy (the ability to understand others) and reality testing (the ability to determine whether you're really dealing with a potential customer or spinning your wheels), assertiveness takes you a long way down the road to success.

EQ in Sales

We know you're dying to hear about the collection agents, but hang on just a second. First, we'd like to mention insurance sales, a field we were drawn to because of a classic study conducted by the psychologist Martin Seligman at Metropolitan Life in New York.[15] He convinced this firm to grant him access to their new employees and administered not only personality and IQ tests but also a new test he'd devised himself that he hoped would measure optimism. Also, he arranged to follow the employees' progress during their first year, to gauge the effectiveness of MetLife's training procedures. At the end of that time, he found that the traditional tests did not predict success, but that the salespeople who scored high in optimism sold 33 percent more insurance than those who scored low. He also found that, after two years, the optimistic group members were more than 50 percent more likely than their lower-scoring peers to be thriving on the job. Optimism, then, seemed to be a strong indication of not only sales success but of an inclination to remain with the firm.

Naturally, when we began administering the EQ-i to workers in various fields, salespeople were high on our list. We found that optimism was still a predictor of success, but it wasn't right up there at the top. In our first study, we looked at 90 insurance people, broken into two groups—those who were doing well and salespeople who were underachieving. Their scores varied significantly—an average of 108 and 97, respectively. The factors that most set the two groups apart were, in order, assertiveness, happiness, self-regard, self-actualization, stress tolerance, and optimism.

We might expect that assertiveness would contribute to sales success. The better you can express your thoughts, feelings, and beliefs in a tactful way, the more your customers will view you as authentic and worth dealing with. It also does wonders when you come, as you must, to closing the sale.

Happiness may seem at first glance more obscure, but ask yourself: who wants to buy life insurance from someone who mopes around and behaves more like an undertaker? An upbeat disposition appears to take the insurance salesperson far, and allows him or her to cast the product (which after all is concerned with death) in a positive light.

As for self-regard, it imparts a sense of confidence and assurance, a sense that the salesperson knows the product inside out, but never gives way to cockiness. Dealing with stress is also an important part of the job description. But how many insurance companies actively seek to recruit people who possess these skills? Based on our informal surveys of audiences at our seminars, it seems that—despite the evidence—very few firms take advantage of these findings.

EQ and the Collection Agency

And now, as promised: EQ and collection agents. Several studies have been conducted in this field by the psychologist John Bachman, who, while working as corporate psychologist at Commercial Financial Services, a large collection agency, administered the EQ-i to its staff.

What would you think it takes to be adept at this hard-nosed task? With visions of enforcers and well-muscled repo men dancing in our heads, we might think first of aggressiveness, toughness, and a willingness to be downright rude.

Wrong. According to Bachman, the secret to success in recovering clients' money is to avoid destructive encounters. He postulated the theory that two pairs of emotional intelligence factors could be key to this kinder, gentler strategy. He thought that emotional self-awareness and empathy would permit collectors to keep tabs on their own emotions while monitoring the debtor's, thus keeping matters on an even keel. He also thought that impulse control and flexibility would allow collectors to negotiate without falling victim to the debtor's evasive, helpless, desperate, or surly comments.

In order to test these theories, Bachman administered the EQ-i to the best performers (as identified by their supervisors) and to their less successful co-workers. He was gratified to find that the group scores were 110 and 102 respectively, with the most effective collectors doing particularly well when it came to independence, stress tolerance, self-awareness, self-actualization, and optimism.

On closer inspection, Bachman found that the more productive group's scores were accounted for not by two, but by three pairs of emotional intelligence factors. The first was assertiveness and independence, which enabled the self-reliant collectors to work autonomously, secure in their ability to express themselves in a non-aggressive but highly effective way. The second was self-actualization and problem solving, which enabled them to work toward fulfillment of their goals by means of time management, information processing, and enhanced communication and negotiation capabilities. The third was optimism and happiness, which imparted a stable mood that overcame the job's inherent stress, rejection, frustration, and disappointment.

Finally, the successful group coupled sufficient (but not too much) empathy with a rather elastic sense of impulse control. The right degree of empathy allowed these collectors to negotiate in a businesslike though humanistic way, without going overboard into excessive sympathy with the debtor's plight or (alternatively) with the client's rightful demands. A little less impulse control than average, it seems, allowed them to retain a sense of urgency—to maintain their edge and keep procrastination at bay.

The results were twofold. Over a six-month period, it was found that the superior collectors raked in 100 percent of their quotas, compared with their less successful peers, who languished at 47 percent. After Bachman had created a statistical formula to help the firm select new recruits based on his findings, another study kept tabs on their performance over the first three months on the job. Remarkably, those who'd been hired on the basis of their high scores (and others, who'd been given special training) collected 163 percent of their quotas, while low scorers managed to come up with a still respectable 80 percent.[16]

The Role of EQ in Leadership

There has been a lot of discussion about emotional intelligence and leadership. Unfortunately, most of what we've seen has been based on speculation or revisionist science. Wild estimates have been proposed—for example, that emotional intelligence accounts for 80 to 90 percent of leadership skills. We think these estimates, based on flimsy evidence, can be harmful to the true research and understanding of the role of emotional intelligence. They run the risk of destroying the credibility of serious researchers in the field. Looking at interviews conducted many years ago on leaders of yesterday's companies may be interesting, but it does not shed much light on what makes today's leaders successful. Also, without standardized testing, the reliability of the information is suspect. Interviews and ratings by peers and subordinates are often full of biases. Many of today's 360-degree (multi-rater) measures are heavily influenced by a desire to please one's boss, or alternatively a wish to replace him or her. Moreover, it is difficult to judge accurately the internal emotions of someone with whom you work.

Our testing of a large group of members of the Young Presidents' Organization, or YPO (along with some other CEO membership groups we've tested), is the first valid study that looks at the relationship between emotional intelligence and leadership. This select group of top business achievers has strict rules for membership: to belong, one must be 39 years old or younger and be president or CEO of a company that employs 60 or more people and generates $5 million or more a year in revenue.

One of us (Steven) was invited to speak at a regional meeting of the YPO, which carefully screens its presenters in order to avoid sales pitches and ensure some take-home value to its members. For us, this invitation offered a unique opportunity to collect some very interesting data. After all, it is not easy to get access to groups with such well-defined criteria for success. In exchange for speaking about emotional intelligence, the YPO agreed to let us test willing members with the EQ-i. This would make the presentation more interesting for them and provide useful research material for us. Each member would get his or her own personal scores, and we would incorporate the "group profile" as part of the presentation. To make it even more interesting, we came up with three naturally occurring subgroups that characterized the YPO's membership. Comparing these three groups gave us yet another dimension to explore.

The first group consisted of "Founders." These were the individuals who had started the companies they managed. As young entrepreneurs with an idea for a small business, they had seen their dreams grow, often beyond their wildest expectations. The second group we called "Family Business." These were individuals who, for one reason or another, took charge of an enterprise that had been started by a parent, uncle, or other close relative. The third group we referred to as "Professional Managers" or, more colloquially, "Hired Guns." These individuals, perhaps as early as age 25, had demonstrated a great deal of managerial competence. In some cases they would go on to head companies generating more than $50 million per year in revenue.

Another area of great interest to many of the members was the potential gender differences that we might uncover. How would the EQ scores of successful entrepreneurial men compare to those of equally successful women? While there were considerably more male members, we still felt that comparing them to the female members would be of great value. What could we learn from the emotional skill sets of these successful businesswomen?

As we began, we had no idea how many of these very busy young executives would have the time to complete our inventory and get back to us by the deadline. Competing with extremely hectic schedules running companies that, in some cases, generated hundreds of millions of dollars in sales, we did not expect a huge return. In most surveys of business people, a return rate of 33 percent is considered quite good. So we were shocked when the responses started to roll in: the return rate was more than 92 percent. And the results were impressive.

The YPO group scored significantly higher than our large sample of norms. In fact, they were high in comparison to the hundreds of group scores we have processed.

What were the specific emotional skills that set this successful group of entrepreneurs apart?

The first was their high level of flexibility. These individuals are characterized by their ability to see opportunities and grasp them. They are ready and able to move quickly when needed, to take advantage of the opportunities they encounter.

Another characteristic that stood out in the successful young entrepreneurs was their independence—a crucial component of effective decision making. We discovered 22-year-olds who had started and continued to manage companies generating more than $20 million in sales. In some cases these individuals far surpassed any of their families or friends in income. They had no role models they could go to, to discuss issues and problems. But one of the benefits of the YPO is their "mentoring" program, which gives these 22-year-old millionaires the opportunity to learn from older, more experienced entrepreneurs who manage $100-million companies. One young millionaire told us he would go to his mentor to discuss business issues, difficulties, and decisions. While the mentor would freely give advice, the student was, in fact, quite selective about which bits of information to heed. That is the essence of independence: listen to others, weigh the advice, then go out and make your own decisions.

How did Founders compare with Professional Managers and Family Business? Only one factor differentiated them. The Founders were significantly more assertive than the other two groups. And what about the young female presidents? Interestingly, they performed as well as their male counterparts in all areas except for two: they scored significantly higher in interpersonal relationships and empathy.

Does emotional intelligence have any relationship to how much money we make? Our colleagues Drs. Jan Derksen and Theodore Bogels in The Netherlands carried out the world's first study looking at the relationship between income and EQ. They tested a large, carefully selected sample of the Dutch population with the EQ-i and related it to income. As you can see in Figure 19-1 (below), they found a significant relationship: people with higher EQ earned more money (we converted their findings into approximate U.S. dollars).

EQ and Journalists

We've had the chance to test another group of people who affect (for better or worse) our lives—print and broadcast journalists. We found that they scored quite high in self-regard and optimism, but did somewhat more poorly in impulse control and (ominously, since their job is to dig for the truth behind the headlines) reality testing. Surprisingly, they also registered average scores in empathy and social responsibility.

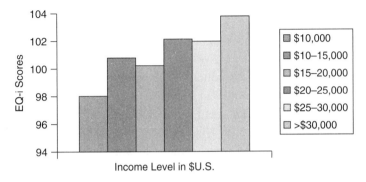

Figure 19-1:   Income and EQ Chart

Reprinted with permission of PEN Test Publishers, The Netherlands.

That final point puzzled a friend of ours, herself a journalist who had thought that most of her peers would be more overtly civic-minded. Her only explanation was that media people express their social responsibility through their work, and are hesitant to involve themselves in their communities, for fear that their objectivity might be clouded if they later had to cover news events relating to these organizations. (Interestingly enough, radio and television broadcasters tended to be more independent and optimistic than their print colleagues. They also showed an ability to be more self-directed and self-controlled.)

EQ Goes To Court

Another group we've had the opportunity to study in some detail is lawyers. In fact, we've administered the EQ-i to more than 130 criminal and corporate practitioners, as well as to judges. Overall, most of them tended to score in the average range, but some—the star performers—stood out from the rest. Among these, we'd like to mention two: Alan Gold and Don Jack.

Alan, as befitted a past president of the Criminal Lawyers' Association in Canada, was cautious at first. He'd had occasion to attack a number of psychological tests in the courtroom and had given a number of expert psychological witnesses a hard time. Nonetheless, we persisted, and finally he agreed to complete the EQ-i.

When we met to discuss the results, however, Alan launched into a dismissal of the entire concept of emotional intelligence. He'd been a good sport, he said, but he doubted that any conclusions we'd draw from his answers would hold water.

So we decided to shift gears. We began by asking him to forget about the test, the questions, the terminology that surrounds the field, and go back to what he knew best. Instead, we asked what makes a top-notch lawyer. Would he, for example, if he were charged with a crime, necessarily want to be defended by the person who stood first in his graduating class?

"The smartest in class?" he replied. "You're kidding. No way."

Of course, we asked him why not. Surely that person would know the law inside and out. But Alan quickly set us straight. He said that knowing the law isn't all-important. Rather, it's a matter of knowing where and how to find out what you need to know—getting the answers to vital questions as they arise.

He also talked about the importance of communication, being able to get your point across quickly and understandably without wasting words or straying off topic, and of conveying an air of competence and confidence. He then remarked that in 80 percent of all cases, the lawyer's skill is probably irrelevant—that is, the issue is decided on points of law. In the remaining 20 percent, a lawyer can influence the outcome, but not always positively. In other words, a lawyer's performance can lose a case rather than win it.

Even though he'd begun by attacking our field, what impressed us about Alan was his total lack of arrogance. He's at the top of his game, and presents a challenge and a target to his adversaries, who quite often will make the mistake of going into full-blown attack mode. But he makes it a point never to respond in kind. In court, he's respectful, courteous, and businesslike, even if he dislikes the person on the other side. This enables him to score points; if the opposition isn't in command of his or her emotions, Alan can turn it to his client's advantage. He keeps his cool, is always under control, and uses anger sparingly, for effect.

As well, visualization is an important feature of the legal arsenal. Alan sees a case unfolding in his mind before he sets foot in court (just like the athlete before a playoff game), dealing with crises before they happen and anticipating how his adversary might present an argument.

Not surprisingly, Alan's EQ-i score was significantly higher than that of the average lawyer. His individual component scores were illustrative too—highest in independence (as befits a senior partner in his own firm), followed by self-awareness and interpersonal relationships, assertiveness, and problem solving.

After we'd run this down, we asked Alan if he saw the connection between reading other people well, being a good communicator, and being calm, courteous, in control, and confident—all components of emotional intelligence—and his success, and he admitted that, despite his misgivings, perhaps our field made a good deal of sense after all.

Our second legal star performer is Don Jack, a corporate litigator who, when he took the EQ-i, had just been involved in a class-action suit against Bre-X, one of the most complex stock market frauds of the 1990s. Our first impression was that he was a true gentleman. We were struck by his warm manners and sensitivity to others, but a mutual friend set us straight. "Don't be fooled," he said. "He's the person you want on your side." We later learned that in the courtroom Don's habitual courtesy is tempered by pit-bull tenacity, and witnesses are almost reduced to tears by his probing examinations.

He, too, scored high on the EQ-i, excelling in self-regard, self-actualization, and stress tolerance. And he, too, although he attended Oxford University, will tell you that it takes more than academic achievement to excel. One factor in his success is the ability to grasp the most complex picture, identify the most relevant details, and go for the jugular. He also sees the need to control his emotions and have a game plan, while reading the emotions of the judge, the opposing lawyer, and the witnesses on the stand. We'd compare his courtroom performance to that of the conductor of an orchestra, or perhaps a chess master who's always thinking a dozen moves ahead.

EQ in the Classroom

All of us may not wind up in a courtroom, but many of us have kids, and one of the most frequently asked questions at our lectures is "What makes a great teacher?" This is because today's consumers of education (for which, read parents and students) are becoming much more demanding in their expectations.

In response, we've administered the EQ-i to thousands of teachers, and we're often asked to give presentations and workshops to teachers' groups and to schools, as part of their professional development programs. For example, we had the opportunity to test the entire staff of a medium-size private school, all of whom are evaluated each year and must make a presentation (including a case study of a student who's excelled) to an administrative committee, outlining what their classes have accomplished over the school term. The school had identified the five top-rated teachers, and when our testing was completed, we compared their results with those of their peers.

We found that these top teachers scored significantly higher than the other teachers in several categories, but—once again—we were mildly surprised by which categories these were. Often, we'll ask teachers to identify what they believe to be the most important factors in their work, perhaps by describing the best and most effective teachers they themselves had when they were young. But the factor that came out as the most important in our study never made the top of their lists.

This was self-awareness. Why would it stand out? Because, as we've seen, being in touch with your emotions is the first step toward their effective management. It's also the way you motivate yourself to do your best, week after week, faced with a classroom full of students with wildly varying needs and abilities, different interest levels and attention spans. Few of us, it's safe to say, encounter so daunting a challenge on a daily basis.

In another study, we administered the EQ-i to 257 elementary and 157 secondary-school teachers. We also asked them to rate their own perceived performance on the job. Thirteen percent of the elementary teachers rated themselves as average or below, 60 percent considered themselves average, and 27 percent claimed to be above average. What EQ factors differentiated these three groups? The biggest difference was their scores when it came to optimism; the teachers who proclaimed themselves better than average were significantly more optimistic than others. They also scored considerably higher in problem solving, self-actualization, stress tolerance, and happiness. When we repeated this procedure with secondary-school teachers, we found that the factor that set the more self-reportedly successful educators apart was self-actualization—the ability to enjoy their duties to the full, to get involved in extracurricular activities, and to constantly strive for excellence—followed by problem solving, self-awareness, and happiness.

But what about poor teachers? At the elementary level, you might guess that they were lacking in optimism, but you'd be mistaken. The factor that limited their success was a lack of impulse control, which led to problems with their temper, lack of patience, and poor organizational skills. At the secondary level, teachers who were less satisfied with their performance were distinguished by their low scores in flexibility. An excess of rigidity is not the way to an adolescent's heart, and the surest way to guarantee that your message doesn't get across is to follow the rules at any cost, without bending and with a focus on enforcing discipline and maintaining your authority. For some teachers, flexibility is the most difficult ability to achieve, but it's necessary. Winning the battle for students' hearts, over the long run, will get teachers much further than fighting over who's the boss on a given day. We suspect that, in or out of the classroom, highly regimented environments are increasingly becoming a thing of the past.

EQ and The Power To Heal

We've also been able to test quite a number of physicians, who scored —alas—lower than average. Their highest scores were in stress tolerance, flexibility, and reality testing; their lowest, in empathy, followed by happiness and social responsibility.[17]

One of us (Steven) happened to be on a national radio show with the head of the family practice training program at a major medical school, and mentioned our findings with a degree of trepidation, fearing that she'd jump all over us or challenge our methodology. But she said she wasn't in the least surprised. In her opinion, medical schools are taking a bunch of intelligent and caring young people and ripping the caring right out of them. No wonder holistic medicine is growing by leaps and bounds at the expense of more traditional disciplines, or lawsuits against medical doctors have risen dramatically over the past 20 years, in large part because of a lack of communication between doctor and patient.

Just how important are these factors? Well, a recent study found that diabetic patients in the care of physicians with higher empathy scores were better able to control their blood sugar and cholesterol levels than patients whose doctors were lower in empathy. The study, carried out at Thomas Jefferson University in Philadelphia, included 891 diabetic patients treated between 2006 and 2009 by 29 doctors. According to the authors of the study, empathy contributes to higher patient satisfaction, trust and compliance, which lead to more desirable clinical outcomes.[18]

Still on the subject of health, we might add that we've asked 3,829 people who took the EQ-i about their ability to cope with health-related issues. Of these, 2,715 thought they were dealing with them successfully, and 1,114 said they thought they could do better. As you might imagine, their scores differed significantly—those who felt they'd coped well averaged 10 points higher across the board. The skills and attitudes that most differentiated the two groups were stress tolerance, optimism, flexibility, self-regard, and happiness, in that order.

Again, this is no great surprise. Illness is stressful, and the way we respond to it is in itself physiological and can compound our discomfort. We not only feel and act ill, but our reactions to the illness slow down our body's natural attempts to deal with disease. It's bad enough to be ill, but to stress ourselves out only compounds the problems we're experiencing. Optimism helps us get through this adversity, just as it helps us deal with other woes. Focusing on how well you can cope with illness and believing that it will eventually go away makes it easier to deal with. As does flexibility: rigidly refusing to do things that will help you get better will only prolong your misery.

Interestingly, another study looked directly at the connection between emotional intelligence and health habits using the EQ-i. It was found that there was a direct relationship between health habits of college students and emotional intelligence.[19]

In 1996 Jenny Dunkley, a graduate psychology student in South Africa, carried out a study comparing the EQ-i scores of 58 patients who had recently suffered heart attacks with a control group who'd had no history of heart disease. As she'd thought, the recovering patients scored much lower, particularly in stress tolerance, flexibility, and self-actualization. But, to her surprise, they actually scored higher in social responsibility. Perhaps a brush with death served to refocus them on one of the most important and rewarding things in life—generosity toward one's fellow men and women.

But Dunkley didn't stop there. She knew that 22 of the patients had participated in a program designed to help them manage stress better, while 16 had not. She compared their scores, and found significant differences in the overall scores, and in every component score except interpersonal relationships and self-regard. Those who'd gone through the program were re-tested after five weeks of training and had increased their total score by an average of 9 points, registering the greatest improvements in stress tolerance, self-regard, flexibility, happiness, reality testing, self-actualization, problem solving, and impulse control.[20]

EQ and the Job-Challenged

What about the unemployed? With the help of Rose-Marie Nigli at the YWCA in Toronto, we collected EQ-i data on a large sample of chronically unemployed people between the ages of 18 and 50. Overall, this group achieved below-average scores in the self-perception, self-expression, and decision-making realms. Their lowest scores were in assertiveness, optimism, emotional self-awareness, reality testing, and happiness. Scores were also below average in self-regard and independence.

These results may help explain the unemployed individual's lack of success in finding and keeping a job. Continued failure reinforces these underdeveloped emotional skills, creating a chronic situation. Notably, however, individuals in this group scored higher than average on empathy and social responsibility. Perhaps receiving government assistance increases one's awareness of and consideration toward others who are less fortunate.

About 50 of these individuals participated in a six-week skills-enhancement group that focused on increasing assertiveness, being more realistic in job choices, and improving general life skills (such as coping with challenges and being more optimistic). The group had classroom instruction, life-skills training, and vocational-management and/or technical-skills training. More than 90 percent of the participants found work following the training. When they were re-tested on the EQ-i, their scores showed significant increases on several scales. The skills that changed the most were assertiveness, reality testing, and emotional self-awareness.[21]

EQ and Marital Bliss

Finally, what's the relationship between emotional intelligence and marital satisfaction?

To find out, we administered the EQ-i to more than 1,100 people and asked them to rate themselves in this regard. As expected, people who were satisfied with their relationships scored an average 5 points higher than those who weren't. Differences cropped up across all five realms of emotional intelligence, as well as among its 15 components, but which do you suppose played the greatest role in determining whether or not a person was happy in his or her union? Many of us might name interpersonal relationship skills, empathy, or flexibility. Instead, happiness led the list, followed by self-regard, self-awareness, self-actualization, and reality testing. Only then did interpersonal relationships per se come into force.

Whenever happiness appears to play a significant role in one of our studies, someone always wonders whether (as in this particular case) satisfactory marriages lead to higher happiness scores or vice versa. We think that happiness is the key, because people who score high in this component tend to be happy in a wide variety of situations, throughout good times and bad (or, as the marriage vows put it, for better or for worse). As we hope you have learned from this book, happiness comes from the inside out.

Self-regard is obviously important in a marriage, dealing as it does with both strengths and weaknesses. Viewing yourself with clarity will help you be less prickly and defensive. (After all, other than your mother, it's most likely your spouse who will criticize you the most in life. Being secure will help you deal constructively with that criticism by looking at it honestly and, if it's valid, doing something about it instead of yelling at the messenger.) As for self-awareness, it gives you the chance to monitor and control your internal thermometer; self-actualization, while it adds spice to every element of our lives, is especially vital when it comes to intimate relationships.

Chapter 20

More Star Performers

It's hard to believe how much the world changed between the time we wrote the first edition of this book and the first update five years later. In the second edition, we speculated that, in the future, the world will be divided between those who remember where they were the morning of September 11, 2001, and those who were either too young to remember or were born after that tragic event. Similarly, many of us of a certain age grew up with the clear memory of where we were when we heard about John F. Kennedy's assassination.

Not too long after 9/11, one of us (Steven) received a surprising phone call from Robert Fazio. He began to tell an amazing story. At 9 a.m. one Tuesday morning, his brother called to tell him their father was okay. Robert, quite puzzled, replied, "Well, why wouldn't he be?" His brother immediately told him to turn on the TV. Their father worked in the South Tower of the World Trade Center.

Robert turned on the TV in time to see the second plane hit the towers. His father had called his mother shortly after the North Tower was hit to tell her that he loved her and that he was safe. Robert and his family had every reason to believe that his father made it safely out of the tower that day. In fact, it took Robert three weeks to finally accept the fact that his father had not survived the attack on the towers.

After dealing with the grief and unanswered questions, Robert eventually found out more about his father's fate. What he learned would change his life and the lives of many other people. Robert discovered from a number of his father's colleagues that he was last seen literally holding the door open so that others could safely leave the building and return home to their loved ones.

As a result of this, Robert started a nonprofit organization called "Hold the Door for Others," whose mission is to provide resources and create opportunities that connect people, to empower them to grow through loss and to achieve their dreams.[1] We were more than happy to help out when Rob asked us to supply the EQ-i tests to support his research work which centered on those family members who had lost loved ones on September 11. Specifically he wanted to look at the importance of emotional intelligence and resilience in predicting post-traumatic growth—that is, those people who successfully grow and move forward with their lives after experiencing a traumatic loss.

Robert's results were fascinating. Specifically, he found a connection between post-traumatic growth and three areas of emotional intelligence: interpersonal relationship, intrapersonal (now known as self-perception and self-expression), and general mood. Two of these realms (interpersonal and intrapersonal) were mediated by resilience. In other words, people high in these two areas of emotional intelligence were more resilient and therefore more effective in dealing with the trauma.[2]

EQ and Law Enforcement

One of the questions we have been asked many times since the release of the first edition of this book has been about the potential effect of emotional intelligence on policing or law enforcement in general. Sometimes questions would take the form of "What would the world be like if we developed emotionally intelligent police forces?" Well, it may have seemed far-fetched at first, but we've now seen some great progress in this area thanks to the work of Special Agent Tim Turner, formerly of the FBI Academy. Tim came to learn more about emotional intelligence at one of our training sessions. He was able to quickly connect the dots on where emotional intelligence fits in with law enforcement.

Tim went back and carried out the largest study we've seen looking specifically at the role of emotional intelligence and police officers. As a leadership trainer at the FBI Academy at Quantico, Virginia, Tim worked with high-potential police officers who were selected from forces not only from throughout the U.S., but around the world. He tested and compared the emotional intelligence test scores of 424 law enforcement leaders who were selected to attend the FBI National Academy against a matched set of law-enforcement leaders who were not so selected. There are many fascinating findings of this study relating emotional intelligence and the backgrounds of the officers, whether they were from rural or urban districts, what gender they were, and so on. Unfortunately, we don't have enough space here to cover all of these groundbreaking results, but here are a few.

One of the most exciting findings was in the differentiation of the "star performer" officers—those who were sent to the Academy. Tim used a complicated statistical procedure (regression analysis) to see which of the many factors best differentiated this group. One might expect that top performers are less flexible (better at following orders), or perhaps they were the toughest cops (more aggressive).

Well, we want to dispel those myths of what a high-performing police officer is all about. The most significant factor was social responsibility. As we are finding in other studies of top leaders, social responsibility, we believe, will be a defining characteristic of tomorrow's leaders (much the way flexibility characterizes today's leaders). Socially responsible police officers are able to see the greater good—what's best for their division, what's best for their force, what's best for their community, and yes, what's best for the world.

The second most important defining factor was problem solving. High performers in this area are good at solving problems—defining the problem, generating solutions, and acting on the solution using emotions as opposed to letting them get in the way. Tim had pointed out to us early on that top cops are good problem solvers.

The third area, one that comes up in many of our job studies, is self-actualization. People with healthy self-actualization really enjoy their work. They are also good goal-setters—able to set and achieve what they want in life. Our high-performing police officers really love the work they do and have a game plan for where they are going both in their career and in life.

Finally, and it should not be a surprise, these people excel in their interpersonal relationships. Being successful in this area requires being a good people person. Knowing how to make and keep good relationships is a big part of what makes these leaders successful.[3]

EQ in the Legal Community

There have been a number of new studies looking at the role emotional intelligence plays in the performance of various professionals over the past few years. One of the areas that has been getting a lot of attention is the importance of emotional intelligence in high-performing lawyers. In an interesting series of articles in the Canadian legal magazine *LEXPERT*, Irene Taylor, a reporter and consultant, profiled the emotional intelligence of some of Canada's top lawyers.[4]

High-performing lawyers were selected through a voting process that involved thousands of legal professionals from across Canada. Irene profiled the top 25 corporate litigators, top 40 under 40, top 30 corporate deal makers, top 25 women lawyers, and top 25 general counsels. In each of these groups, the average EQ-i scores were significantly higher than our database of several hundred lawyers.

What are the emotional skills that characterize these star performers? Well, they differ somewhat depending on the type of lawyer. While there were far too many findings to report in the space we have here, we'll highlight a few of the major ones. For example, when we think of top litigators, most of us think of pit bulls ready to pounce or scare the opposition away. While the psychological profiling found them fiercely independent self-starters, they were also sensitive, private introverts. Surprisingly, these attorneys are not driven by money or power, but rather by self-actualization and mastery, making a contribution, peer recognition, and winning "good" fights.[5]

The top litigators had higher than average emotional intelligence. Their key strengths were independence, optimism, reality testing, and stress tolerance. Their lowest scores were in flexibility, impulse control, and interpersonal relationships.

What about our top 40 under 40? These were an impressive crop of up-and-coming lawyers, destined for great things. Many of them had truly outstanding accomplishments, working with multi-billion-dollar accounts. What are the factors that differentiated this group of young achievers? Well, those such as birth order and family background were not significant. Also, these lawyers look different from the top litigators. They are more effective team players, less sensitive, and very pragmatic in action. Also, their motivation is different; rather than seeing law as a calling, they see it as a means to an end.

Emotional intelligence, once again, was a differentiator for this group. Scoring significantly higher than the general population and our database of lawyers, three factors stood out in this group. First, they were highly independent—self-starters with a great deal of initiative. Second, they had very strong stress tolerance—a great ability to work well under pressure. Third, they were very optimistic—able to see themselves get through the most challenging of situations.[6]

The next group, the top 30 dealmakers, represents a different type of legal professional. These are the skilled individuals who believe there is a solution for every problem—and they work until they find it. In interviews they were quoted using terms such as "adrenaline rush," "in play," "life-death choices," "one clear shot," "flanking tactic," "hooked-up," "risk," "fun," and "win."[7]

There were three strengths that really characterized this group. First, they had high levels of self-awareness, really knowing their strengths and weaknesses. Second, they had high raw intelligence. Third, they had a very strong drive to succeed. Their highest areas of emotional intelligence were independence, stress tolerance, problem solving, and optimism. Again, their overall scores were higher than the general population and other lawyers.

We also found out a lot from Canada's top female lawyers. One of the big lessons we wanted to learn from this group was how they deal with work-life balance issues. As with the previous attorney groups, these women scored significantly higher than our general population and our lawyer normative groups. The three highest scores for this group were in independence, stress tolerance, and assertiveness. They were also very high in optimism.

What advice did these women leaders give us on balancing a demanding career and a busy home life? Well first, it's important to love what you do. If your work is not exciting and challenging, then it will seem like pure drudgery. Second, they recommend that women change their definition of success. They correctly point out that for most men career is the measure of success. But, successful women redefine the criteria, putting the priority on mother, spouse, individual, and then career. Well, if these women rate career as fourth on their list, can you imagine how difficult that must be for all the male lawyers they outperform?

Third, these female lawyers have come to realize that you can't have it all. So, they pick their priorities, focusing on only a few things at a time that they can really succeed in. In many cases, they learn to compromise, and to develop new sets of rules. For example, where a client may insist that certain information be compiled by the next day, they may show the client that only some of what they want immediately is important, and the rest of the information can be more carefully collected over a longer period of time.

Another characteristic of some of these women was to see adversity as a challenge. In more than one case when difficult life challenges were experienced, they were not just resigned to accept them, but rather took the bull by the horns and reorganized their lives and surroundings to deal with the challenges.

All of these higher performers keep physically active. In spite of their very busy schedules they find time to run, hike, ski, and pursue other physical activities. They definitely were not couch potatoes.

Many of them also, at some point in their career, made a point of seeking a mentor. They identified someone in their field for whom they had a great deal of respect and would use them as a sounding board and advice-giver. The mentor provided invaluable help in their careers goals.

Managing time well was also volunteered as a critical aspect of success. While not all of them use the same time-management techniques, they all seem to have perfected systems that work for their situation. After all, time management is the bottom line of work-life balance. One of the rules mentioned as something never to be broken was, "Don't cancel family vacations."[8]

The last group of lawyers we'll look at are general counsel or in-house lawyers. There has been a move among many organizations to bring in their own corporate counsel. This is partly due to the high cost of sending out legal work, as well as the benefit of having a lawyer who understands a company's specific business issues. The trends toward corporate consolidations, global growth, an increasingly litigious environment, and the requirements of Sarbanes-Oxley have also contributed.

As in the previous groups, there are clear areas of strength reflected in their EQ scores. The highest scores, in order, are: assertiveness, independence and stress tolerance (tied in second place), and problem solving. This means that as a group these are "take charge" people who push to get things done. They are highly independent (in thinking, decision making, and action), can withstand high levels of stressful/tough situations, and are highly competent working through complex issues.[9]

EQ and Your Dentist and Doctor

While we're on the topic of professional groups, another interesting call came to us from psychologist Dr. Dana Ackley suggesting we explore the emotional intelligence of dentists. "How would emotional intelligence affect dental practice?" we asked.

Dana has been working with dentists for quite some time. In fact, he was working with the Pankey Institute in Florida, a world-famous training center for dentists. He wanted our help in carrying out a study looking at the relationship between the success of Pankey Institute graduates and their emotional intelligence. Together with dentists Drs. Irwin Becker and Richard Green of the Pankey Institute, he tested the EQ of 144 dentists who had taken training at the center.

They also created a Survey of Progress (SOP) scale that evaluated dentists' actual practice following their training at the Institute. They found that emotional intelligence (as measured by the EQ-i) was directly related to success in implementing practice initiatives as identified by the SOP.

They then identified the specific EQ factors that were most important, using a complex statistical (multiple regression) equation. The most important skills associated with dental practice success were emotional self-awareness, reality testing, assertiveness, and self-actualization. The investigators then related how these factors specifically contribute to successful dental practice.[10]

For example, highly skilled professionals in technical fields such as engineering and dentistry tend to think of emotions as frivolous or unimportant. They want to appear objective. However, being objective is not always what the patient wants. Denying that feelings exist does not help either. Dana gives the example of the dentist who is tired at the end of a long day's work. The last patient of the afternoon needs some unexpected dental procedures that exceed the time allowed, but the work needs to be done. The dentist, frustrated, may vent his or her frustration by being curt, maybe even impolite. The self-aware dentist knows that this kind of behavior is likely to upset the patient and may erode the dentist's long-range ability to influence the patient's dental health. Only by paying attention to and dealing with these internal cues will the dentist be more assured of a positive patient relationship.

Another area we get many calls about is the role of emotional intelligence in medical practice. Our early data in this area raised a lot of concerns regarding the low levels of emotional intelligence among many physicians. A recent study by Peggy Wagner and her colleagues at the Medical College of Georgia helps shed more light on how this relationship plays out.[11]

They tested the emotional intelligence of 30 physicians (including faculty and residents) with the EQ-i. They also developed a patient satisfaction scale that contained eight items and assessed patients' satisfaction with their individual physicians as well as their overall satisfaction with healthcare. They had both a "total satisfaction" score and a "relationship satisfaction" score.

There were 232 patients included in this study and an average of seven patients rated each physician. Overall, the patient satisfaction scores were quite high, ranging from averages of 3.69 to 3.94 (out of 4) per item. There were no differences in satisfaction scores for gender, although there was a positive trend for satisfaction with faculty over residents.

There were no differences in EQ-i scores between faculty and residents. However, while female physicians scored higher than males in all scores, they were only significantly higher in stress tolerance. This is quite interesting, because in the general population women tend to score lower than men on this scale.

Comparisons were made between physicians of patients who were 100 percent satisfied and those who were less than 100 percent satisfied (138 out of 232 rated their physicians as excellent—4 points—on all eight satisfaction items). The most significant finding on the EQ subscales was that physicians with higher patient ratings scored significantly higher on the happiness subscale. In other words, patients were more satisfied with doctors who were happy. The best-rated doctors were also somewhat higher in social responsibility and optimism. Interestingly, as you will see later in this chapter, social responsibility and optimism are significant areas for leaders.

The authors of the study suggest helping medical students learn the importance of personal happiness and life satisfaction as a starting point for EI coaching and intervention during training. So, the next time you see your doctor, you may want to see how happy she or he is.

EQ and the Principal's Office

Since the first release of this book in 2000, there has been a surging interest in emotional intelligence and education. In the last chapter we presented some of our findings on the role emotional intelligence plays with teachers. Now we have some groundbreaking studies of school principals.

An ambitious study looking at leadership in education was recently carried out by Howard Stone, James Parker, and Laura Wood.[12] In this study, funded by the former Ontario Ministry of Education and Training in Canada, 464 principals or vice-principals from nine different school boards in the province of Ontario were tested with the EQ-i. Two hundred and twenty-six of the participants were elementary school principals, 84 were elementary school vice-principals, 43 were secondary school principals, and 57 were secondary school vice-principals.

Participants also had their immediate supervisor and three staff members complete a specifically designed leadership questionnaire. The 21 items that were related to leadership ability measured two broad categories: task-oriented leadership (e.g., "comes well prepared for meetings") and relationship-oriented leadership (e.g., "seeks consensus among staff members"). Building relationships and getting things done are widely accepted as two key components of leadership.

A "leadership score" was calculated for each participant that included scores of supervisors and staff. This was used to identify "below average" (20th percentile or lower) and "above average" (80th percentile or higher) leaders.

What factors would you predict differentiate the highly rated principals? Do you think they are friendlier or higher in interpersonal relationships? Are they more assertive and therefore more direct with their staff? Well, if that's what you thought you'd be partly right. The above-average leadership group scored significantly higher on emotional self-awareness, self-actualization, empathy, interpersonal relationship, flexibility, problem solving, and impulse control. Interestingly, these skills were equally important for males and females, and principals and vice-principals. The authors go on to discuss the relative importance of the different components, as well as training issues.[13]

Here's how they summarized their findings:

> ...Professional development programs would be wise to focus on promoting or developing the following abilities: emotional self-awareness (the ability to recognize and understand one's feelings and emotions); self-actualization (ability to tap potential capacities and skills in order to improve oneself); empathy (ability to be attentive to, understand, and appreciate the feelings of others); interpersonal relationships (ability to establish and maintain mutually satisfying relationships); flexibility (ability to

adjust one's emotions, thoughts, and behavior to changing situations and conditions); problem solving (ability to identify and define problems as well as to generate potentially effective solutions); and impulse control (ability to resist or delay emotional behaviors). Since there were no differences on these EI dimensions when principals or vice-principals were compared, or when supervisors who were working in an elementary school were compared to individuals working in a secondary school, professional development programs that developed these abilities would benefit a broad range of school administrators.[14]

EQ and Sales Talent

We've also profiled salespeople for a large, well-known national U.S. electronics chain. Unfortunately, we can't divulge the names of the players in this case, but we screened thousands of job applicants—all online—to see which applicants came closest to matching the electronics chain's star performers. We see this as the selection method of the future. By creating a formula based on star performers in a company, we can use the statistical algorithm to see to what degree applicants come close to this ideal candidate. Applicants are rank ordered, after their skills, availability, location, and various knockout criteria (such as poor language skills) are taken into account. They are then screened, with a brief phone interview that "checks" their skills in the areas that the star performer analysis found to be important.

The most appropriate applicants as confirmed by a post-phone interview are then invited for a more in-depth one-to-two-hour interview with the most relevant people in the organization. This process not only saves hundreds of hours in the selection process, but tens of thousands of dollars as well. Just as important, it prevents people from accepting jobs that they are highly likely to fail in—avoiding a waste of their time as well as the humiliation of being let go.

In this case, we looked at cell phone salespeople. We started by testing 91 of the chain's employees throughout the country with the EQ-i, and an online ability test measuring vocabulary and arithmetic. Then individual managers ranked all employees based on a combination of sales, attitude, and attendance to create a performance rating. These ratings were categorized into three groups: "top performers," "average performers," and "bottom performers."

We then used a complex statistical analysis that analyzed the relationship between EQ-i responses and performance ratings. We found that self-actualization, empathy, problem solving, and happiness were all positively related to performance in this group. Several other EQ-i components or subcomponents also were significant.

These EQ-i factors were extremely effective in differentiating top performers from the other two performance groups, although a bit less effective in distinguishing average from bottom performers. For example, using our formula to predict performance, 8 percent of top performers, and 78 percent of bottom performers were correctly identified. On the other hand, 13 percent of average performers were incorrectly identified as top performers, and 8 percent of bottom performers were wrongly identified as top performers. None of the top performers was classified as a bottom performer.

The measures of cognitive ability (vocabulary and arithmetic) did not contribute to our predictive model. These results were then used to create a formula that compared all new applicants to the top performers. People often worry about cheaters when online testing is used as part of the selection process. The difficulty, however, is that nobody outside of the selection group knows which specific factors are important for this job. Most people who cheat are likely to cheat across the board, on all scales, which would not be helpful in beating the selection formula. Also, the results of cheating likely won't help get the job. Cheaters may get screened out after the initial interview, or after the in-depth interview. Even if they fooled everyone in the interviews and got hired, chances are their performance will not be very good (but if it is, we're glad they cheated), or they will end up being unhappy performing a job they really aren't suited for.

The effects of this program led to hiring a much better caliber of salesperson. It also streamlined the selection process, saving a great deal of time and money.

EQ and Leadership

Another study in star performers was carried out by an MHS team led by Diana Durek for a major telecom company. The company wanted to understand the relationship between EQ-i and leadership competencies to enhance training and coaching of leaders in their organization.

In this star performer model, the EQ-i accounted for 48 percent of what differentiated the high- and low-performing leaders. This means that one-half of the skill set required for successful execution of this organization's leadership competencies is comprised of emotional and social skills. Twenty-four percent of the difference between high and low performers was accounted for by the happiness subscale, 13 percent by the self-regard subscale, 9 percent by self-actualization, 2 percent by interpersonal relationship, and 1 percent by optimism. When we ran a classification test, the resultant model was accurate in predicting star performers nine out of 10 times.

These results have powerful implications for selection and development initiatives in this organization. The EQ-i subscales that account for the difference in performance are incorporated into the competency training, thus strengthening their training results. The selection process could be enhanced significantly with the creation of an algorithm that will evaluate a candidate's EQ-i match against high performers in the position, generating a value to predict the likelihood of an individual becoming a star performer.

So far, the largest and best designed study looking at emotional intelligence and leadership was carried out by Dr. Marian Ruderman and her colleagues at the Center for Creative Leadership (CCL) in Greensboro, North Carolina.[15] The CCL is a world-famous leadership training center with a long history of research into what makes leaders great.

In the CCL's study, 302 leaders and senior managers, some who were quite successful and others who were struggling, were tested for emotional intelligence with the EQ-i, and for their on-the-job (leadership) performance with Benchmarks®, a tool designed to get a clear picture of leadership performance from superiors, peers, and subordinates.

One of Dr. Ruderman's findings was that emotional intelligence accounted for approximately 28 percent of leadership performance. This finding is consistent with a number of other studies we've reported on previously.

Based on their work, we've identified four pillars or competencies that are important for successful leadership. These are: 1) being centered and grounded; 2) having the ability to take action; 3) having a participative management style; and 4) being tough-minded. Each of these pillars was significantly related to specific aspects of emotional intelligence as measured by EQ-i.

The first pillar of leadership success involves being centered and grounded. High performers are in control of themselves. They are seen by people around them as having a stable mood and they don't fly off the handle when things get tough. You can predict how these leaders are going to react to things. You don't come in to work, say good morning, and then get berated for something you neglected to do the day before.

Also, the successful leaders were more aware of their strengths and weaknesses. The most dangerous leaders are the ones who propose to know it all. While it's important to know your strengths and use them wisely, it's equally important to know your weaknesses and not inflict them on everyone around you. We find that not all leaders are willing to invest the time in improving their weaknesses; however, the next best alternative is to surround yourself with people strong in the skills you lack.

Another aspect of this pillar is the ability to balance work life and personal life. While in the past there has been an overemphasis on the workaholic lifestyle of leaders, we find that balance is associated with better-performing leaders. If you can manage your own life well—managing stress, home life, fitness, diet—then chances are higher that the workplace is well managed.

Successful leaders are also straightforward and self-aware. People know where these leaders stand on issues, as they tend not to be vague or wishy-washy. As well, they are aware of their own feelings and motivators. They are consistent in their approach to issues because they know how and what they feel and believe about those issues.

Finally, these leaders are composed under pressure. They do not flare up or lose control even under difficult circumstances. The most important emotional intelligence skills in this pillar are social responsibility, stress tolerance, impulse control, and optimism.

The second pillar of leadership success is action-taking and includes the ability to be decisive. Successful leaders can make decisions and have a track record of making good decisions. These leaders take into account the views of others, but, in the end, make the best decision they can with all available information.

They don't give up easily once they have decided on a course of action. They realize follow-through is a critical part of the decision-making process. As well, they will evaluate the effectiveness of the decision throughout the process and learn from their mistakes.

This competency was directly related to three factors of emotional intelligence, which are assertiveness, independence, and optimism.

Participative management style is the third pillar. Command and control are no longer in style in today's military, let alone in business environments. People resent being told what to do and certainly do not appreciate being ignored. Successful leaders today focus on winning the hearts and minds of the people around them. Without getting buy-in for their ideas, plans, and tactics, there's little incentive for those around them to perform optimally. People want to be involved in the plans and their implementation. As well, they have to feel they contributed. After all, if people feel they have some ownership of the initiative, they are more likely to want to see it succeed.

The ability to succeed in this aspect of leadership involves having good listening and communication skills. While many leaders know how to present their ideas and directions to others, fewer know how to actively listen to their people to ensure they are on board. Good leaders are sensitive to what may seem to be minimal objections to ideas and requests. They can pull out the objections and attempt to deal with them, even adjusting plans when flaws are pointed out. The leader must aim for what is best for the whole organization, not just what may meet his or her own ego.

Great leaders can put people at ease. Bad leaders scare people. When people are at ease, they are more likely to freely speak their mind and offer suggestions and ideas. Great leaders give people credit for their contributions and make them feel like an important part of the team. Even greater leaders take responsibility for bad decisions and mistakes.

The important work of building consensus follows hearing everyone out. Successful leaders, after ensuring they are aware of people's positions, both pro and con, use their skills to get everyone on board with whatever decision is made. If team members feel that they participated in the process, presented their case, and got a fair hearing, they are more likely to go with the prevailing consensus.

What was surprising about this cornerstone of leadership was the nature of its relationship to specific factors of emotional intelligence. While related to several aspects of emotional intelligence, the strongest relationships were with empathy and social responsibility. Empathic leaders can hear what others are saying and feeling. Leaders who are socially responsible, that is, those who care about their community and less fortunate people, and respect society's rules, are more participatory in their leadership style. These leaders also have better interpersonal relationships, better impulse control, and are happier.

The fourth pillar of successful leadership has to do with being tough-minded. These leaders show resiliency following difficult situations. They manage to persevere in the face of obstacles, overcome challenges, and handle pressure well. These people have an air of confidence as they lead the way through difficult times.

The emotional intelligence skills that relate to this competency are self-regard, stress tolerance, and impulse control.

EQ and the CEO

Continuing our work on the emotional intelligence of CEOs, described in the previous chapter in relation to the Young Presidents' Organization (YPO), we've tested many more high-performing CEOs. One group we'll focus on is the Innovators Alliance (IA). Members of this group, an organization of CEOs of fast-growing companies in Ontario, were tested for emotional intelligence and asked to complete a survey.

These CEOs are an elite group in Canada. Members must be a company CEO or president; run a company with a minimum cumulative revenue growth rate of 35 percent over three years; generate $2 million (CDN) or more in annual revenue; employ between 10 and 500 people; and maintain an Ontario-based head office. The sample we tested included 76 IA members—61 males and 15 females. Their average age was 44, with 50 percent of them 45 years old or younger.

In Figure 20-1, you can see that their results are almost identical to the YPO group of leaders. We consistently find that CEOs are very high in independence, assertiveness, and stress tolerance. Interestingly, they scored lower than average in social responsibility and impulse control.

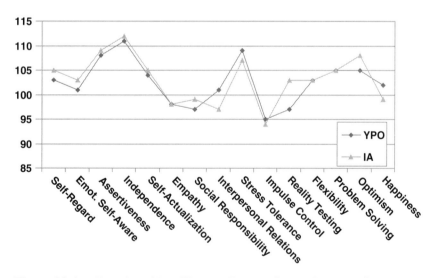

Figure 20-1: Emotional Intelligence Scores of Two Groups of CEOs

Another analysis we did with the IA group was truly unique. We separated the "top CEOs" from the rest based on what we thought to be the most important measure of success for this group—profitability. We compared the most profitable CEOs to the least profitable based on data we collected. We then did a complex statistical analysis to see if there were any EQ factors that differentiated these groups. We thought that being really good at managing stress would predict business success. Or, perhaps, the more successful CEOs would be happier than their less profitable counterparts.

Well, we were wrong. In fact, there were three factors that differentiated the high performers. First, they were more empathic. These leaders were better at listening and reading their employees. Second, they had higher self-regard: they were surer of themselves and had a better handle on their strengths and weaknesses. Finally, they were more assertive. People around them know where they stand and what they expect. They are not about hidden agendas or bullying people into submission. Our work in the area of CEO leadership and emotional intelligence has been published in a peer-reviewed journal.[16]

As a result of these and other studies with leaders, there is a special version of the EQ-i that looks specifically at leadership skills. One special feature is the breakdown of specific leadership skills into three areas. The first is people oriented. This looks at a leader's ability to motivate staff and work as a team. The second area is process oriented. This measures the ability to get things done, set and attain goals, and meet timelines. Finally, there are the organization-oriented skills. These include understanding and working in the corporate structure and knowing who to contact and what resources are available.[16]

EQ and Lessons from Reality TV

At this point it probably comes as no surprise that emotional intelligence is needed to survive in any organization. Maybe that's why the EQ-i was used as part of the selection process for the reality show *Survivor*. California psychologist Dr. Richard Levak is the psychologist involved in pre-selection testing for *Survivor*, *The Apprentice*, *Big Brother*, and *The Amazing Race*. The EQ-i was used in all of these shows as part of the selection process. We learned from Dr. Levak that some of the people fired first on *The Apprentice* had the highest IQ, but lowest EQ, scores. The ones who managed really well had the greatest EQ. In his experience, having a high IQ and a low EQ is like having a powerful sports car with bad steering.

The EQ-i was also used (by Steven) to screen candidates for a Canadian reality TV show called *From the Ground Up* starring Debbie Travis, a home designer and TV personality. The idea is that a group of young twenty-somethings, who have been struggling in life and career, may be ripe for working in the trades. The show dispels the myth that you need to be a professional to be successful in the world. The contestants, who were carefully screened, worked on building a house—from the ground up. Expert trades-people mentored the contestants in a variety of different skills required in home construction and design. The winners are selected from the first half of the series by Debbie, and for the last half by votes from Canadians across the country. Suffice it to say, the predictions made using the EQ-i scores were surprisingly accurate regarding the outcomes of the various contestants.

EQ and the Graduate

Imagine if we could predict who will complete their college education. Surprisingly, it is not academic ability that separates who will graduate from who will not. In an interesting set of studies with hundreds of college students, Dr. James Parker and his colleagues at Trent University in Canada have come a long way in helping us understand college retention. In one study they tested the EQ of all incoming students at a small Ontario university. They also had the school grades of all the students. They found a significant relationship between their EQ and school grades at the end of the first year.[17]

They continued to follow up on these college students. The main reasons students drop out of college are to change their program of study, personal problems, and economic or health problems. The main personal problems tend to be difficulties making new relationships, problems changing existing relationships (living apart), difficulties learning new study habits, and problems learning to be independent. There were consistent findings that emotional intelligence scores were significant predictors of which students dropped out of college. Dr. Parker has been working on developing interventions to help students stay in school.

In another study that included close to 1,500 students attending four universities located in Mississippi, North Carolina, and West Virginia, Parker found nearly identical results.[18] A strong link was found between academic achievement and several dimensions of emotional intelligence. Specifically, the academically successful students had higher levels of interpersonal, adaptability, and stress-management abilities, as well as overall emotional intelligence. According to their research, these skills are what students need in order to be successful in forming new relationships, modifying existing relationships, learning new study habits, adjusting to increased academic demands, and learning to live more independently.

EQ in the Movies

We had a few calls from some sharp-eyed movie fans who carefully watched the movie *The Recruit* (2003) starring Al Pacino, Colin Farrell, and Bridget Moynahan. The movie deals with recruiting and training bright young people into the CIA. A significant part of the story takes place when the young applicants are completing a paper-and-pencil test as part of the selection process for CIA agents. During the testing, one young hopeful is caught cheating and gets thrown out of the room. The commotion causes the brash young James Douglas Clayton (Colin Farrell) to turn around where he locks eyes with the beautiful young recruit Layla Moore (Bridget Moynahan). We have to admit that during the filming of this scene, Steven was actually on the set with one of his daughters, who was excited about seeing Colin Farrell.

The next scene shows the test answer sheets of the person who cheated, next to the one that he cheated from. If you look carefully at the top of the test form, you'll notice the EQ-i logo. We were amazed that some EQ-i users out there were on the ball and caught it. One of the messages of the film is that "life is a test." So they not only used paper-and-pencil tests to aid in making their selection, but incorporated "on the job" challenges to help select the best. Were they successful in their selections? Well, you'll have to go see the movie for the answer to that. And as for the other question we're often asked, "Does the real CIA use the EQ-i?"—sorry, we're afraid we can't answer that one.

EQ and Aboriginal Culture

The cultural adaptation of emotional intelligence is still a topic of great interest. Having given presentations throughout North America, Europe, Africa, Australia, and Asia, it has been gratifying to see how well the topic has fit so many cultures. One fascinating example has been the work one of us

(Steven) has done in Thompson, Manitoba, with the Burntwood Regional Health Authority. Responsible for health care throughout northern Manitoba up to Hudson Bay, this organization services large groups of First Nations Cree and Métis indigenous to that region.

Karen McClelland, former president of the Regional Health Authority, has a strong commitment to serving the First Nations people in a culturally sensitive way. All new staff (including Steven) are required to undergo an intensive two-day Northern Cultures course so that employees can become attuned to the special needs and cultural issues of this northern part of Canada.

Part of the training includes the vice-president of Aboriginal Affairs for the Authority, Lloyd Martin. He is also known by his aboriginal name, OSAWIKEESIK, which means "Blue Sky." In the process we learned that the medicine wheel, which dates back to early aboriginal culture, is right on track with the "modern" concept of emotional intelligence. For example, Figure 20-2 is a version of the medicine wheel as used in the Cree culture. Notice the importance of looking after yourself first—by the "me" and "fire" in the center. Without the energy to take care of ourselves, we're unable to look after others.

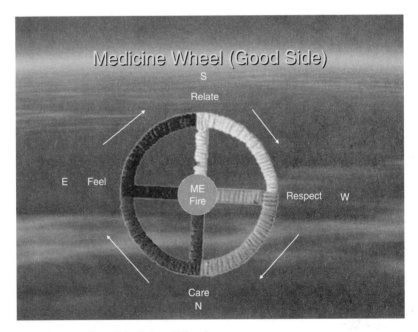

Figure 20-2:   Cree Medicine Wheel

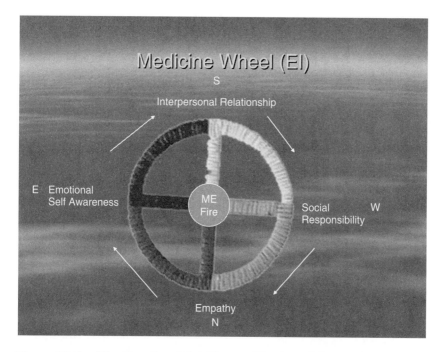

Figure 20-3: The Emotional Intelligence Version of the Medicine Wheel

Then we start with caring at the bottom of the wheel. It's important to care for ourselves and others. This leads to our ability to feel and then relate to others. Finally, we learn to respect those around us.

With just a little translation we have the EI version above in Figure 20-3. This version begins with empathy—understanding others—at the bottom. It then moves to emotional self-awareness—our ability of be aware of our own feelings. Using this to develop interpersonal relationships takes us to the top, and then we become socially responsible human beings.

Chapter 21

The EQ Research Continues

"Science is organized knowledge."

—HERBERT SPENCER (1820–1903) ENGLISH PHILOSOPHER

One of the reasons we continue updating this book is to keep readers informed of new developments in the emotional intelligence field and the EQ-i 2.0 in particular. In this chapter we will briefly outline a few of the many interesting studies that have been carried out since the publication of the previous edition *The EQ Edge*. These studies range from developments in the fields of leadership to teamwork, education, and early interventions strategies. We hope you find these new studies as fascinating as we do.

EI Studies in Business

What role does EI play in making someone a good leader?

One of the most popular topics for continuing research in emotional intelligence includes getting a better understanding of successful leadership behaviors. Are good leaders born that way or can they be created? What leadership behaviors are important for specific types of leaders—business, religious, sports, non-profit, public service, and so on? In one study, looking at leadership in non-profit, faith-based organizations in Colorado, Cheryl Meredith found that emotional intelligence was highly related to transformational leadership. In this type of leadership, leaders create a vision of what's to be accomplished, and inspire action of others toward this vision. This has been found to be one of the most productive ways of leading others.

In her study she found that the most important EQ-i factors related to transformational leadership were optimism, self-actualization, empathy, problem solving, and assertiveness. These results parallel and support the findings with leaders across a variety of different organizations and industries.[1]

Another study in leadership compared the emotional intelligence scores of leaders in non-profit health and human service agencies with those of leaders of profit organizations in the business arena. The study, carried out by Michelle Morehouse, evaluated 32 non-profit leaders and 32 business leaders. She found significant differences between these two groups. There were differences in overall emotional intelligence scores as well as differences in the subscales of stress management and adaptability. These results could be important in training future leaders for the type of organization they will be working in.[2]

We get a lot of questions about identifying high-potential future leaders and managers. We are pleased to report that there are now studies available that have explored this area. One interesting study was carried out at Vrije University in Brussels by Nicky Dries and Roland Pepermans. They looked at 51 high potentials in organizations and matched them to 51 "regular" managers, based on managerial level, gender, and age.

All of these managers were administered a battery of tests which included the EQ-i. A number of EQ-i scales differentiated the high-potential managers. These included assertiveness, independence, optimism, flexibility, and social responsibility. This helps confirm some of our other work looking at successful leadership. Note that social responsibility pops up as one of those factors we predicted would become increasingly important for tomorrow's leaders.[3]

There have been many studies looking at the role of emotional intelligence in school leaders (administrators). One question often asked is whether school leaders who are emotionally intelligent are more resilient and better leaders. That was the focus of Aileen Thompson Bumphus's study at the University of Southern Mississippi. She tested 63 public school principals and surveyed their respective professional colleagues. Those sampled came from across five states—Florida, Georgia, Louisiana, Mississippi, and Texas.

She found that emotional intelligence was a big part of a principal's resilience and good leadership. General mood on the EQ-i (optimism and happiness) was a strong predictor of resilience. Good leaders had higher scores in intrapersonal (self-perception and self-expression) and interpersonal scales.[4]

There has also been interest in leadership and emotional intelligence in early childhood educators. These professionals have a significant effect on the children in their care and can be very influential in shaping their future. Karen Jerome at the University of Oklahoma conducted a study with 203 Department of Defense children and youth program managers, who were tested for emotional intelligence and leadership style. She found the EQ-i a strong predictor of leadership style for these professionals.[5]

And the investigation of emotional intelligence doesn't stop at the level of school principal. There's also been research looking at school district superintendents. Richard Hansen at Capella University in Minneapolis, Minnesota, carried out a study that began by surveying 1,019 school superintendents in the states of Michigan, Indiana, and Ohio. He ended up getting a response rate of 13 percent from those superintendents who were tested with the EQ-i, a measure of transformational leadership, and other questionnaires. As in the previously mentioned studies he found a strong link between emotional intelligence and transformational leadership among these professionals. Once again it was found that there were no differences in emotional intelligence due to age, race, or gender.[6]

What does it take to be a good team player?

What makes a good team? Are some teams more successful than others? There has been a lot of discussion about the role of emotional intelligence in successful team functioning in the workplace. There have also been studies looking at some of the specific emotional intelligence ingredients that make up good teams. One study looking at this was carried out at Eastern Michigan University by Crissie Frye and her colleagues.

The researchers wanted to explore the relationship between the emotional intelligence of self-directed teams and two dimensions of team interpersonal process—team task orientation and team maintenance function. These basically have to do with how well a team focuses on its goal and carries out the work to achieve that goal without becoming distracted or moving off-target, and how well the team members support and motivate one another over time. The EQ-i was administered to all members of 33 work teams. There is a program that computes the average EQ-i scores along each of the factors for each of the teams. This study looked at the average scores for each of the teams.

They used a regression analysis, which allowed them to predict which of the EQ-i factors were most important in each of the team areas. They found that the interpersonal relationship factor best predicted the team maintenance factor. In other words, having high interpersonal skills among each of the team members leads to a team that functions well together over time. They also found that both interpersonal relationship and general mood predicted how well the team did in team task orientation. Emotional intelligence comes out as an important element in enabling people to work together towards their goals.[7]

Is your workplace a diverse one?

Increasingly our workplaces are becoming more diverse with a greater number of people from different backgrounds and cultures needing to work together. How do we manage this diversity? What are the characteristics of people who manage different people well? Emotional intelligence is beginning to play a more important role in diversity training programs.

In a study at the University of North Florida, Jarik Edwardo Conrad investigated the role of emotional intelligence in intercultural diversity among 70 graduates of Leadership Jacksonville. Using a mixed-method design which included testing and interviews, some factors were identified in working successfully with culturally diverse populations.

Some of the emotional intelligence factors that were found to be important in this study included general mood, empathy, problem solving/decision making, social responsibility, and interpersonal relationship. The study concludes that leaders seeking to manage diversity would greatly benefit from integrating elements of emotional intelligence into their professional development.[8]

What does it take to be a good project manager?

What does it take to manage complex projects? Since the beginning of time, humans have had to manage projects in order to get things done. Only in the past few years has project management been recognized as a distinct professional field. A study done at Pepperdine University in California by Grazyna Maria Gasiorowska looked at the ability to manage projects and emotional intelligence.

In the study, both the EQ-i and the MSCEIT were administered to 23 experienced professional project managers from various parts of the United States. As project managers are constantly challenged by ongoing demands, their people skills and emotions are at the forefront of what they do. This calls for high levels of emotional intelligence.

Significant factors were found in both measures for project managers. For the MSCEIT, the strategic areas proved most important, which included the abilities to understand and manage emotions. The most important EQ-i skills for this group included assertiveness, self-actualization, and problem solving. It would seem that successful project managers need to know how to give direction to others, need to be organized and focused on where they are going, and require constant problem solving to get past the ongoing challenges of bringing projects to fruition. Hopefully this study will contribute to bringing emotional intelligence into the formal training of this group of professionals.[9]

Another study of project managers focused on specific leadership skills. While it is widely accepted that successful project managers require both transformational leadership skills as well as technical skills for success, there is still more to learn. In this study, done at Walden University in Minneapolis, Minnesota, Dereje Befekadu Tessema wanted to further explore those factors known to be at the bottom of many failed projects—lack of communication and leadership skills and their relationship to emotional intelligence.

The EQ-i was administered to 578 project managers along with other questionnaires, including the Multifactor Leadership Questionnaire. Eight of the emotional intelligence skills were found to be highly related to transformational leadership in this study. Suggestions are provided that can help develop the right emotional skills needed by project managers.[10]

EI and a Midlife Career Crisis

Some interesting work by Elva Keem Wong-Fong at Capella University has looked at the role emotional intelligence (using the EQ-i) plays in women who decide to change careers at midlife. She found that the need for a career change in these women was often driven by the need for a secondary household income. This was influenced by an underlying desire to do fulfilling, meaningful work, wanting to make a difference, needing to follow one's passion, moving forward on a conscious level, overcoming fears, and believing in oneself.

The key emotional intelligence findings involved the role played by emotional self-awareness, influences on self-regard, and the impact of self-actualization. These EI factors, when paid attention to, can help focus midlife career changes and guide a person in meaningful ways.[11]

But then there are others who desire career change for different reasons. The importance of emotional intelligence over and above traditional skills, abilities, competencies, personality, and interests is finally being recognized. People who are happiest at work are those who have the right "emotional fit" with what they do.

Researchers in Italy at the Università degli Studi di Firenze in Florence, used the EQ-i along with a number of other tests, including personality and interest, with 296 interns. They found that emotional intelligence played a significant role over and above personality in finding the right career fit.[12]

EI and Business Advice

In many jurisdictions the government sets up business development centers to help entrepreneurs and owners of small businesses get established. What should you look for in a business counselor when setting up your own business? Well, now there's research that can help you look for the right emotional skills in a business advisor.

A study by Michael Farlow focused on looking at the emotional intelligence of Small Business Development Center (SBDC) counselors and directors throughout regions in the state of Texas. He administered the EQ-i to 103 counselors in the different areas. He then looked at the average group score at each center and related that to how successful that group was in various outcomes, such as number of jobs created, access to capital loans, and new business starts. He found some interesting relationships with outcomes and emotional intelligence. Specifically, higher-performing centers had counselors that were stronger in empathy, reality testing, social responsibility, and stress tolerance.[13]

EI and Early Intervention

We've often been asked what can be done about early intervention with emotional intelligence. Can we detect early warning signs in kids before behavioral problems get out of hand? That was part of the focus of a study carried out with the youth version of the EQ-i (EQ-i YV) at the University of Akron. Amanda Rovnak tested 684 students in seventh and eighth grade across 19 schools in Ohio.

She found interesting trends in the scores of both males and females, but more importantly she found that the EI scores were important predictors of academic and mental health issues. By using an inexpensive screener, we can use early detection to help intervene when there's a good chance of problems down the road.[14]

Along the same theme, but with older students, an interesting study was carried out at West Virginia University, looking at college students and binge drinking. What role does emotional intelligence play in the problems caused—both to oneself and to others—through the misuse of alcohol? This study looked at 309 undergraduate students.

Basically, the author, Jeffrey Dulko, found that emotional intelligence played a significant role in binge drinking. The number of binge drinking consequences (getting sick, getting into fights, etc.) was related to one's over-all score in EI. That is, the higher your EI, the fewer negative consequences of binge drinking you had. The specific factors of emotional intelligence that predicted outcomes in this area included intrapersonal (self-perception and self-expression), stress management, and interpersonal skills. So by inter-vening and improving EI skills in college students we may be able to lessen the negative effects of binge drinking.[15]

Taking prevention to an even younger level, a Japanese study carried out by Junko Tsujino and Mayumi Oyama-Higa at Kwansei Gakuin University in Hyogo, Japan, looked at the emotional intelligence of mothers and the development of their children. The project, using the EQ-i, looked at 65 mothers from the time their child was a fetus, and when the child was two, three, four, and five years of age. The researchers found a strong correlation between deficits in certain emotional intelligence skills of the mother and problem behaviors in their children; that is, higher emotional intelligence in the mother was related to fewer child behavior problems.[16]

And can EI play a role in the early detection of addictive or exces-sive gambling? As you've probably noticed, with the widespread use of the Internet there have been increases in gambling addictions. Would emotional intelligence help protect young people from getting in over their heads with gambling? That's a question that James Parker and his colleagues at Trent University in Canada looked at in different samples of adolescents. They used the EQ-i YV with two groups—209 13- to 15-year-olds and 458 16- to 18-year-olds.

Basically, they found that emotional intelligence was a good predictor of addiction-related behaviors in both groups of adolescents. They went on to discuss some of the implications of these findings in setting up preventative programs for youth at risk for gambling addictions.[17]

We often get asked about the cross-cultural aspects of EI and specifically around the use of the EQ-i and EQ-i YV. It amazes us whenever we see the amount of activity around emotional intelligence all over the world and in different cultures. One study looking at adolescent EI and its relationship to other factors—such as academic achievement and ability to cope with stress—was completed in Bahrain.

Jihan Alumran and Raija-Leena Punamäki tested 112 adolescents in the Bahraini school system to explore these factors. Among their main findings was that gender, but not age, was associated with levels of EI and the coping styles of these adolescents. EI contributed to the variance in all three coping styles that were looked at. Here, as in many different cultures around the world, the EQ-i helps us better understand our ability to deal with others.[18]

Adding to the international research on EI, a study in Mexico looked at adolescence from a different perspective. Instead of looking at what goes wrong with teens, this study, from the University of Guanajuato in central Mexico, looked at what differentiates highly popular teenagers from those who are less popular. María Alicia Zavala and her colleagues were interested in why some adolescents are more socially accepted by their peers than others.

Through a series of surveys they were able to identify 62 adolescents who were rated among the most popular in their peer groups. These teens, averaging aged 13, were administered a number of tests including the youth version of the EQ-i. The study also tested 331 other students who were neither high nor low in their level of popularity. The more popular group was significantly higher in their emotional intelligence scores. Interestingly, they also measured social skills, which were not universally higher in the popular group. The study raises some interesting questions and proposes a number of ideas for helping adolescents become more popular through their emotional and social intelligence skills.[19]

An American study looking at middle school students finds a connection between emotional intelligence, discipline problems, and school grades.

The study, carried out by Karen Michelle Kohaut at Widener University in Pennsylvania, used the EQ-i Youth Version and compared it with students' final grades for the year and the number of discipline referrals taken from school records.

Karen found significant relationships between the youths' emotional intelligence scores and both academic performance and number of school discipline problems. Interestingly, she found no difference between students' ethnic or racial origin and their EQ-i YV scores.[20]

EI and Education

Can high school students increase their emotional intelligence?

Continuing with international work in emotional intelligence and youth, researchers in Iran at Mahabad Azad University, Alzahra University, and Tehran Azad University used the EQ-i with Iranian high school students. Esmaiel Sadri and his colleagues tested 40 male students and randomly assigned them to treatment or control groups. The experimental group went through a 12-session training program in emotional intelligence. At the end of the program both groups were retested with the EQ-i. Only the group receiving the training showed a significant increase in their scores.[21]

Can emotional intelligence help you get through college?

There have been many studies demonstrating the importance of emotional intelligence in students who successfully complete college. But, just in case you're not quite convinced, here is yet another.

Larry Sparkman at the University of Southern Mississippi tested 783 students with the EQ-i and followed them up looking at enrollment status, graduation status, and cumulative college grade point average. The best predictors of college completion (or graduation) were the emotional intelligence scales of empathy, social responsibility, flexibility, and impulse control. Of these scales, the strongest predictors were social responsibility, followed by impulse control and empathy. Interestingly, too much flexibility got in the way of completing college. A certain amount of routine and discipline is required to complete assignments, prepare for tests and exams, and make it to class on a regular basis.

Cumulative grade college grade point average was best predicted by self-actualization, social responsibility, and happiness. There was an interesting qualifier here as well. Too-high scores in independence and interpersonal relationships tended to bring down the grade point average. So students who are too dependent on others may be at a disadvantage in getting better grades.

In addition to the emotional intelligence scores, high school grade point average was a stable predictor of continued enrollment, college grade point average, and graduation; and ACT scores predicted graduation and college grade point average.[22]

Can college students increase their emotional intelligence?

We now know how important emotional intelligence is for getting through college. One question that comes up a lot is whether or not you can improve emotional intelligence in college students. A study completed at the University of Hawaii by Kelly Chang evaluated a program designed to improve the emotional intelligence of college students.

In the study two groups of students—79 in a treatment group and 74 in a control group—were assessed for their emotional intelligence using both the EQ-i and the MSCEIT. The program used behavioral self-modification techniques that included training in assertiveness, empathy, self-regard, and emotional management. After the training there were significant increases in test scores for the treatment group and no change in scores for the control group. Hopefully, these types of training programs are likely to become more integrated into college courses.[23]

Can medical students increase their emotional intelligence?

An area we get many questions about revolves around the emotional intelligence of physicians and other health professionals. How do health professionals compare to other professional groups? Can they improve their emotional intelligence? Can we teach emotional intelligence as part of the training of health professionals? A British study carried out at the University of Liverpool focused on teaching empathy to third-year medical students.

Ian Fletcher and his colleagues tested 36 control group and 50 intervention group medical students with the EQ-i. Not all of the students completed the seven-month training program. However, by the end of the training period the intervention group increased their EQ-i scores while the control group's scores decreased slightly.[24]

EI and Lifelong Learning

Does emotional intelligence affect the way that adult students learn? Do academic programs need to take into account various "non-academic" factors? A study done in Phoenix, Arizona, by R. Dean Colston looked at what role EI might play in adult learning. He investigated academic achievement among 115 male and female adult nontraditional undergraduate students. They were all administered the EQ-i among other measures, and their GPA was noted.

In this group of learners there was a significant relationship between EI scores and their performance based on GPA. Learners with a higher EI score were found to also have a higher GPA. The study made some suggestions on how EI could be integrated into the curriculum to benefit these learners.[25]

EI and Athleticism

The EQ-i is widely used with athletes at both Olympic and professional levels of competition. An important question for developing athletes may be how aware their coach is about the importance of emotional intelligence in nurturing athletic performance. One athlete who is interested in this question is Leith Drury, who completed her dissertation in this area at the University of Toronto in Canada.

She was interested in athletic coaches' perceptions of EI and its influence in the coaching process. She surveyed 60 coaches of elite adult athletes and administered the EQ-i to further explore this area. She looked at both male and female coaches, and individual and team sports. Basically, she found that most coaches were unfamiliar with the concept of emotional and social intelligence. As well, their coaching style tended to be focused on maintaining unilateral control or power over the athletes they coached.

Some of the athletes rated their coach's EI using the 360 rating form of the EQ-i. Interestingly, they saw their coaches quite differently from the way the coaches perceived themselves. The athlete's level of satisfaction with their coach and type of relating styles were strongly influenced by the coach's levels of emotional and social intelligence. Leith has a lot of suggestions on how EI can be successfully integrated into the coaching–athlete relationship.[26]

In an earlier chapter we discussed Steven's work with a professional sports team, the Toronto Maple Leafs hockey team. Another study was carried out by Trevor Halverson and Arthur Perlini that also looked at emotional intelligence in professional hockey players. They tested 79 players from 24 different teams in the National Hockey League.

They were also interested in the role that emotional intelligence might play in the performance of professional athletes. Among their findings they found that the years-since-draft was the strongest predictor of performance, and draft rank was the weakest predictor of performance. This implies that those players who are able to stick it out the longest—that is, have the most staying power—tend to do the best. Also, being a top draft pick can be a bad omen. Perhaps the pressure around being picked early can influence performance in a negative way by increasing the pressure on the player.

Interestingly, emotional intelligence had a role to play in these athletes' success. The researchers found that both intrapersonal competency (now known as self-perception and self-expression) and general mood were significant predictors of the number of NHL points won and the number of games played. So it seems likely that emotionally intelligent players are more likely to have the staying power that leads to success as an athlete. This is something that professional coaches, scouts, and trainers in all areas of sport should take note of.[27]

El and Your Health

Is emotional intelligence good for your health?
We continue to see research that demonstrates the importance of emotional intelligence to your health. A number of studies have looked at whether training people to improve their emotional intelligence can affect their health status. One interesting study, carried out in the Faculty of Medicine and Department of Psychology at Ondokuz Mayis University in Turkey, focused on people with Type 2 diabetes.

Bektas Murat Yalcin and his colleagues collected data from 184 patients with Type 2 diabetes who volunteered to participate in the study. They amassed a vast array of information that included health status, psychological well-being, and emotional intelligence. They selected 36 patients with the lowest scores on the health status questionnaires.

These patients were then randomly assigned into either a treatment group or a control group (18 patients in each group). The treatment group went through a 12-week program in emotional intelligence training. The control group wasn't part of any special intervention. All of the patients were retested at the end of the program, and three and six months later. Only the group that went through the emotional intelligence training increased in their reported quality of life, well-being, and emotional intelligence. An increasing number of studies are finding that patients, even with chronic health problems, can benefit from developing their emotional intelligence.[28]

There have been so many studies looking at the relationships between emotional intelligence and health that researchers have begun doing major reviews looking at all the studies in order to summarize their findings. One analysis of the research was published by Nicola Schutte at the University of New England in Maine. She and her colleagues analyzed the effects in 44 studies looking at this connection. They found significant relationships between emotional intelligence and mental health, psychosomatic health, and physical health. The EQ-i plays a prominent role in this area of research.[29]

Are you getting the amount of exercise you need?

Would increasing your emotional intelligence help with your exercise plan? What's the role of emotional intelligence in exercise behavior? Well, a study carried out at the University of Calgary in Canada and the University of Edinburgh in the U.K. has looked at the role of personality and emotional intelligence in exercise behavior.

Psychologists Donald Saklofske, Elizabeth Austin, and their colleagues tested 497 Canadian university students with a personality test and the EQ-i and had them monitor their exercise behavior. It seems that extroverts and people high in emotional intelligence exercise more frequently. Personality factors were seen as distinct from emotional intelligence skills in terms of their influence of exercise.[30]

Are you getting enough sleep?

The folks at Walter Reed Army Institute of Research in Maryland have been doing some very interesting research related to sleep deprivation. What happens when you're overtired? Are you more likely to do things that you wouldn't normally do? William Killgore and his colleagues at Walter Reed looked at what happens when you face a moral dilemma after 53 hours of not sleeping. Twenty-six healthy adults took part in the research. The results are fascinating.

After being deprived of sleep your response latency increases—it takes longer for you to make a decision—but only when it comes to moral dilemmas that are personally significant. In other words, only those dilemmas that are emotionally important to you are affected. Impersonal dilemmas (those that don't arouse your emotions—or matter that much) and non-moral dilemmas don't show the same delays.

Interestingly, emotional intelligence as measured by the EQ-i played a role in determining the willingness of someone deprived of sleep to violate their personally held moral beliefs. So people with higher emotional intelligence are better able to keep their personal moral beliefs intact under trying circumstances.[31] Maybe this helps us better understand those politicians (who maybe have lower EQ) who go against their moral beliefs and have extra-marital affairs—although they may not be sleep deprived.

Where in the brain does your emotional intelligence reside?

While there is most likely no single point in the brain that is responsible for emotional intelligence, we are getting a better understanding of which parts of the brain may play a role. University of Southern California neuroscientist Antonio Damasio proposed a theory in which a neural array in the brain called the "somatic marker" is where a lot of what we call emotional intelligence is based.

Damasio proposed that a number of sections of the brain—the ventromedial prefrontal, parietal, and cingulate areas—all contribute, as well as the right amygdala and insula. His work, based on studying people with lesions in these areas, demonstrated that they had emotional and social deficits. For example, they had problems reading social and emotional cues in other people.

In some fascinating research carried out at Walter Reed Army Institute of Research and McLean Hospital at Harvard Medical School, brain imaging was used in normal subjects to get a better picture of emotional functioning.

The researchers, William Killgore and Deborah Yurgelun-Todd, administered the EQ-i Youth Version to 16 adolescents. They chose adolescents because that is a prime time for the development of emotional and social competencies. Each of these teenagers was subjected to functional magnetic resonance imaging (fMRI) where their brain waves were carefully monitored while they were exposed to a series of fearful faces.

The researchers were able to find significant relationships between the EQ scores and brain activity. Specifically, the EQ scores were related to activity in the cerebellum and visual association cortex. The level of emotional intelligence on the EQ-i YV was inversely related to the efficiency of neural processing within the somatic marker circuitry during the emotional stimulation.

Here's a quote from their study that summarizes these findings:

> During the perception of fearful faces, higher levels of EQ in adolescent children were associated with greater activity in the cerebellum and visual association cortex, as well as with decreased activity in a variety of emotion-related limbic and paralimbic regions, including the insula, cingulate, ventromedial prefrontal cortex, amygdala, hippocampus, and parahippocampal gyrus. These findings suggest that EQ in adolescent children may involve greater neural efficiency of these key emotional-processing structures and, therefore, may lead to reduced reactivity in response to emotional provocation within the somatic marker circuitry believed to mediate the integration of somatic states and cognition during decision making.[32]

Interestingly, these areas of the brain are quite distinct from the areas where most of the functions of cognitive intelligence are triggered.

Another study looking at emotional intelligence and the brain focused on people undergoing temporal lobe resections, which is a surgical procedure used with people suffering from certain types of epilepsy who are not benefitting from medication. The research was carried out at Dalhousie University in Canada by Jodie Gawryluk and Jeannette McGlone. They administered a battery of tests to 38 patients who underwent this type of surgery in the temporal lobe area of the brain.

The EQ-i scores of patients were affected after the surgery. The EQ-i scores were also related to the patient's psychosocial adjustment, in that higher EI scores reflected better post-surgical coping in these areas. The

EQ-i scores were not differentially affected by which side of the brain the operation occurred.[33]

* * *

So as we have seen, emotional and social intelligence involve widely accepted and adaptable principles of human behavior. We've seen how it applies across cultures, occupational groups, work functions, developmental levels, health issues, psychological well-being, and many other facets of human performance. In the next chapter we will briefly discuss new developments in the ability model of emotional intelligence.

Chapter 22

Emotional Intelligence as Ability

"It is a fine thing to have ability, but the ability to discover ability in others is the true test."

—LOU HOLTZ

Much of what we've focused on in this book has involved the expression of emotional and social intelligence. In other words, we've explored the ways in which emotional and social intelligence are expressed through how we feel, think, or behave in the world. If we compare this to school performance, think of your school grades. Your grades were based on how well you performed on your assignments, essays, quizzes, exams, and maybe even on how big a star you were in the classroom. However, you may remember taking certain ability tests, like the SAT. These tests were designed to understand your ability to succeed in certain areas, such as in verbal or numerical endeavors. They didn't really tell you how you were actually performing, but had more to do with your potential.

One of the leading models of emotional intelligence is based on an ability model. As mentioned at the beginning of this book, Drs. John (Jack) Mayer and Peter Salovey were the pioneers who, in the late 1980s, first developed the term emotional intelligence that we use today.[1] Their model of emotional intelligence can be found in Figure 22-1.

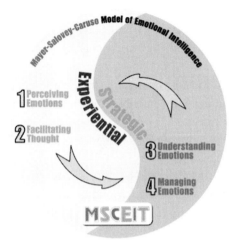

Figure 22-1:   The Mayer-Salovey-Caruso model of emotional intelligence

Reprinted with permission of Multi-Health Systems, Inc., Toronto, Canada. www.mhs.com (2005).

Dr. Salovey is currently the Yale University Provost and Chris Argyris Professor (Psychology) at Yale University, and Dr. Mayer is a psychology professor at the University of New Hampshire. They began the current interest in this field by looking at emotions as an intelligence. Their model includes four specific areas or branches. The first branch, *Perceiving* (or identifying) *Emotions*, involves your ability to successfully read other people's emotions. It also includes your ability to express emotions accurately to others in order to be an effective communicator.

The second branch, *Facilitating Thought*, or using emotions, involves using your emotions to get you in the mood. The way we feel has a big influence on how we think. Also, emotions can help us focus our attention and guide us as we solve problems.

The third branch, *Understanding Emotions*, helps us use our emotions to predict our future. Knowing our emotions helps us navigate through life. It helps to understand why we feel sad, angry, or giddy. For example, feeling angry because of bad traffic in the morning and taking that anger out on your co-workers is not going to help you at work. Understanding where your anger comes from makes it easier to deal with it.

Finally, the last branch involves *Managing Emotions*. This is where you can really put your emotions to your advantage. By managing the way you feel, you can get along better with others, solve problems more easily, make sounder judgments, and manage your behavior more effectively.

So what is emotional intelligence, according to these researchers? Well, emotional intelligence consists of these four abilities: to identify how people feel; to use emotions to help you think; to understand the causes of emotions; and to include and manage emotions in your decision making to select optimal choices in life.

The more formal definition they use goes as follows:

> [Emotional intelligence is] the ability to perceive emotions, to access and generate emotions so as to assist thought, to understand emotions and emotional knowledge, and to regulate emotions as to promote emotional and intellectual growth.[2]

Just like any good theory in psychology, you need data to validate it. In order to validate the ability model, you need a way to measure emotional intelligence as an ability. Peter and Jack teamed up with their colleague Dr. David Caruso to develop the Mayer-Salovey-Caruso Emotional Intelligence Test (MSCEIT). The MSCEIT is an ability-based test that measures the four branches of emotional intelligence.[3]

The MSCEIT is a well-validated instrument with many scientifically published articles supporting it. In fact, since its publication in 2002, an amazing number of scientific articles have appeared featuring the MSCEIT. In this brief chapter we'll highlight just a few of the interesting studies that have used it.

Researchers are constantly pushing the envelope to see how emotional intelligence affects our lives in meaningful ways. For some people, what can be more meaningful than the size of their paychecks? Seriously though, one study brings a unique look at how emotional intelligence—as measured by the MSCEIT—relates to positive work outcomes.

Researchers Paulo Lopes (University of Surrey), Stéphane Côté (Rotman School of Management, University of Toronto), Daisy Grewal and Jessica Kadis (Yale University), Michelle Gall (MG Executive Coaching), and Peter Salovey (Yale University) carried out a project at the finance department of a Fortune 500 insurance company. They looked at 44 analysts and clerical employees who worked in teams. Team members rated each other on a number of emotion-related factors such as how well they manage stress, their awareness of the feelings of others, and so on. Supervisors at the company also rated employees on similar items.

The authors tested the analysts and clerical employees with the MSCEIT and a battery of other tests so that they could also look at the role of cognitive intelligence (IQ), personality, and positive and negative moods over time. They looked at job performance which was based on salary, percent merit increase, and company rank from company records. The average percent merit increase was calculated for the period 2000 to 2002. There were also peer and supervisor reports made on job performance.

Their study found that emotional intelligence was related to several indicators of job performance, interpersonal relationships, mood, and attitudes. Most of these relationships were more important than other factors such as verbal ability and personality. In fact, all four emotional intelligence subscales of the MSCEIT, but especially the managing-emotions branch, were related to the outcomes.

For example, employees who scored higher on the MSCEIT had higher ratings from both peers and supervisors. They also had fewer conflicts at work and were seen as creating a positive atmosphere. According to supervisors (who were unaware of the MSCEIT scores), the higher-scoring employees were rated as more interpersonally sensitive, sociable, tolerant of stress, and having more leadership potential. Perhaps the most surprising finding of the study was that higher scores were directly related to higher pay in the company.[4]

The importance of emotional intelligence in making and keeping good relationships was supported in another study that was also led by Dr. Lopes. German college students were asked to keep diaries that described their everyday interactions with each other over two weeks. For every interaction they had that was 10 minutes or longer, they recorded the gender of the person they met with, their feelings about the interaction, and the degree to which they made the kind of impression they wanted to make on the person.

All the students had taken the MSCEIT. The branch measuring facilitating thought—or using emotions to predict—was directly related to how enjoyable and interesting students found their interactions to be. The managing-emotions branch was most important in how successful students felt they were in relationships with the opposite sex. It was directly related to how much they enjoyed these relationships in addition to how well they felt they had made the right impression on the opposite-sex person.[5]

Leadership is an area where there is a growing number of studies looking for the links to emotional intelligence. In Australia David Rosete at the University of Wollongong carried out a study that helps shed some light in this area.[6] His research looked at the degree to which emotional intelligence predicts leadership performance over and above traditional personality and reasoning measures.

He tested 117 executives from a large Australian public service organization for personality and IQ, and also used the MSCEIT. As well, he got ratings of leadership effectiveness from the managers' annual feedback discussions with their supervisors. These ratings basically boiled down to two main areas: 1) *what* had been achieved and 2) *how* it had been achieved. The first part of the ratings focused on deliverable and measurable outcomes. The second focused on the way in which leaders behaved to get these results.

David found that personality factors were not related to the managers' performance ratings. He did find, however, that the MSCEIT showed some interesting relationships with performance. The MSCEIT overall score was significantly related to the "what" and the "how" of getting things done.

While it may not seem like much, of all the measures used, the MSCEIT was the best predictor of what was achieved, accounting for 5 percent of the variance above the other measures. In terms of the "how" measure, once again, the personality measure was not significant. The MSCEIT, however, helped account for 22 percent of the variance. These findings confirm that there is a role for emotional intelligence as an ability among leaders.

An important aspect of leadership involves the aptitude to motivate others. Developing an effective vision statement is an important part of that process. A study was carried out looking at the relative effects of personality and emotional intelligence on vision statements produced by 137 women and men by Drs. Stéphane Côté, Paulo Lopes, and Peter Salovey. The MSCEIT predicted a better-quality vision statement far more effectively than personality.[7]

What's the importance of a leader's emotional intelligence to those people lower down in the organization? In a study carried out at the University of New South Wales in Australia looking at two small groups of managers (13 each from a public and private organization) along with 108 people reporting to them, S. Giles found a significant relationship between the employees' commitment to the organization and the managers' emotional intelligence.

The specific branches that were important were emotional management and emotional understanding (i.e., using emotions).[8]

In another study looking at the emotional intelligence of supervisors by Jay Janovics and Neil Christiansen, it was found that supervisors with high emotional intelligence scores were better rated by the 78 employed undergraduate students who worked for them. This rating of emotional intelligence was more important than the cognitive intelligence (IQ) measures used.[9]

What does it take to be a successful real estate sales agent? Also, what's the relationship between the MSCEIT and the EQ-i? A study by Selina Tombs at York University in Toronto looked at the relative contribution of personality, IQ, and different measures of emotional intelligence for successful real estate sales.[10] While her study had several parts, we'll just focus on one of a number of very interesting sets of findings. Selina selected and tested 69 real estate sales agents from a major Canadian real estate firm. They completed personality, vocabulary, and abstract thinking tests, the EQ-i and MSCEIT.

Among those in the industry who were consulted, the best success criterion for real estate agents was agreed to be earned commission over the year. Controlling for age, gender, ethnicity, years of experience, and English proficiency, she looked at the contribution of the different test scores to sales success through a complex statistical analysis (regression analyses).

The EQ-i and MSCEIT scores were in the same direction, but they were not exactly the same. There were some complicated but significant findings regarding the predictions of success. For example, the EQ-i total score predicted sales commission. This finding was not as strong when the formula also included how extroverted the salesperson was, the number of hours per week they worked, and their number of years' experience. Upon further analysis, it was found that sales commission was positively related to MSCEIT facilitating thought scores, and EQ-i interpersonal relationship and general mood scores. Further analysis revealed the MSCEIT facilitation score (using emotions to get you in the mood) to be the most significant in predicting scales.

Once again, the MSCEIT facilitation scale looks at how you use emotion to help you think. This ability involves using your emotions to help you solve problems, make decisions, and be creative. On the actual test people are asked to rate the degree of similarity between certain emotions and internal sensations (e.g., tastes), and to assess the usefulness of certain moods for improving performance on tasks (such as following a complex recipe).

Another important aspect of this study is that it once again shows that emotional intelligence contributes to our understanding of performance beyond personality and cognitive intelligence. In this regard, the study shows that both the MSCEIT and the EQ-i can be useful.

On occasion people have asked us if being high in emotional intelligence means having a better sense of humor. Well, thankfully, someone has actually examined this. Jeremy Yip and Rod Martin carried out a study at the University of Western Ontario in Canada, looking at relationships among emotional intelligence, social competence, and sense of humor.[11] They tested 111 undergraduate university students with two tests measuring their sense of humor, a test of emotional intelligence (MSCEIT), and a measure of social competence.

It turns out there is more than one type of humor. They found that the ability to manage emotions was related to having a *self-enhancing* sense of humor. Also, the ability to accurately perceive emotions was higher in people who were less likely to use aggressive and self-defeating humor.

People who had bad moods over long periods of time scored lower in three out of four MSCEIT branches. People who had a positive style of humor (e.g., a positive outlook on life) were better at initiating relationships and self-disclosure, but people with a negative sense of humor (e.g., sarcasm, hostility) had poorer interpersonal skills with problems in assertiveness, emotional support, and managing conflicts.

The emotional-management branch of the MSCEIT was directly related to being socially competent. People with higher scores were better at initiating relationships, providing emotional support, and managing conflicts.

One of the more interesting findings matches something many of us have probably already suspected. People who use negative humor a lot—sarcasm, hostile or racist jokes—are less liked by others. In this study these people were found to have more difficulty in perceiving emotion in themselves and others. Maybe this helps explain why these people use humor inappropriately—teasing or disparaging others. They seem to have problems realizing that others may not appreciate their humor. This, in turn, weakens their relationships with others.

The authors of the MSCEIT are now in the final process of developing an ability measure of emotional intelligence for children and adolescents. There are many reasons to believe, based on our preliminary research with this tool, that it will lead to significant findings in understanding and working with youth. Watch out for further developments in this area.

We hope we have given you a good introduction to the wide range of current and potential future directions of the world's leading work in emotional intelligence. There are now hundreds of studies that we're sure will open new vistas of understanding of human performance. Stay tuned for more.

The Case of Sabrina and Workplace Inclusion

Sabrina worked in a team at a large appliance distribution center. The senior management had been more concerned about productivity than usual due to the economic downturn and its effect in the industry. The team Sabrina worked on came under scrutiny due to some unimpressive performance statistics during the previous quarter. In addition, there were higher than average absences among that group.

Sabrina was relatively new to the team. It didn't take long for someone interacting with the team to realize she was not fully accepted by the group. It was generally assumed that Sabrina was not intelligent enough for the work and should be let go. As part of an exercise, each member of the team took the MSCEIT and an IQ-type assessment.

Interestingly, Sabrina's IQ score was higher than most of the other members of the team. While most of the team members had rather average MSCEIT scores, Sabrina scored lower than average in perceiving and understanding emotions. It was discovered during follow-up that Sabrina missed many emotional cues that the others picked up when interacting. She seemed to be left out of socializing and the usual office gossip. The exclusion really hurt her and made it difficult for her to come to work each morning. Some of the emotional misunderstanding may have, in fact, been cultural.

Fortunately, a coaching opportunity was provide by the company to Sabrina. The coach, using the test scores, realized there were issues in her picking up and understanding emotional cues. The coach spent time working with Sabrina on real and artificial office situations, teaching her to observe and think through the possible meanings that could be attributed to the words and behaviors of others. She learned to pay more attention to facial expressions, subtleties in voice inflection and other potential cues that would help her interpret the situation. She also learned how to probe what was intended in certain interactions by asking the right questions. She was assigned various movies and TV shows to watch that would help her focus on some of these cues. In time Sabrina was able to better integrate with her teammates, and their productivity increased as a result.

The Case of Harry and Emotional Management

Harry was part of a high-profile sales team in his organization. Their focus was on developing new prospects, closing sales, and maintaining long-term relationships with large customer accounts. While Harry was good at prospecting and initiating new client accounts, he failed to maintain long-standing relationships. Even his supervisor found it difficult to deal with Harry and would often avoid having the difficult conversations with Harry he knew he had to have.

Things came to a head when Harry learned that a competitor was courting one of his largest customers. When Harry found out, his anxiety level went up and he went into overdrive. He immediately called his contact at the company. After exchanging some pleasantries, he suddenly panicked and began probing directly about the meetings he heard about. His contact, caught completely off-guard, tried to change the subject and then asked Harry if he could review his price quotes from a recent proposal and e-mail him some justification for the costs.

After hanging up Harry flew into a rage. There was nothing he hated more than being low-balled by a competitor. He went back and forth with the sales manager and accounting department to try and trim his offer. As the e-mails went back and forth through the process of fine-tuning the proposal, Harry had inserted a comment about how cheap his client was and how ignorant he was of the importance of the quality of their product in comparison to the competitor. Included in the missive was a derogatory name that he used to refer to his client.

As a result of either his anxiety about the account, his anger at the competitor, the exhaustion in altering the proposal, or a combination of all these factors, the proposal that was sent to the client included Harry's diatribe. Not only did he lose the account, but a note went to his supervisor from the now ex-client that included Harry's rant. Had Harry been better able to manage his emotions he could have dealt with this situation more calmly and productively. In fact, even if he had simply waited a day or so before dealing with it, he might have been able to cool down and handle it more rationally.

* * *

We hope that the concepts and exercises in this book have helped you develop your emotional intelligence. We firmly believe that there is no one who would not benefit from enhancing the skills that comprise EQ. Be it at work, during play, or within relationships, when your emotional intelligence is strong, you are better poised for success in life. Remember—it's never too late to make a change for the better.

Appendix A | # The EQ-i 2.0

Since the development of the Emotional Quotient Inventory (EQ-i), a number of surveys and testing procedures have appeared that claim to evaluate emotional intelligence. But it takes several years of research and development to develop a serious test, one that can be trustworthy and effective in the workplace, in schools, and in therapeutic settings. To our knowledge, the EQ-i 2.0, which accurately defines and assesses the 15 skills that constitute emotional intelligence, is the only self-report test that's been normed on a representative stratified sample from across the United States and Canada, and has been scientifically demonstrated to be both reliable and valid—criteria that all psychological, mental health, and vocational tests must meet in order to be worthwhile. Most of the information in this chapter is reported in more detail in the *EQ-i 2.0 Technical Manual*.[1]

Also, the MSCEIT (Mayer-Salovey-Caruso Emotional Intelligence Test) is the only ability-based test of emotional intelligence that has been nationally normed and validated. Information on the norms, reliability, and validity of the MSCEIT are well documented in the *MSCEIT Technical Manual*.[2]

Reliability and validity are easily defined. For a test to be considered reliable, it must yield similar results each time it's used by the same person, at least over the short term. (Over time, as we shall see, certain changes are to be expected.) For example, if your bathroom scale registers the same weight three times within half an hour, you can rely on these readings. If it registers different weights, something's wrong. Suppose, however, that it registers the same weight each time, but you know—because you've just come from the doctor's office—that this weight is wrong. In this case, the readings, although consistent, are invalid, because the scale isn't doing what it's supposed to do—that is, accurately measure your weight.

The EQ-i 2.0 holds up on both counts. It's consistent in the results that it produces, and those results are meaningful because the test has been proven to measure what it purports to measure—that is, emotional intelligence.

We know the EQ-i 2.0 is valid because it was developed according to the guidelines of the American Psychological Association (APA).[3] To meet these guidelines, a test must conform to three main standards:

- While under development, it must be administered to a large sample of people who represent sufficiently diverse socioeconomic groups and embody a number of regional differences. Most often this procedure takes place only in the United States, but the original EQ-i went even further, collecting data from Canada, Israel, Germany, South Africa, Nigeria, Sweden, the Netherlands, India, Argentina, France, Singapore, and Japan, with more countries continually being added. While most APA-standard tests are published after 1,000 people have been sampled, the EQ-i had been administered to four times that number when it was commercially released. Also, putting a test online and counting every completed response does not constitute norming. There needs to be representative responses from throughout the country. We know of more than one person who trolls test sites using fabricated names and fake responses to complete a variety of online tests. The EQ-i 2.0 went even further in ensuring that the North American norms were representative of the population with an even larger, more representative sample. As well, numerous translations have been underway ensuring both linguistic and cultural adaptations of the EQ-i 2.0 for countries around the world.
- In order to demonstrate reliability, researchers must test and retest a sample group. Usually this is done only once, within six weeks or less, but the EQ-i was re-administered twice—once after one month, and again after four months. To ensure reliability was maintained in the new version, the EQ-i 2.0 had one group of people take the test again after two to four weeks and a separate group retake the tests after an eight-week interval.

- In addition, an APA-standard test must demonstrate several different sorts of validity, which are outlined below. Not only do recent online "quick" tests tend to be weak in validity, but they tend to be too shallow to give you any meaningful results or interpretations. When the short version of the EQ-i was created, a great deal of research went into its development. For clarity's sake, we'll relate these criteria to the specific format of the EQ-i 2.0.

    Content validity demands that each item must help capture the essence of what one of the 15 scales is supposed to measure. Thus, the first task (with the EQ-i) was to settle on a precise definition of each scale, from emotional self-awareness to happiness. Then hundreds of potential questions were created by Reuven Bar-On, by a team of international researchers, and by a panel of five expert psychologists and psychiatrists. Eventually, more than 1,000 questions were whittled down to the final 133. This was done by examining each question to make sure it best represented one and only one particular scale. Those that made the cut were put to a large group of people, which led to further modifications and the elimination of overlaps and redundancies. The content for the EQ-i 2.0 was subject to even further analysis and item renewal by the team of highly talented professional test developers at Multi-Health Systems.

    Face validity concerns the degree to which each question can be identified as helping to measure what the test is all about. Let's say, for example, that we'd created a test designed to aid you in determining whether you ought to become an auto mechanic. If it asked you questions about your relationship with your mother or your preference in ice cream, you'd quite rightly conclude that you were wasting your time. You're much less likely to take seriously or honestly complete a test that seems to have nothing to do with the matter at hand. During its developmental stages, the EQ-i and EQ-i 2.0 went through several face validity studies, which examined all potential questions for grammar, syntax, and relevance to the definition of a particular scale. Eventually, only those that were strongly and unequivocally related to the scale remained.

Next, the EQ-i and EQ-i 2.0 was subjected to factor analysis, a series of statistical procedures that assess whether the inventory's entire structure seems to make sense—that is, whether the scales "hold up and hang together." During this process, a computer crunched the responses of thousands of people. Only those items that best suited a particular scale were left in place.

Construct validity refers to how well a test as a whole measures what it's supposed to. It would have been useless to develop items that read well, grouped together well, and fit nicely within a specific definition, if they didn't advance the cause of determining someone's emotional intelligence. Let's say, for example, that we'd come up with a test designed to measure success as a football quarterback. Then let's suppose that we gave the test to a group of quarterbacks and found absolutely no relationship between the results and their performance. The test's construct validity would have gone out the window. Thus, the EQ-i and EQ-i 2.0 were compared, in their early stages, to numerous other widely administered and long-established tests that measured personality and mood. These studies—which took place in six different countries—found that the EQ-i and EQ-i 2.0 did indeed measure a number of characteristics and relevant areas that were already covered by the existing tests. But the overlaps weren't too high, which meant that the EQ-i and EQ-i 2.0 were not duplicating the materials already available.

Convergent validity looks at the extent to which a test comes up with the same assessment of the test-taker as would an impartial outside observer. During this stage of development, people who had completed the EQ-i were interviewed by an experienced psychologist. These interviews covered all the areas measured by the test. Later, three clinical psychologists listened to tapes of the interviews, and—based solely on these—rated each person on all the scales of the EQ-i. Then the judges' ratings were averaged to produce a single score per scale for each person tested. The average scores corresponded very closely with the actual test results, especially those for the assertiveness, problem-solving, and reality-testing scales. Social responsibility proved the hardest for the judges to rate. In addition, the people tested rated themselves on each of the EQ-i scales by reading its definition and choosing a number between one and seven that best reflected how they saw their performance in that regard. These results also showed a high correspondence with their actual scores.

Divergent validity means simply that, when working on a new test, you have to make sure it isn't inadvertently measuring something completely different. For example, let's suppose that we suddenly discovered that everyone who registered a high EQ also had a high IQ, and that everyone who scored low also had a low IQ. If so, we'd simply have created another IQ test. To guard against this, the EQ-i and EQ-i 2.0 were given to large numbers of people, along with IQ and personality tests, in search of areas that might overlap. For example, it was suggested that problem solving, as an EQ skill, might be related to the "abstract reasoning" measured by IQ tests. On close examination, however, the two proved to be quite distinctly different. The more socially oriented and day-to-day solutions that are part of emotional intelligence are only remotely related to academic and (the word sums it up) abstract mental processes. Other scales were examined as well, and it was found that assertiveness had nothing to do with hostility; social responsibility didn't translate as submissiveness, obedience, or undue conformity; flexibility wasn't instability; impulse control was distinct from a tendency to be unspontaneous or restricted; and happiness (to everyone's relief) didn't mean frivolity or mania.

Criterion group validity means that any test worth its salt must be able to differentiate between groups of people who share the characteristics the test is designed to measure. Let's say, for example, that we started to administer a hypothetical test that was supposed to measure the success of football quarterbacks. If we found that high-school tackles and NFL quarterbacks (all of whom play football, but are otherwise entirely dissimilar) all scored the same, we would have to go back to the drawing board. Thus, great pains were taken to make sure the EQ-i and EQ-i 2.0 would apply to—but be capable of pinpointing the differences between—a wide variety of groups, all of whom have in common (as does everyone) some degree of emotional intelligence.

That is why, over the past 15 or so years, one single test has enabled us to develop distinct and meaningful profiles for such disparate groups as the chronically unemployed; psychiatric patients and individuals with serious substance abuse problems; men who've battered their spouses; the chief financial officers of Fortune 500 companies; the students of a prestigious military academy; hardened criminals; highly paid professional athletes;

recovering cardiac patients; United States Air Force recruiters; and people who have successfully emigrated and integrated into a new culture. All these and many more have been captured and accurately measured by the EQ-i and now the EQ-i 2.0.

> *Predictive validity* is, for many people, the proof in the pudding. Does the EQ-i or EQ-i 2.0 enable us to look forward in time and speak confidently to someone's chances of success in a particular area? Can we make use of it to determine which draft pick will set the National Hockey League on fire; which employees will make superior managers; which patients will benefit from their treatment; which salesperson will break all previous quotas; which parent will prove the most caring or which spouse the most sharing? Although the EQ-i and EQ-i 2.0 is still in its relative infancy, it has already logged an impressive predictive record, as we believe the preceding chapters have demonstrated.

All that having been said, should you consider being tested? Perhaps a degree of doubt and skepticism remains. In particular, perhaps you wonder about the validity of a self-report procedure. Sight unseen, the idea of 133 items that purport to capture your emotional intelligence may seem unnecessarily laborious. If we want to know how emotionally smart someone is, why don't we simply buy him a coffee, sit him down in a comfortable chair and ask him if he's emotionally smart? We don't do this because it wouldn't work; the person's response would be wildly subjective and impossible to substantiate. Self-reporting—that is, responding truthfully to the EQ-i 2.0's 133 questions—does work.

We're certain that it works in general, because this same procedure has been common practice in the field of psychological testing for almost 100 years. It works in the case of the EQ-i 2.0 because of the validation procedures described above, and because a person who takes the test doesn't self-score or self-interpret it.

To understand why self-interpretation would be a mistake, let's look at a specific example. Jodie, a journalist, is viewed by everyone who knows her as an empathetic and socially responsible person. When she completes the EQ-i 2.0, however, her scores in these scales are found to be more or less average. She is surprised, but—as the rest of her responses makes clear—she tends to be extremely self-critical and sets impossibly high standards for herself. When responding to the EQ-i 2.0's items, she answers quite truthfully, but in her mind she was comparing herself to people whom she admires and considers to be ideal embodiments of empathy and responsibility.

That same day, Harry, a factory worker, completes the test as well. He doesn't have all that many role models when it comes to these two scales. He listens patiently to his co-workers' problems, gives money to charities and spare change to the homeless, and is involved in a church group, but he's certainly no paragon. Most of his friends would probably agree—he's a nice guy who tries to do his best, but he's nothing special. Harry, however, views himself as very empathetic and socially responsible, especially when compared to some of the people he knows. As a result, his answers—again, totally truthful ones—will result in a higher score than Jodie's.

Does this mean that Harry is in fact more empathetic and socially responsible than Jodie? Not necessarily. Their results speak to the way they perceive themselves. And when it comes to emotional intelligence, these perceptions may be more important than the objective reality. Remember that EQ is a set of ways in which we interact with our environment, a set of beliefs about the world and our place in it. Jodie sees herself as an underachiever—she wishes she could do much more. Harry thinks he's doing just fine, and better than most. Their subjective views will affect how they conduct their personal relationships, cope with health issues, deal with fellow employees, and perform in competitive situations. And, in fact, ordinary-guy Harry may be more successful within his own frame of reference in achieving the goals he sets and the life he desires, even though, in everyone else's estimation, Jodie may be the more fully functioning individual.

Now imagine what might have happened had Jodie been self-scoring her EQ-i 2.0. Two average (but in her eyes, hopelessly low) results in areas she held dear would have realized her darkest fears. Perhaps she'd have tried to remedy this alleged failing by charging off in the wrong direction. Fortunately, by placing these scores in context and interpreting the test results as a whole, we can help her gain deeper insight and pursue more useful courses.

One or two final points should be mentioned. We're frequently asked whether a person's EQ-i 2.0 scores will vary over time. Indeed they will—less so than the results of tests that measure moods or states of mind (which fluctuate from day to day, if not hour to hour), but more so than the results of personality tests, which measure characteristics or traits such as honesty and introversion that tend to remain relatively stable throughout one's lifetime. Since emotional skills change with age and experience,

EQ-i 2.0 scores can be expected to change also—even without coaching, training, or conscious effort on our part.

Periodic retesting of a number of sample groups has borne this out. In general, the differences in scores after one month are very small. After four months, specific scales showed more fluctuation than others—particularly stress tolerance, reality testing, and assertiveness. The most stable scales tended to be flexibility, self-actualization, and problem solving.

A final (though all too common) question, which speaks to the outlaw lurking within us all, is whether you can fool the EQ-i 2.0 by replying falsely to its items. The short answer is you can't. Or, more accurately, it would be more difficult than you can guess. You can sabotage a test, similar to lying in an interview or on your résumé, but chances are higher that it will be detected. A number of safeguards are built into the test that set off alarm bells if you try to make yourself appear more (or less) emotionally intelligent than you are. The positive-impression index catches those who try to paint too rosy a picture of themselves. A negative-impression index detects those who go out of their way to score too low. (Why would anybody do so? It might be in their best interests if, for example, they were seeking an insurance or workplace injury-compensation settlement.) There's also an inconsistency index and a few more early warning signals that we have no intention of describing, in case someone decides to take up the challenge and attempt to beat the odds.

Our advice is to be as honest as possible when taking the EQ-i 2.0 or any other test. Attempt to cheat, and you deceive—not to mention shortchange—only yourself. The EQ-i 2.0, properly administered and interpreted, will help you develop your strengths and overcome your weaknesses. If it's being used as a part of a job selection process, trying to cook up a bogus score can only act against you. Even if you succeed in "fooling" the testers and are hired partly on the basis of faked results, chances are the job won't mesh with your real skills—in which case, nobody winds up the winner.

EQ and Work Success

"The secret of success is to do the common things uncommonly well."

—JOHN D. ROCKEFELLER

What does it take to be successful at work?

What follows is a brief summary of the first research in the world that uses a valid measure of emotional and social intelligence to explore this issue. While there is no easy answer to the above question, our studies have found that EQ can account for between 15 percent and 45 percent of work success. Using the EQ-i, we tested 4,888 working people in various occupations and asked them to report on how successful they believed they were at their jobs. While we cannot be sure that all of them were completely accurate in their estimates of success, we do feel this self-report acts as a useful guideline. Please keep in mind, when going through this list, that these are estimates.

These data were all collected by Multi-Health Systems from people throughout North America. All were asked to complete the EQ-i and rate how successful they felt they were at their jobs. Some of the groups were smaller than others, and only data where statistical significance was found were reported. That is, only if successful people scored significantly higher in their EQ scores than unsuccessful people was that group included. Within each occupational group we have presented the top five factors, in order of importance, for differentiating between the high performers and the low performers.

Some groups may not seem to make sense at first. For example, you might expect high-performing engineers to be better at reality testing than low performers. However, as it turns out, all of the engineers are relatively high in reality testing, so that does not distinguish their performance. Rather, it is other skills, as shown below, that separate high from low performers.

Think of these as recipes for a cake. We are trying to produce recipes (or combinations of factors) for the best-tasting cakes. In our more sophisticated analysis, we create a formula that actually indicates the amount of each factor to look for. Using a process called logistical regression we have identified ideal combinations of EQ factors for many occupational groups. These have paid big dividends for employers and employees who want to find the best and most satisfying fit between people and jobs. People who are most satisfied in their work tend to be those whose emotional skills fit the formula for that work.

Listed in the next pages are the five most important factors (if at least five were significant) for each occupation. The numbers in parentheses indicate the sample size for each group.

Overall Work Success (4,888)

1. Self-Actualization
2. Happiness
3. Optimism
4. Self-Regard
5. Assertiveness

General Sales (524)

1. Self-Actualization
2. Assertiveness
3. Happiness
4. Optimism
5. Self-Regard

Insurance Salespeople (97)

1. Assertiveness
2. Self-Regard
3. Happiness
4. Stress Tolerance
5. Self-Actualization

Business Services Salespeople (53)

1. Self-Regard
2. Reality Testing
3. Assertiveness
4. Stress Tolerance
5. Optimism

Marketing Professionals (99)

1. Optimism
2. Reality Testing
3. Independence
4. Impulse Control
5. Social Responsibility

Retail/Sales Clerks (109)

1. Self-Actualization
2. Assertiveness
3. Happiness
4. Emotional Self-Awareness
5. Interpersonal Relationships

Other Sales (100)

1. Self-Regard
2. Self-Actualization
3. Happiness
4. Optimism
5. Assertiveness

Cashiers/Bank Tellers (35)

1. Stress Tolerance
2. Optimism
3. Self-Regard
4. Self-Actualization
5. Reality Testing

Financial Services Professionals (40)

1. Assertiveness
2. Interpersonal Relationships
3. Problem Solving
4. Happiness
5. Empathy

Customer Service Representatives (72)

1. Stress Tolerance
2. Assertiveness
3. Happiness
4. Interpersonal Relationships
5. Self-Actualization

Employment Counselors (94)

1. Self-Actualization
2. Reality Testing
3. Stress Tolerance
4. Optimism
5. Interpersonal Relationships

Personnel and Human Resources Administrators (104)

1. Happiness
2. Self-Actualization
3. Optimism
4. Assertiveness
5. Stress Tolerance

Management Consultants (252)

1. Assertiveness
2. Emotional Self-Awareness
3. Reality Testing
4. Self-Actualization
5. Happiness

Senior Managers (260)

1. Self-Regard
2. Happiness
3. Interpersonal Relationships
4. Reality Testing
5. Self-Actualization

Production Planning Managers (75)

1. Flexibility
2. Problem Solving
3. Independence
4. Impulse Control
5. Self-Actualization

Business Managers (General) (145)

1. Interpersonal Relationships
2. Assertiveness
3. Happiness
4. Self-Regard
5. Emotional Self-Awareness

Accountants (57)

1. Problem Solving
2. Interpersonal Relationships
3. Happiness
4. Self-Regard
5. Emotional Self-Awareness

Nurses (126)

1. Self-Actualization
2. Independence

Medical Staff (Technical) (78)

1. Self-Regard
2. Optimism
3. Reality Testing
4. Self-Actualization
5. Independence

Commercial Artists/Graphic Designers (36)

1. Flexibility
2. Self-Actualization

Education Workers (Administrative) (168)

1. Interpersonal Relationships
2. Reality Testing
3. Optimism

4. Happiness
5. Self-Regard

Secondary-School Teachers (200)

1. Empathy
2. Self-Actualization
3. Stress Tolerance

Elementary-School Teachers (347)

1. Optimism
2. Self-Regard
3. Independence
4. Stress Tolerance
5. Happiness

Public Servants (141)

1. Optimism
2. Self-Actualization
3. Self-Regard
4. Independence
5. Assertiveness

Religious Workers (Clerics, Ministers) (79)

1. Self-Actualization
2. Interpersonal Relationships
3. Assertiveness
4. Stress Tolerance
5. Self-Regard

Social Workers (52)

1. Independence
2. Stress Tolerance
3. Assertiveness

4. Impulse Control
5. Optimism

Government Social Services Workers (91)
1. Self-Awareness
2. Interpersonal Relationships
3. Empathy
4. Stress Tolerance
5. Happiness

Physicians/Surgeons (19)
1. Independence
2. Stress Tolerance
3. Empathy
4. Impulse Control
5. Flexibility

Lawyers (26)
1. Self-Actualization

2. Happiness
3. Stress Tolerance
4. Assertiveness
5. Social Responsibility

Engineers (86)
1. Self-Actualization
2. Happiness
3. Optimism
4. Empathy
5. Interpersonal Relationships

Psychologists/Clinical Psychiatrists (52)
1. Reality Testing
2. Independence
3. Happiness
4. Stress Tolerance
5. Flexibility

The Emotional Intelligence Skills Assessment (EISA)

"Look well into thyself; there is a source of strength which will always spring up if thou wilt always look there."

—MARCUS AURELIUS

"I think self-awareness is probably the most important thing towards being a champion."

—BILLIE JEAN KING

There has been an exciting new development since the last edition of *The EQ Edge* was published. Together with colleagues Derek Mann, Peter Papadogiannis, and Wendy Gordon at MHS, we have developed a brief self-test of emotional intelligence. Instead of an in-depth and comprehensive assessment like the EQ-i 2.0 or the MSCEIT, the Emotional Intelligence Skills Assessment (EISA) gives you a snapshot in five areas that tap your emotional skills. You can take the EISA free of charge when you purchase the book *EQ: Maximize Your Emotional Skills* by Steven J. Stein and Derek Mann.

For the purposes of the EISA assessment, we define emotional intelligence as the ability to identify and manage emotional information in oneself and others, and to focus energy on required behaviors. The EISA is a brief tool designed for personal development and training. It measures adult emotional intelligence on five scales: Perceiving, Managing, Decision Making, Achieving, and Influencing.

The EISA Self-Assessment helps you achieve better awareness of your ability to manage and perceive emotions, and improve your understanding of how your own emotions impact you—and others. This knowledge can open the door to increased emotional and social functioning by directing your developmental efforts to the areas of greatest opportunity and potential for growth.

The EISA was developed using standard test development procedures to ensure its effectiveness as a tool for personal and professional growth. It derives its theoretical roots from the vast amount of EI literature and research in the EI and training communities. The EISA measures and addresses emotional intelligence on these key scales:

Perceiving
The ability to accurately recognize, attend to, and understand emotion.

Managing
The ability to effectively manage, control, and express emotion.

Decision Making
The application of emotion to manage, change, and solve problems.

Achieving
The ability to generate the necessary emotions to self-motivate in the pursuit of realistic and meaningful objectives.

Influencing
The ability to recognize, manage, and evoke emotion within oneself and others to promote change.

Why was the EISA developed?

The EISA is a tool for personal development. It provides a means to accurately assess individual strengths and opportunities, and implement various strategies to increase intra- and interpersonal awareness.

When people better understand themselves and others, they're able to work more effectively, they're happier doing it, and they're able to foster more winning outcomes in the workplace.

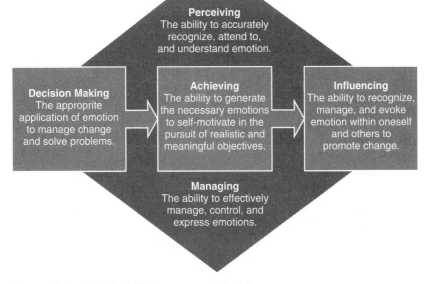

Figure C-1: EISA Self-Assessment Model

The EISA was developed to quickly and accurately measure emotional intelligence skills and provide a framework for discussion, coaching, and growth.

In order for people to improve their emotional skills and abilities, they must first be able to recognize their strengths and identify areas in which they may require improvement. Thus, the EISA program has the following specific goals:

1. To familiarize participants with the components of emotional intelligence and their relevance in the workplace.
2. To aid participants in the identification of emotionally intelligent actions and behaviors.
3. To help participants improve their own emotional intelligence by understanding and practicing effective behaviors.

It takes approximately 10 minutes to finish the items on the EISA, which can be completed online.

What is the EISA designed to measure?

The EISA is designed to measure a participant's current level of emotional and social functioning, which enables him or her to better understand how these skills impact personal and professional performance. The EISA is designed to provide participants with feedback on their perceived or self-described frequency of emotionally and socially intelligent behavior across five behavioral dimensions.

The EISA comprises 50 questions that are designed to identify the frequency and level of functioning of emotionally intelligent behavior.

The assessment is scored on a five-point scale. Pfeiffer Online Assessments (the online assessment administration system) automatically computes scores for all online Self- and 360 Assessments. A report with the respondent's results is included in the cost of the assessment.

Respondents taking the EISA (self-report) online will receive a summary of their results. The report provides numerical and graphical representations of the participant's results. Reports also provide a definition of each scale, and a discussion of the implications of the participant's results. The EISA-360 report includes the respondent's self-report results together with the aggregate results of their raters.

Endnotes

Introduction

1. Goleman, D., *Emotional Intelligence: Why It Can Matter More than IQ* (New York: Bantam, 1995). See also Goleman, D., *Working with Emotional Intelligence* (New York: Bantam, 1998); Goleman, D., Boyatzis, R., and McKee, A., *Primal Leadership: Realizing the Power of Emotional Intelligence* (Boston: Harvard Business School Press, 2002).

2. Herrnstein, R., and C. Murray, *The Bell Curve: Intelligence and Class Structure in American Life* (New York: Free Press, 1994).

Chapter 1: Exploring Emotional Intelligence

1. Bar-On, R, Bar-On Emotional Quotient (EQ-i) *Inventory Technical Manual* (Toronto: Multi-Health Systems Inc., 1997).

2. Mayer, J.D., P. Salovey, and D. Caruso, Mayer-Salovey-Caruso Emotional Intelligence Tests (MSCEIT) *User's Manual* (Toronto: Multi-Health Systems Inc., 2002).

3. MHS Staff, Emotional Quotient Inventory 2.0 (EQ-i 2.0) *Technical Manual* (Toronto: Multi-Health Systems Inc., 2011).

4. Darwin, C., *The Expression of the Emotions in Man and Animals* (Chicago: University of Chicago Press, 1965 [originally published in 1872]).

5. Thorndike, E. L., "Intelligence and its Uses," *Harper's Magazine*, 140 (1920): 227–235. See also Thorndike, E. L., "Intelligence and its Measurement: A Symposium," *Journal of Educational Psychology*, 12(3, 1921): 124–127; Thorndike, R. L., "Factor Analysis of Social and Abstract Intelligence," *Journal of Educational Psychology*, 27 (1936): 231–233; Thorndike, R. L., and S. Stein, "An Evaluation of the Attempts to Measure Social Intelligence," *Psychological Bulletin*, 34 (1937): 275–285.

6. Weschler, D., "Nonintellective Factors in General Intelligence," *Psychological Bulletin*, 37 (1940): 444–445. See also Wechsler, D., "Nonintellective Factors in General Intelligence," *Journal of Abnormal Psychology*, 38 (1943): 100–104.

7. Leeper, R.W., "A Motivational Theory of Emotions to Replace 'Emotions as Disorganized Responses'," *Psychological Review*, 55 (1948): 5–21.

8. Ellis, Albert, "New Approaches to Psychotherapy Techniques," *Journal of Clinical Psychology*, 11 (1955): 207–260.

9. Gardner, Howard, *Frames of Mind* (New York: Basic Books, 1983). See also Gardner, H., *Multiple Intelligences: The Theory in Practice* (New York: Basic Books, 1993); Gardner, H., "Reflections on Multiple Intelligences: Myths and Messages," *Phi Delta Kappan*, 77(3), (1995): 200–203, 206–209; Gardner, H., *Intelligence Refrained: Multiple Intelligences for the 21st Century* (New York: Basic Books, 1999).

10. Bar-On, Reuven, *The Development of a Concept of Psychological Well-Being,* draft copy of an unpublished doctoral dissertation presented in 1985 (Rhodes University, South Africa, 1988). See also Bar-On, R., *The Development of a Concept and Test of Emotional Intelligence,* unpublished manuscript, 1992 [published as part of the *Bar-On Emotional Quotient Inventory (EQ-i) Technical Manual* (Toronto: Multi-Health Systems Inc., 1997)]; Bar-On, R., *The Era of the EQ: Defining and Assessing Emotional Intelligence*, poster session at the 104th Annual Convention of the American Psychological Association, Toronto, Ontario, 1996.

11. Salovey P., and J.D. Mayer, "Emotional Intelligence," *Imagination, Cognition and Personality*, 9 (1990): 185–211.

12. Mayer, J.D., P. Salovey, and D. Caruso, *Mayer-Salovey-Caruso Emotional Intelligence Tests (MSCEIT) User's Manual* (Toronto: Multi-Health Systems Inc., 2002).

13. Binet, A., "Les Premiers Mots de la Thèse Idéaliste," *Revue Philosophique.*, 61 (1906): 599–618. See also Binet-Sanglé, C., "Racine," *Chronique Medical* XII (1905): 12–13; Binet, A., and T. Simon, "Conclusions," *L'Année Psychologique*, 16 (1910): 361–371; Johnston, K.L., "M. Binet's Method for the Measurement of Intelligence," *Report of the British Association for the Advancement of Science*, 80 (1910): 806–808; Huey, Edmund B., "The Binet Scale for Measuring Intelligence and Retardation," *Journal of Educational Psychology*, 1(8), (Sept. 1910): 435–444.

14. Goddard, H.H., "The Binet and Simon Tests of Intellectual Capacity," *Training School Bulletin*, 5 (1908): 3–6. See also Goddard, H.H., "Two Thousand Normal Children Measured by the Binet Measuring Scale of Intelligence," *Pedagogical Seminary*, 18 (1911): 232–259.

15. Terman, L.M., "The Binet-Simon Scale for Measuring Intelligence: Impressions Gained by its Application," *Psychological Clinic*, 5 (1911): 199–206. See also Terman, Lewis M., and H.G. Childs, "A Tentative Revision and Extension of the Binet-Simon Measuring Scale of Intelligence. Part III. Summary and Criticisms," *Journal of Educational Psychology*, 3(5), (May 1912): 277–289.

16. Wagner, Richard K., "Intelligence, Training, and Employment," *American Psychologist*, 52(10), (Oct. 1997): 1059–1069. This review article points out that the average observed validity coefficient or correlation between cognitive ability test scores and job performance is between .20 and .30, which amounts to between 4 percent and 9 percent of the variance. That leaves somewhere between 91 percent to 96 percent of job performance due to other factors.

17. Stanley, Thomas, *The Millionaire Mind* (New York: Andrews McMeel Publishing, 2001).

18. MHS Staff (2011). *Emotional Quotients Inventory 2.0 (EQ-i 2.0) Technical Manual*. Toronto: Multi-Health Systems.

19. Auletta, K., *The Highwaymen: Warriors of the Information Superhighway* (New York: Random House, 1997).

20. "Employers Want Common Sense," *Toronto Star* (Oct. 21, 1996); *Employability Skills for British Columbia*, Human Resource Development Canada, The British Columbia Labour Force Development Board, and The British Columbia Institute of Technology, Oct. 1996.

Part II: The Self-Perception Realm

1. Definition adapted from Bar-On, R., *Bar-On Emotional Quotient Inventory Technical Manual* (Toronto: Multi-Health Systems Inc., 1997), p. 44. See also MHS Staff, *Emotional Quotient Inventory 2.0 (EQ-i 2.0) Technical Manual* (Toronto: Multi-Health Systems Inc., 2011).

Chapter 3: Emotional Self-Awareness

2. Definition adapted from Bar-On, R., *Bar-On Emotional Quotient Inventory Technical Manual* (Toronto: Multi-Health Systems Inc., 1997), p. 15. See also MHS Staff, *Emotional Quotient Inventory 2.0 (EQ-i 2.0) Technical Manual* (Toronto: Multi-Health Systems Inc., 2011).

Chapter 4: Self-Regard

1. Definition adapted from Bar-On, R., *Bar-On Emotional Quotient Inventory Technical Manual* (Toronto: Multi-Health Systems Inc., 1997), p. 16. See also MHS Staff, *Emotional Quotient Inventory 2.0 (EQ-i 2.0) Technical Manual* (Toronto: Multi-Health Systems Inc., 2011).

2. Hare, Robert, *Without Conscience: The Psychopaths Among Us* (New York: The Guilford Press, 1999).

Chapter 5: Self-Actualization

1. Definition adapted from Bar-On, R., *Bar-On Emotional Quotient Inventory Technical Manual* (Toronto: Multi-Health Systems Inc., 1997), p. 16. See also MHS Staff, *Emotional Quotient Inventory 2.0 (EQ-i 2.0) Technical Manual* (Toronto: Multi-Health Systems Inc., 2011).

2. Murphy, Shane, *The Achievement Zone: 8 Skills for Winning All the Time from the Playing Field to the Boardroom* (New York: Putnam Publishing Group, 1996).

3. Vargas, Jose Antonio, "The Face of Facebook," *The New Yorker* (Sept. 20, 2010).

4. See Costanza, Mike, *The Real Seinfeld* (New York: Worldwise Books, 1998); Oppenheimer, Jerry, *Seinfeld: The Making of an American Icon* (New York: HarperCollins, (2002).

Chapter 6: Emotional Expression

1. Definition adapted from Bar-On, R., *Bar-On Emotional Quotient Inventory Technical Manual* (Toronto: Multi-Health Systems Inc., 1997), p. 44. See also MHS Staff, *Emotional Quotient Inventory 2.0 (EQ-i 2.0) Technical Manual* (Toronto: Multi-Health Systems Inc., 2011).

2. Mehrabian, Albert, *Silent Messages* (Oxford, England: Wadsworth, 1971)

3. Dion, Karen, Ellen Berscheid, and Elaine Walster, "What Is Beautiful is Good," *Journal of Personality and Social Psychology*, 24 (Dec. 1972): 285–290, doi: 10.1037/h0033731.

4. Ritts, Vicki, Miles, L. Patterson, and Mark E. Tubbs, "Expectations, Impressions, and Judgements of Physically Attractive Students: A Review," *Review of Educational Research*, 62 (Winter 1992): 413–426, doi: 10.2307/1170486.

5. Dion, Karen K., and Steven Stein, "Physical Attractiveness and Interpersonal Influence," *Journal of Experimental Social Psychology*, 14 (Jan. 1978): 97–108, doi: 10.1016/0022-1031(78)90063-X.

6. Webb, Tim, "BP Boss Admits Job on the Line Over Gulf Oil Spill," *The Guardian*, UK, May 13, 2010. www.guardian.co.uk/business/2010/may/13/bp-boss-admits-mistakes-gulf-oil-spill. (accessed May 13, 2010).

7. "BP's CEO Tony Hayward Takes a Walk on Oil-Covered Beach," CNN via *YouTube*, May 25, 2010, www.youtube.com/watch?v=_2U0z2gCnIs (accessed May 30, 2010).

8. "BP's Tony Hayward: 'I'd Like My Life Back'," *USA Today*, June 1, 2010. www.content.usatoday.com/communities/greenhouse/post/2010/06/bp-tony-hayward-apology/1 (accessed June 1, 2010).

Chapter 7: Independence

1. Definition adapted from Bar-On, R., *Bar-On Emotional Quotient Inventory Technical Manual* (Toronto: Multi-Health Systems Inc., 1997), p. 16. See also MHS Staff, *Emotional Quotient Inventory 2.0 (EQ-i 2.0) Technical Manual* (Toronto: Multi-Health Systems Inc., 2011).

Chapter 8: Assertiveness

1. Definition adapted from Bar-On, R., *Bar-On Emotional Quotient Inventory Technical Manual* (Toronto: Multi-Health Systems Inc., 1997), p. 15–16. See also MHS Staff, *Emotional Quotient Inventory 2.0 (EQ-i 2.0) Technical Manual* (Toronto: Multi-Health Systems Inc., 2011).

2. See Smith, T.W., Glazer, K., Ruiz, J.M., and Gallo, L.C., "Hostility, Anger, Aggressiveness, and Coronary Heart Disease: An Interpersonal Perspective on Personality, Emotion and Health," *Journal of Personality*, 72(6), (Dec. 2004): 1217–1270. See also Sirois, B.C., and Burg, M.M., "Negative Emotion and Heart Disease: A Review," *Behavior Modification*, 27(1), (Jan. 2003): 83–102. A newspaper article titled "Study Links Cheerfulness to Lower Heart Attack Risk: 'Type D' Personalities Called More Vulnerable" reported in the *Medical Tribune News Service* describes a study carried out at the University of Antwerp. In a 10-year study it found that patients who don't express their emotions were at greater risk of a second heart attack than people with a more cheerful disposition. Fifty-two percent of patients with what they called a "Type D" personality had a repeat heart attack in comparison to 12 percent who were non-type-D.

Part IV: The Interpersonal Realm

1. Definition adapted from Bar-On, R., *Bar-On Emotional Quotient Inventory Technical Manual* (Toronto: Multi-Health Systems Inc., 1997), p. 44. See also MHS Staff, *Emotional Quotient Inventory 2.0 (EQ-i 2.0) Technical Manual* (Toronto: Multi-Health Systems Inc., 2011).

Chapter 9: Interpersonal Relationships

2. Definition adapted from Bar-On, R., *Bar-On Emotional Quotient Inventory Technical Manual* (Toronto: Multi-Health Systems Inc., 1997), p. 17. See also MHS Staff, *Emotional Quotient Inventory 2.0 (EQ-i 2.0) Technical Manual* (Toronto: Multi-Health Systems Inc., 2011).

3. The complete program is provided in Turner, S.M., D. Beidel, and M. Cooley-Quille, *Social Effectiveness Therapy (SET): A Therapist's Guide* (Toronto: Multi-Health Systems Inc., 1997). See also Beidel, D., S.M. Turner, and T. Morris, *Social Effectiveness Therapy for Children and*

Adolescents (SET-C): A Therapist's Guide (Toronto: Multi-Health Systems Inc., 2003).

Chapter 10: Empathy

1. Definition adapted from Bar-On, R., *Bar-On Emotional Quotient Inventory Technical Manual* (Toronto: Multi-Health Systems Inc., 1997), p. 16. See also MHS Staff, *Emotional Quotient Inventory 2.0 (EQ-i 2.0) Technical Manual* (Toronto: Multi-Health Systems Inc., 2011).

2. Covey, Stephen, *Seven Habits of Highly Effective People* (New York: Free Press, 15th Anniversary Edition, 2004).

3. Book, Howard, "Empathy: Misconceptions and Misuses in Psychotherapy," *American Journal of Psychiatry*, 145(4) (1988): 420–424.

Chapter 11: Social Responsibility

1. Definition adapted from Bar-On, R., *Bar-On Emotional Quotient Inventory Technical Manual* (Toronto: Multi-Health Systems Inc., 1997), p. 17. See also MHS Staff, *Emotional Quotient Inventory 2.0 (EQ-i 2.0) Technical Manual* (Toronto: Multi-Health Systems Inc., 2011).

2. Ibid.

3. Raths, David, "100 Best Corporate Citizens for 2006: Celebrating Companies that Excel at Serving a Variety of Stakeholders Well," *Business Ethics* (2006); project director, Marjorie Kelly; statistical analysis designed by Sandra Waddock and Samuel Graves, Boston College; social data from KLD Research & Analytics Inc.

4. Drohan, Madelaine, "Being Nice Can Pay Off, English Research Shows: But Let People Know About It, Scientist Says," *The Globe and Mail*, describes the research of Professors Martin Nowak of Oxford University and Karl Sigmund of University of Vienna.

Part V: The Decision-Making Realm

1. Definition adapted from Bar-On, R., *Bar-On Emotional Quotient Inventory Technical Manual* (Toronto: Multi-Health Systems Inc., 1997), p. 45. See also MHS Staff, *Emotional Quotient Inventory 2.0 (EQ-i 2.0) Technical Manual* (Toronto: Multi-Health Systems Inc., 2011).

Chapter 12: Reality Testing

2. Definition adapted from Bar-On, R., *Bar-On Emotional Quotient Inventory Technical Manual* (Toronto: Multi-Health Systems Inc., 1997), p. 17–18. See also MHS Staff, *Emotional Quotient Inventory 2.0 (EQ-i 2.0) Technical Manual* (Toronto: Multi-Health Systems Inc., 2011).

3. Ibid.

Chapter 13: Problem Solving

1. Definition adapted from Bar-On, R., *Bar-On Emotional Quotient Inventory Technical Manual* (Toronto: Multi-Health Systems Inc., 1997), p. 17. See also MHS Staff, *Emotional Quotient Inventory 2.0 (EQ-i 2.0) Technical Manual* (Toronto: Multi-Health Systems Inc., 2011).

2. For more information about this work see D'Zurilla, T., and A. Nezu, *Problem-Solving Therapy: A Social Competence Approach to Clinical Intervention* (New York: Springer Series on Behavior Therapy and Behavioral Medicine, 1999). The authors have also developed a test to measure individual social problem-solving ability: D'Zurilla, T., A. Nezu, and A. Maydeau-Olivares, *Social Problem-Solving Inventory– Revised (SPSI–R): Technical Manual* (Toronto: Multi-Health Systems Inc., 2002).

3. Levine, M., *Effective Problem Solving (2nd Edition)* (Englewood Cliffs: Prentice Hall, 1993).

Chapter 14: Impulse Control

1. Definition adapted from Bar-On, R., *Bar-On Emotional Quotient Inventory Technical Manual* (Toronto: Multi-Health Systems Inc., 1997), p. 18. See also MHS Staff, *Emotional Quotient Inventory 2.0 (EQ-i 2.0) Technical Manual* (Toronto: Multi-Health Systems Inc., 2011).

2. Shoda, Yuichi, Walter Mischel, and Philip K. Peake, "Predicting Adolescent Cognitive and Self-Regulatory Competencies from preschool Delay of Gratification: Identifying Diagnostic Conditions," *Developmental Psychology.* 26(6), (Nov, 1990): 978–986. See also Mischel, Walter, Yuichi Shoda, and Monica L. Rodriguez, "Delay of Gratification in Children," *Science*, 244(4907), (May 1989): 933–938.

3. As reported by Goleman, D., based on conversations with Philip Peake, in *Emotional Intelligence: Why it Can Matter More than IQ* (New York: Bantam, 1995).

4. Moffitt, Terrie E., Louise Arseneault, Daniel Belsky, Nigel Dickson, Robert J. Hancox, HonaLee Harrington, Renate Houts, Richie Poulton, Brent W. Roberts, Stephen Ross, Malcolm R. Sears, W. Murray Thomson, and Avshalom Caspi, "A Gradient of Childhood Self-Control Predicts Health, Wealth, and Public Safety," The Proceedings of the National Academy of Sciences USA (PNAS, 2011) www.pnas.org/content/early/2011/01/20/1010076108.full.pdf+html. Also cited by Carly Weeks, "Self-Control at an Early Age Helps Avoid Pitfalls: Study," *The Globe and Mail*, Jan. 24, 2011.

Part VI: The Stress-Management Realm

1. Definition adapted from Bar-On, R., *Bar-On Emotional Quotient Inventory Technical Manual* (Toronto: Multi-Health Systems Inc., 1997), p. 45. See also MHS Staff, *Emotional Quotient Inventory 2.0 (EQ-i 2.0) Technical Manual* (Toronto: Multi-Health Systems Inc., 2011).

Chapter 15: Flexibility

1. Definition adapted from Bar-On, R., *Bar-On Emotional Quotient Inventory Technical Manual* (Toronto: Multi-Health Systems Inc., 1997), p. 45. See also MHS Staff, *Emotional Quotient Inventory 2.0 (EQ-i 2.0) Technical Manual* (Toronto: Multi-Health Systems Inc., 2011).

2. Iaccoca, Lee, "Henry Ford," *Time* magazine, 153 (December 7, 1998).

3. Gates, Bill, www.microsoft.com/billgates/speeches/

4. Gelernter, David, "Bill Gates," *Time* magazine, 153 (December 7, 1998).

Chapter 16: Stress Tolerance

1. Definition adapted from Bar-On, R., *Bar-On Emotional Quotient Inventory Technical Manual* (Toronto: Multi-Health Systems Inc., 1997), p. 18. See also MHS Staff, *Emotional Quotient Inventory 2.0 (EQ-i 2.0) Technical Manual* (Toronto: Multi-Health Systems Inc., 2011).

2. Ibid.

3. Freud, S., "Repression," *Collected Papers*, Vol. 4 (1915): 84–97.

4. Cummings, T., and C.L. Cooper, "A Cybernation Framework for the Study of Occupational Stress," *Human Relations*, 32 (1979): 395–419.

5. See Jacobson, Edmund, "Progressive Relaxation," *American Journal of Psychology*, 100(3–4), (Fall–Winter 1987): 522–537, for a reprint of his original 1925 instructions.

6. Wolpe, Joseph, "Deconditioning and Ad Hoc Uses of Relaxation: An Overview," *Journal of Behavior Therapy and Experimental Psychiatry*, 15(4), (Dec. 1984): 299–304.

Chapter 17: Optimism

1. Definition adapted from Bar-On, R., *Bar-On Emotional Quotient Inventory Technical Manual* (Toronto: Multi-Health Systems Inc., 1997), p. 19. See also MHS Staff, *Emotional Quotient Inventory 2.0 (EQ-i 2.0) Technical Manual* (Toronto: Multi-Health Systems Inc., 2011).

2. Seligman, Martin, *Learned Optimism: How to Change Your Mind and Your Life* (New York: Free Press, 1990 [reissued 1998]). See also Seligman, Martin E.P., Karen Reivich, Lisa Jaycox, and Jane Gillham, *The Optimistic Child* (Boston: Houghton Mifflin Co., 1995).

3. Seligman, Martin, *Learned Optimism: How to Change Your Mind and Your Life* (New York: Free Press, 1990 [reissued 1998]).

Part VII: General Well-Being

1. Definition adapted from Bar-On, R., *Bar-On Emotional Quotient Inventory Technical Manual* (Toronto: Multi-Health Systems Inc., 1997), p. 45. See also MHS Staff, *Emotional Quotient Inventory 2.0 (EQ-i 2.0) Technical Manual* (Toronto: Multi-Health Systems Inc., 2011).

Chapter 18: Happiness

2. Definition adapted from Bar-On, R., *Bar-On Emotional Quotient Inventory Technical Manual* (Toronto: Multi-Health Systems Inc., 1997), p. 18–19. See also MHS Staff, *Emotional Quotient Inventory 2.0 (EQ-i 2.0) Technical Manual* (Toronto: Multi-Health Systems Inc., 2011).

3. Lykken, David, and Auke Tellegen, "Happiness is a Stochastic Phenomenon," *Psychological Science*, 7(3), (May 1996): 186–189.

4. Csikszentmihalyi, Mihaly, "If We Are So Rich, Why Aren't We Happy?" *American Psychologist*, 54(10), (Oct. 1999): 821–827. See also Diener, Ed, "Subjective Well-Being: The Science of Happiness and a Proposal for a National Index," *American Psychologist*, 55(1), (Jan. 2000): 34–43.

5. World Values Study Group (1994), *World Values Survey*, computer file, ICPSR version, (Ann Arbor, MI: Institute for Social Research, 1981–1994 and 1990–1993). www.wvsevsdb.com/wvs/WVSData.jsp

6. Myers, David G., and Ed Diener, "Who is Happy?" *Psychological Science*, 6(1), (Jan. 1995): 10–19. See also Diener, Ed, and Robert Biswas-Diener, "Will Money Increase Subjective Well-Being?" *Social Indicators Research*, 57(2), (Feb. 2002): 119–169; and Diener, Ed, and Martin E.P. Seligman, "Very Happy People," *Psychological Science*, 13(1), (Jan. 2002): 81–84.

7. Covey, Stephen, *Seven Habits of Highly Effective People* (New York: Free Press, 15th Anniversary Edition, 2004).

8. Csikszentmihalyi, Mihaly, Sami Abuhamdeh, Jeanne Elliot Nakamura, J. Andrew (ed), and Carol S. Dweck (ed), *Flow: Handbook of Competence and Motivation* (New York: The Guilford Press, 2005). See also Csikszentmihalyi, Mihaly, "Reflections on enjoyment," *Perspectives in Biology and Medicine*, 28(4), (Summer 1985): 489–497; Csikszentmihalyi, Mihaly (ed), and Isabella Selega Csikszentmihalyi (ed), "The Flow Experience and its Significance for Human Psychology," *Cambridge University Press*, 14 (1988): 416; and Csikszentmihalyi, Mihaly (ed), and Isabella Selega Csikszentmihalyi (ed), "Optimal Experience: Psychological Studies of Flow in Consciousness," *Cambridge University Press*, 14 (1988): 416.

9. Veenhoven, Ruut, *Conditions of Happiness* (Dordrecht/Boston/Lancaster: Kluwer Academic, 1984 [reprinted 1989]) www2.eur.nl/fsw/research/veenhoven/Pub1980s/84a-con.htm

Chapter 19: The Star Performers

1. Dizdarevic, Tin, "'Soft Skills' On Rise: IT Workers Can No Longer Rely on Technical Expertise," *Computer Reseller News* (September 2, 1996): 111. Based on a study by RHI Consulting.

2. Mirsky, Steve, "Separate But EQ," *Scientific American* (April 1997): 25. See also Carey, Elaine, "Women Relate Better, More Aware of Feelings,"

Toronto Star (August 20, 1997): A10; Multi-Health Systems staff, "Men and Women Have Different Kinds and Levels of Emotional Intelligence, EQ for Both Sexes is Key to Workplace Success," Multi-Health Systems Inc., www.emotionalintelligencemhs.com/MenAndWomanEI.asp

3. Carey, Elaine, "Older's Better Emotionally, Test Says," *Toronto Star* (March 5, 1997). See also Multi-Health Systems staff, "According to New Bar-On EQ-i Test Results from Multi-Health Systems, the Older You Get, the More Emotionally Intelligent You Become," Multi-Health Systems Inc., www.emotionalintelligencemhs.com/EIGetsBetter WithAge.asp

4. The EQ-i has been translated (with back translations) into the following languages: Arabic, Arabic (Egyptian), Mandarin, Cantonese, Croatian, Czech, Danish, Dutch, Finnish, French (European), French (PQ), German, Greek, Hebrew, Indonesian, Iranian/Persian, Italian, Japanese, Korean, Norwegian, Portuguese (European), Portuguese (Brazilian), Russian, Serbian, Slovak, Spanish (Mexican), Spanish (European), and Turkish. In addition, large normative samples have been collected in many countries throughout the world. For information on specific languages or countries, contact Multi-Health Systems Inc., translations@mhs.com.

5. Sitarenios, G., and S.J. Stein, *EQ-i Ethnicity Analysis* (Toronto, Canada: Multi-Health Systems. 1998). This study compared samples of African-Americans, Hispanics, Asians, and Caucasians taken from the EQ-i normative sample. Ethnic differences were negligible.

6. Bar-On, R. and J.D.A. Parker, (2000). *Bar-On Emotional Quotient (EQ-i YP) Inventory Youth Version Technical Manual* (Toronto: Multi-Health Systems Inc., 2000).

7. Handley, R., "Emotional Intelligence," *Recruiter* (April 1997): 10–11.

8. US Senate. Report to the subcommittee on Personnel, Committee on Armed Services, *Military Recruiting: DOD Could Improve its Recruiter Selection and Incentive Systems* (Chapter Report, 01/30/98, GAO/NSIAD-98-58).

9. Ibid., p. 15.

10. Ibid., p. 17.

11. U.S. House of Representatives. *Military Attrition: DOD Needs to Better Analyze Reasons for Separation and Improve Recruiting Systems*,

March 12, 1998, (GAO/T-NSIAD-98-117). See also United States House Of Representatives. Department of The Air Force, Presentation To The Committee On National Security Subcommittee On Military Personnel, Subject: Recruiting, Statement of Colonel Peter U. Sutton, Commander, USAF Recruiting Service, United States Air Force, 12 March 1998.

12. Jae, J.H-W., "Emotional Intelligence and Cognitive Ability as Predictors of Job Performance among Bank Employees," unpublished master's thesis (Ateneo De Manila University, Philippines, 1997).

13. Sitarenios, G., and S.J. Stein, *Emotional Intelligence in the Prediction of Sales Success in the Finance Industry* (Toronto, Canada: Multi-Health Systems Inc., 1998).

14. Cannon, Kate, in personal communication to authors, 1998. See also Sitarenios, G., *Pre-Post Analysis: American Express Co. Employees* (Toronto, Canada: Multi-Health Systems Inc., 1998); and Schwartz, Tony, "How Do You Feel?" *Fast Company*, 35 (June 2000): 296. www.fastcompany.com/magazine/35/emotion.html

15. Seligman, Martin E., and Peter Schulman "Explanatory Style as a Predictor of Productivity and Quitting among Life Insurance Sales Agents," *Journal of Personality and Social Psychology*, 50(4), (April 1986): 832–838.

16. Bachman, J., S.J. Stein, K. Campbell, and G. Sitarenios, G, "Emotional Intelligence in the Collection of Debt," *International Journal of Selection and Assessment*, 8 (2000): 176–182.

17. Swift, D., "Do Doctors Have an Emotional Handicap?" *The Medical Post*, (March 9, 1999): 30.

18. Hojat, M., D.Z. Louis, F.W. Markham, R. Wender, C. Rabinowitz, and J.S. Gonnella, "Physicians' Empathy and Clinical Outcomes for Diabetic Patients," *Acad Med.*, 86(3), (March 2011): 359–364.

19. Yates, J.M., "The Relationship Between Emotional Intelligence and Health Habits of Health Education Students," *Dissertation Abstracts International*, 60 (1999): 3284.

20. Dunkley, J., "The Psychological Well-Being of Coronary Heart Disease Patients Before and After an Intervention Program," unpublished master's thesis (University of Pretoria, South Africa, 1996).

21. Nigli, R., Executive Summary of LEAP Program, YWCA of Metropolitan Toronto, Program Review (unpublished manuscript, 1998).

Chapter 20: More Star Performers

1. Fazio, Robert, and Lauren Fazio, "Growth Through Loss: Promoting Healing and Growth in the Face of Trauma, Crisis, and Loss," *Journal of Loss & Trauma*, 10(3), (2005): 221–252.

2. Fazio, Robert J., Steven J. Danish, and Daniel R. Strunk, "Post-Traumatic Growth Following the September 11th Terrorist Attacks: An Examination of Emotional Intelligence and Resilience," paper being submitted for publication.

3. Turner, Timothy W., "Identifying Emotional Intelligence Competencies Differentiating FBI National Academy Graduates from other Law Enforcement Leaders," unpublished dissertation (Faculty of Curry School of Education, University of Virginia, 2005).

4. Taylor, Irene, "Canada's Top 25 Litigators," *LEXPERT* (July/August 2002): 64–89. See also Taylor, Irene, "Top 40 Under 40," *LEXPERT* (September 2002): 62–90; Taylor, Irene, "Canada's Top 30 Corporate Dealmakers," *LEXPERT* (November/December 2002): 58–81; Taylor, Irene, and Stephanie Willson, "Carpe Diem! Canada's Top 25 Women Lawyers," *LEXPERT* (September 2003): 68–98; and Taylor, Irene, "Power Bloc: Canada's Top 25 General Counsel," *LEXPERT* (April 2003): 66–97.

5. Ibid.

6. Ibid.

7. Ibid.

8. Ibid.

9. Ibid.

10. Becker, I.M., D.C. Ackley, and R.A. Green, "New Study: The Value of Emotional Intelligence in Dentistry," *Dentistry Today*, 22 (2003): 106–111.

11. Wagner, Peggy, Ginger, Moseley, Michael Grant, Jonathan Gore, and Christopher Owens, "The Relationship Between Physician, Emotional Intelligence, and Patient Satisfaction," *Family Medicine* (Nov./Dec. 2002).

12. Stone, H., J.D.A. Parker, and L.M. Wood, "Report on the Ontario Principals' Council Leadership Study," *Consortium for Research on Emotional Intelligence in Organizations* (Feb. 2005), www.eiconsortium.org

13. Ibid.

14. Ibid.

15. Ruderman, M.N., K. Hannum, J.B. Leslie, and J.L. Steed, "Leadership Skills and Emotional Intelligence," unpublished manuscript, Center for Creative Leadership, Greensboro, NC (presented at the Applying Emotional Intelligence to Business Solutions & Success Conference, Toronto, August 9–10, 2001).

16. Contact Multi-Health Systems Inc. (www.mhs.com; 800-456-3002 [US]; 800-268-6011 [Canada]; 0845-601-7603 [UK]; or 416-492-2627 [International]) for more information about the EQ-i Leadership Report.

17. Parker, J.A., L.J. Summerfeldt, M.J. Hogan, and S. Majeski, "Emotional Intelligence and Academic Success: Examining the Transition from High School to University," *Personality and Individual Differences*, 36(1), (Jan. 2004): 163–172.

18. Parker, J.D.A., J. Duffy, L.M. Wood, B.J. Bond, and M.J. Hogan, "Academic Achievement and Emotional Intelligence: Predicting the Successful Transition from High School to University," *Journal of First-Year Experience & Students in Transition*, 17 (2005): 67–78.

Chapter 21: The EQ Research Continues

1. Frye, Crissie M., Rebecca J. Bennett, and Sheri Caldwell, "Team Emotional Intelligence and Team Interpersonal Process Effectiveness," *American Journal of Business: Applying Research to Practice*, 21 (Spring 2006): 49–56.

2. Morehouse, Michelle M., "An Exploration of Emotional Intelligence Across Career Arenas," *Leadership & Organization Development Journal*, 28(4), (2007): 296–307, doi: 10.1108/01437730710752184.

3. Dries, Nicky, and Roland Pepermans, "Using Emotional Intelligence to Identify High Potential: A Metacompetency Perspective," *Leadership & Organization Development Journal*, 28(8), (2007): 749–770, doi: 10.1108/01437730710835470.

4. Bumphus, Aileen Thompson, "The Emotional Intelligence and Resilience of School Leaders: An Investigation into Leadership Behaviors," Dissertation Abstracts International Section A: Humanities and Social Sciences, 2009: 3401.

5. Jerome, Karen L., "An Examination of the Relationship Between Emotional Intelligence and the Leadership Styles of Early Childhood Professionals," Dissertation Abstracts International Section A: Humanities and Social Sciences, 2010: 3336.

6. Hansen, Richard A., "A Study of School District Superintendents and the Connection of Emotional Intelligence to Leadership," Dissertation Abstracts International Section A: Humanities and Social Sciences, 2010: 3920.

7. Frye, Crissie M., Rebecca J. Bennett, and Sheri Caldwell, "Team Emotional Intelligence and Team Interpersonal Process Effectiveness," *American Journal of Business: Applying Research to Practice*, 21 (Spring 2006): 49–56.

8. Conrad, Jarik Edwardo, "The Relationship Between Emotional Intelligence and Intercultural Sensitivity," Dissertation Abstracts International Section A: Humanities and Social Sciences, 2007: 846.

9. Gasiorowska, Grazyna Maria, "A Study of Project Managers' Most Dominant Emotional Intelligence Abilities and Skills," Dissertation Abstracts International: Section B: The Sciences and Engineering, 2007: 4129.

10. Tessema, Dereje Befekadu, "The Relationship Between Emotional Intelligence and Transformational Leadership in Project Management: A Quantitative Study," Dissertation Abstracts International Section A: Humanities and Social Sciences, 2010: 1715.

11. Wong-Fong, Elva Keem, "The Relationship Between Emotional Intelligence and a Voluntary Midlife Career Change Among Women," Dissertation Abstracts International: Section B: The Sciences and Engineering, 2008: 2664.

12. Di Fabio, Annamaria, and Letizia Palazzeschi, "Emotional Intelligence, Personality Traits and Career Decision Difficulties," *International Journal for Educational and Vocational Guidance*, 9 (July 2009): 135–146, doi: 10.1007/s10775-009-9162-3.

13. Farlow, Michael J., "The Possible Relationship Between Emotional Intelligence and Performance in Small Business Development Center Regional Groups in Texas," Dissertation Abstracts International: Section B: The Sciences and Engineering, 2010: 7841.

14. Rovnak, Amanda M., "A Psychometric Investigation of the Emotional Quotient Inventory in Adolescents: A Construct Validation and Estimate of Stability," Dissertation Abstracts International Section A: Humanities and Social Sciences, 2008: 3747.

15. Dulko, Jeffrey P., "Application of the Emotional Intelligence Construct to College Student Binge Drinking," Dissertation Abstracts International: Section B: The Sciences and Engineering, 2008: 1321.

16. Tsujino, Junko, and Mayumi Oyama-Higa, "The Relationship Between Emotional Intelligence of Mothers and Problem Behavior in their Young Children: A Longitudinal Analysis," *Journal of Prenatal & Perinatal Psychology & Health*, 21 (Spring 2007): 215–229.

17. Parker, James D.A., Robyn N. Taylor, Jennifer M. Eastabrook, Stacey L. Schell, and Laura M. Wood, "Problem Gambling in Adolescence: Relationships with Internet Misuse, Gaming Abuse and Emotional Intelligence," *Personality and Individual Differences*, 45 (July 2008): 174–180, doi: 10.1016/j.paid.2008.03.018.

18. Alumran, Jihan I.A., and Raija-Leena Punamäki, "Relationship Between Gender, Age, Academic Achievement, Emotional Intelligence, and Coping Styles among Bahraini Adolescents," *Individual Differences Research*, 6 (June 2008): 104–119.

19. Zavala, María Alicia, María Dolores Valadez, and María Carmen Vargas, "Emotional Intelligence and Social Skills in Adolescents with High Social Acceptance," *Electronic Journal of Research in Educational Psychology*, 6 (Sept. 2008): 319–338.

20. Kohaut, Karen Michelle, "Emotional Intelligence as a Predictor of Academic Achievement in Middle School Children," Dissertation Abstracts International: Section B: The Sciences and Engineering, 2010: 2688.

21. Sadri, Esmaiel, Nasrin Akbarzadeh, and Kambiz Poushaneh, "Impact of Social-Emotional Learning Skills Instruction on Emotional Intelligence of Male High School Students," *Psychological Research*, 11 (Winter 2009): 69–83.

22. Sparkman, Larry Austin, "Emotional Intelligence as a Non-Traditional Predictor of College Student Retention and Graduation," Dissertation Abstracts International Section A: Humanities and Social Sciences, 2009: 3068.

23. Chang, Kelly B.T., "Can We Teach Emotional Intelligence?" Dissertation Abstracts International Section A: Humanities and Social Sciences, 2007: 4451.

24. Fletcher, Ian, Peter Leadbetter, Andrew Curran, and Helen O'Sullivan, "A Pilot Study Assessing Emotional Intelligence Training and Communication Skills with Third Year Medical Students," *Patient Education and Counseling*, 76 (Sept. 2009): 376–379, doi: 10.1016/j.pec.2009.07.019.

25. Colston, R. Dean, "The Relationship Between Emotional Intelligence and Academic Achievement: Implications of Birth Order Based on Social Rank for Nontraditional Adult Learners," Dissertation Abstracts International Section A: Humanities and Social Sciences, 2008: 2165.

26. Drury, Leith, "Coaches' Perceptions of Emotional and Social Intelligence," Dissertation Abstracts International: Section B: The Sciences and Engineering, 2008: 3831.

27. Perlini, Arthur H., and Trevor R. Halverson, "Emotional Intelligence in the National Hockey League," *Canadian Journal of Behavioural Science/Revue canadienne des sciences du comportement*, 38 (April 2006): 109–119, doi: 10.1037/cjbs2006001.

28. Yalcin, Bektas Murat, Tevfik Fikret Karahan, Muhittin Ozcelik, and Fusun Artiran Igde, "The Effects of an Emotional Intelligence Program on the Quality of Life and Well-Being of Patients with Type 2 Diabetes Mellitus," The *Diabetes* Educator, 34 (Nov.–Dec. 2008): 1013-1024, doi: 10.1177/0145721708327303.

29. Schutte, Nicola S., John M. Malouff, Einar B. Thorsteinsson, Navjot Bhullar, and Sally E. Rooke, "A Meta-Analytic Investigation of the Relationship Between Emotional Intelligence and Health," *Personality and Individual Differences*, 42 (April 2007): 921–933, doi: 10.1016/j.paid.2006.09.003.

30. Saklofske, Donald H., Elizabeth J. Austin, Betty A. Rohr, and Jac J.W. Andrews, "Personality, Emotional Intelligence and Exercise," *Journal of Health Psychology*, 12 (Nov. 2007): 937–948, doi: 10.1177/1359105307082458.

31. Killgore, William D.S., Desiree B. Killgore, Lisa M. Day, Christopher Li, Gary H. Kamimori, and Thomas J. Balkin, "The Effects of 53 Hours of Sleep Deprivation on Moral Judgment," Sleep: *Journal of Sleep and Sleep Disorders Research*, 30 (Mar. 2007): 345–352.

32. Killgore, William D.S., and Deborah A. Yurgelun-Todd, "Neural Correlates of Emotional Intelligence in Adolescent Children," *Cognitive, Affective & Behavioral Neuroscience*, 7 (June 2007): 140–151, doi: 10.3758/CABN.7.2.140.

33. Gawryluk, Jodie R., and Jeannette McGlone, "Does the Concept of Emotional Intelligence Contribute to our Understanding of Temporal Lobe Resections?" *Epilepsy & Behavior*, 11 (Nov. 2007): 421–426, doi: 10.1016/j.yebeh.2007.06.002.

Chapter 22: Emotional Intelligence as Ability

1. Salovey, P., and J.D. Mayer, "Emotional Intelligence," *Imagination, Cognition, and Personality*, 9 (1990): 185–211. See also Mayer, J.D. and J.D. Salovey, "What is emotional intelligence?" in P. Salovey (ed) and D. Sluyter (ed), *Emotional Development and Emotional Intelligence: Educational Implications* (New York: Basic Books, 1997).

2. Mayer, J.D. and J.D. Salovey, "What is emotional intelligence?" in P. Salovey (ed) and D. Sluyter (ed), *Emotional Development and Emotional Intelligence: Educational Implications* (New York: Basic Books, 1997): 3–31. See also Mayer, J.D., P. Salovey, and D.R. Caruso, "Emotional Intelligence: Theory, Findings, and Implications," *Psychological Inquiry*, 15(3), (2004): 197–215.

3. Mayer, J.D., P. Salovey, and D.R. Caruso, *Mayer-Salovey-Caruso Emotional Intelligence Tests (MSCEIT) User's Manual* (Toronto: Multi-Health Systems Inc., 2002).

4. Lopes, P.N., S. Côté, D. Grewal, J. Kadis, M. Gall, and P. Salovey, "Evidence That Emotional Intelligence is Related to Job Performance, Interpersonal Facilitation, Affect and Attitudes at Work, and Leadership Potential," submitted for publication.

5. Lopes. P.N., A. Brackett, J. Nezlek, A. Schutz, I. Sellin, and P. Salovey, "Emotional Intelligence and Social Interaction," *Personality and Social Psychology Bulletin*, 30 (2004): 1018–1034.

6. Rosete, D., and J. Ciarrochi, "Emotional Intelligence and Its Relationship to Workplace Performance Outcomes of Leadership Effectiveness," *Leadership & Organizational Development Journal*, 26(5), (2005): 388–399.

7. Côté, S., P.N. Lopes, and P. Salovey, "Emotional Intelligence and Vision Formulation and Articulation" (2003), manual submitted for publication. Cited in Mayer, JD., P. Salovey, and D. Caruso, "Emotional Intelligence: Theory, Findings, and Implications," *Psychological Inquiry*, 15(3), (2004): 197–215.

8. Giles, S.J.S., "The Role of Supervisory Emotional Intelligence in Direct Report Organizational Commitment," unpublished master's thesis (University of New South Wales, Sydney, Australia, 2001).

9. Janovics, J., and N.D. Christiansen, "Emotional Intelligence in the Workplace." Paper presented at the 16th Annual Conference of the Society of Industrial and Organizational Psychology, San Diego, CA: May 2002.

10. Tombs, S., "Challenging the Bell Curve: An Assessment of the Role of Emotional Intelligence in Career Placement and Performance." Unpublished doctoral dissertation (York University, Toronto, 2004).

11. Yip, J.A., and R.A. Martin, "Sense of Humor, Emotional Intelligence, and Social Competence," (in press), *Journal of Research in Personality*.

Appendix 1: The EQ-i 2.0

1. Bar-On, R., *Bar-On Emotional Quotient Inventory Technical Manual* (Toronto: Multi-Health Systems Inc., 1997). See also MHS Staff, *Emotional Quotient Inventory 2.0 (EQ-i 2.0) Technical Manual* (Toronto: Multi-Health Systems Inc., 2011).

2. *Standards for Educational and Psychological Testing* (1985), American Psychological Association, Washington, DC. Other references that are important in testing: Equal Employment Opportunity Commission, Civil Service Commission, Department of Labor, & Department of Justice (1978); adoption by four agencies of uniform guidelines on employee selection procedures; *Federal Register*, 43 (166), 38290–38315; Society for Industrial and Organizational Psychology, Inc. (1987); *Principles for the Validation and Use of Personnel Selection Procedures* (3rd edition), College Park, MD; Code of Fair Testing Practices in Education (2004), Joint Committee on Testing Practices (JCTP); 2002 American Psychological Association, Ethical Principles of Psychologists and Code of Conduct, American Psychological Association, Washington, DC, www.apa.org/ethics/code2002.html

Index